"Many people are afraid of where the world is going, and Christians often seem as fearful as anyone. Daniel's visions showed his hearers why they didn't need to be afraid, and the stories about him and his friends modeled what it meant to be brave, forthright, and faithful. Chris Wright has often preached on Daniel, and he's therefore just the person to help us hear the book's message for the pressing context of our lives today."

JOHN GOLDINGAY, Professor, Fuller Theological Seminary

"Chris Wright's Old Testament scholarship, his superb expository gift, and ability to apply it in a relevant, practical way combine to produce this excellent book on Daniel. Any one committed to live faithfully in a culture which increasingly seems alien to followers of Christ will find invaluable help here."

PETER MAIDEN, International Director Emeritus, Operation Mobilisation; Minister at Large, Keswick Ministries

"Like his great mentor and friend, John Stott, before him, Chris Wright has an all-too-rare ability to expound God's Word and God's world in the same breath. Pastors, small group leaders, and Christians in general will find in this gem both a clear explanation of the text of Daniel—no easy thing—and a wealth of insights into how believers can confidently live as a pressured minority in a secularising world. This book made me want to reread Daniel and preach its treasures in my own setting. And the international flavour of Chris's writing means that others are sure to feel the same wherever they live."

THE REV'D DR JOHN DICKSON, author and speaker; Founding Director of the Centre for Public Christianity; Senior Minister of St Andrew's Roseville; Honor of Ancient History, Macquarie

"This eminently accessible volume shows how Daniel, far from being a children's book or a biblical oddity, speaks directly to the most difficult ethical questions for contemporary Christians. Wright's careful attention to words and literary details, as well as his pastorally informed imagination, enable him to draw a genuine connection between Scripture and the lived experience of people in both Majority-world and Minority-world cultures, so that we may 'know the story we are in.'"

ELLEN F. DAVIS, Amos Ragan Kearns Professor of Bible and
Practical Theology, The Divinity School, Duke University

"This is the kind of book I like to recommend to preachers. It is firmly rooted in sound biblical scholarship yet it is in the service of listening to God's address through Daniel to his own contemporaries so we can hear that address today. The message of Daniel comes alive as we hear what the Spirit is saying to us in our own missionary setting. Chris Wright does not just tell us what the text says but shows us what the text is trying to do – shape a distinctive people in the midst of a hostile culture then and now. This delightful book helps us read and preach Daniel in a way that is both faithful to the original context and relevant to the present."

MICHAEL W. GOHEEN, Theological Director, Missional Training
Center; Scholar in Residence, Surge Network, Phoenix, AZ

HEARING THE MESSAGE OF DANIEL

HEARING THE MESSAGE OF DANIEL

SUSTAINING FAITH IN TODAY'S WORLD

CHRISTOPHER
J. H. WRIGHT

ZONDERVAN

Hearing the Message of Daniel
Copyright © 2017 by Langham Partnership International

This title is also available as a Zondervan ebook.

Requests for information should be addressed to:
Zondervan, *3900 Sparks Dr. SE, Grand Rapids, Michigan 49546*

ISBN 978-0-310-28464-2

Cover design: Studio Gearbox
Cover imagery: Shutterstock
Interior design: Kait Lamphere

Printed in the United States of America

17 18 19 20 21 22 23 24 /DHV/ 15 14 13 12 11 10 9 8 7 6 5 4 3 2 1

To
David and Rosemary Harley
". . . but even if not . . ."

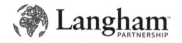

TABLE OF CONTENTS

PREFACE

"All Nations, January—March 1986" are the words scribbled at the top of the first page of a set of well-worn handwritten notes. They are my notes from the first time I preached through Daniel 1–7 in the weekly chapel services at All Nations Christian College during a period of home leave from India, where I was serving with my family at the Union Biblical Seminary. All Nations kindly gave us accommodation for those months, and part of the deal was that I should do some lectures and deliver a series of expositions on Daniel each Wednesday morning.

The principal of All Nations at that time was David Harley, who later went on to be the International Director of OMF International in Singapore. Ever since our days at All Nations, when David and his wife Rosemary have greeted me on any occasion when the paths of our travels cross, they remind me of the words, "But even if not. . . ." Apparently my preaching of those words in the mouths of Shadrach, Meshach, and Abednego in Daniel 3:17–18 made a deep impression on many of the students at that time (or at least they did on David and Rosemary). So since this book owes its distant origin to that invitation from the Harleys, it is dedicated to them with affection and gratitude for our shared ministries.

As often happens, expositions are recycled, revisited, revised, extended, updated, and delivered on other occasions as the years go by. I preached again on Daniel at the Union Biblical Seminary, then again at All Nations a few years later after we returned from India. The expositions of chapters 1–6 were published in 1993 by Scripture Union in a small contribution to their series, Word for Today, under the title *Tested by Fire: Daniel 1–6: Solid Faith in*

Today's World. That book has been out of print for years (though I see it is available on Amazon for a penny), so I am grateful also to Katya Covrett and Zondervan for inviting me to bring it back to life by updating it once more and adding chapters on the rest of the book of Daniel, and to Nancy Erickson for her meticulous editing of the final text.

Two further comments need to be made.

First, this is not a commentary on the book of Daniel. There are a good number of excellent commentaries on the book, with detailed exegesis of the complex text and thorough exploration of all the issues that the book raises. Anyone wanting to study Daniel in depth needs to go to those sources. The book in your hands had its origin in preaching, and it retains much of that style, though now smoothed out in written form. It tries, as expository preaching should do, to be faithful to the thrust and purpose of the text, to explain what needs to be explained (and omit what doesn't—always a subjective judgment), and to explore what response to the text is appropriate for us in our own historical and cultural context.

Second, this book takes no position on the critical questions of the unity of Daniel, or the dating of its later chapters, or of the book as a whole. Clearly the entire book is intended to be an encouragement to God's people in the midst of hostile and threatening cultures and to affirm God's sovereign control of all that happens, even as fallen human beings "do as they please" in exercising their own rebellious wills in opposition to God and his people. So I have sought to read and expound the book from within its own perspective and from the angle of its own visions. Those who want to explore the scholarly debate over whether the visions of the later chapters are truly predictive or a prophetic interpretation of past and present events need to consult larger commentaries.

Among the most helpful and thorough in recent years are:

Baldwin, Joyce. *Daniel: Tyndale Old Testament Commentaries.* Leicester: Inter-Varsity Press; Downers Grove, IL: InterVarsity Press, 1978;

Goldingay, John E. *Daniel*. Word Biblical Commentary 30. Dallas: Word, 1989;

Lucas, Ernest C. *Daniel*. Apollos Old Testament Commentary. Leicester: Apollos, 2002;

Wells, Samuel and George Sumner. *Esther and Daniel*. Brazos Theological Commentary on the Bible. Grand Rapids: Brazos, 2013.

At a more popular level of exposition, similar to this book, I have found the following helpful:

Wallace, Ronald S. *The Message of Daniel: The Lord is King*. The Bible Speaks Today. Leicester: Inter-Varsity Press, 1979;

Fernando, Ajith. *Spiritual Living in a Secular World: Applying the Book of Daniel Today*. London: Monarch, 2002;

Reid, Andrew. *Kingdoms in Conflict: Reading Daniel Today*. Sydney: Aquila Press, 1993.

INTRODUCTION

After giving up my childhood attempts to learn the piano properly, I found as a teenager that I could play it by ear. I used to play the piano for all the songs and choruses in our Belfast church youth group in the early sixties—murdering most of the tunes and straining most of the singers by playing them all in the only two or three keys I had mastered. One old song was very popular and very easy for a ham pianist like me to play, "This World Is Not My Home."[1]

I enjoyed playing the catchy tune, but that was partly because it got me out of having to sing the words. Because, frankly, I didn't like them at all. They seemed sloppy and only half true. They seemed sheer escapism to my youthful idealism. This world *is* my home, I remember thinking, and God has put me here for a purpose. So the angels can go and beckon somebody else if they want. I'm staying.

And yet, of course, the song is partly right. This world *is* alien territory for the Christian in one sense: not planet earth itself, which is part of God's good creation and very much the home that God intended for us in creation, but "the world" as it is sometimes described in the Bible, the world of humanity organized without reference to God and in rebellion against him; the world as a place of fallenness and curse, of evil and sin. *That* is the world from which we have been saved and yet in which we still have to live. That is the world in which we should not "feel at home."

So in a sense, yes, we are "a-passing through" that world of sin and rebellion against God. The language of pilgrimage has a good pedigree in the Bible. We are on a journey to somewhere better, though the Bible describes it as not just heaven up above when you die but

1. Jim Reeves, "This World Is Not My Home" in *We Thank Thee* (RCA, 1962).

as a whole new creation, a new heaven and a new earth. So we are living *in* this world but in the light of a destiny that lies beyond it, a new world liberated from the curse of sin and evil, a world in which we can truly be at home as God intended.

The New Testament puts a sharp edge on this tension by talking about the kingdom of God in contrast and conflict with the kingdom of Satan or the kingdoms of this world. This is the primary tension that the Christian has to live with. We are "in the world but not of it"—at home in the world because it is still God's world yet alienated from the world because the world itself is so alienated from God.

How then can the believer live as a citizen of the kingdom of God while having to live in an earthly kingdom? More specifically, how can the believer witness to his or her faith (or preserve it at all) in the midst of an alien and non-Christian culture, whether that means the culture of some other religion (e.g., in Islamic countries) or the culture of the secular, increasingly pagan West? Especially, how can the believer do this if it involves a high cost in misunderstanding, suffering, threat, or even death?

I have been told by some Christians in India, in all seriousness, that it is simply impossible to be in business and maintain fully biblical standards of integrity. Whatever you may *want* to do, business simply cannot function without the bribery and corruption that goes on behind the scenes. Or quite openly, others have told me that it *is* possible but only with a lot of faith and courage. In some parts of India, Christians who refuse to participate in neighbourhood Hindu festivals or to contribute financially to them face personal intimidation and serious vandalism against their homes and property.

Teachers in Britain point to the climate of hostility and sometimes the threat of disciplinary action that hangs over any overt Christian faith commitment that can be smeared with charges of indoctrination or intolerance. Any kind of Christian commitment is now assumed to imply intolerance, especially in the area of sexual ethics. And it is being openly said in the UK at present, by political leaders, that "we will not tolerate intolerance." I know a Christian woman who gave up her job when it became clear that among the expectations of her employers was that she should accept the sexual advances of business clients as part of the process of bargaining for contracts. In Northern Ireland, a bakery run by a Christian couple was condemned in court as guilty of breaking the "equality" legislation because they declined to bake a wedding cake for a same-sex couple with the words "Support Gay Marriage" iced on the top. It may mean the loss of their business if they cannot operate in accordance with their conscience. Many more examples of this kind of low-grade hostility and exclusion could be given. And of course they are pin-pricks in comparison with the vicious and murderous assaults on Christian believers in Pakistan, Nigeria, Kenya, Egypt, Syria and Iraq, and elsewhere.

Such issues are not new. Christians have faced them ever since Nero's lions and even before that. Jews also have faced the same questions all through their history, most tragically sometimes enduring horrendous persecution from states claiming to be Christian. So it is not surprising that the Bible gives a lot of attention to these questions. The book of Daniel tackles the problem head on, both in the stories of Daniel and his friends and in the visions he received. A major theme of the book is how people who worship the one, true, living God—the God of Israel—can live and work and survive in the midst of a nation, a culture, and a government that are hostile and sometimes life-threatening. And that will be our focus in this book. What does it mean to live as believers in the midst of a non-Christian state and culture? How can we live "in the world" and yet not let the world own us and squeeze us into the shape of its own fallen values and assumptions?

The book of Daniel, of course, has been used for many other purposes, especially by those with a gift for arithmetic and a fascination for describing the end of the world in advance. That is not our concern here. People who go in for complicated biblical arithmetic to make detailed predictions always seem to have to revise their sums. There are nearly as many versions of the meaning of all the numbers in the book as there are numbers. In any case the New Testament tells us that "the end of the world" (which is not really a very helpful expression) will be a surprising and unpredictable event, perhaps most of all for those who have it timetabled so precisely. In the 1970s there were many confident "end-times" predictions, based with clever plausibility on readings of Daniel and Ezekiel, that the Soviet Union would invade Israel, heralding the last great battle of Armageddon. We seem to have missed that since the Soviet Union no longer exists. But the "end-times" prediction industry rolls on regardless.

So we shall leave such future-gazing to the astrologers and magicians like the ones who cross the stage of the book of Daniel with such contemptible futility and wrestle instead with the questions of our life and mission as God's people in the here and now, as Daniel and his three friends did. The book was written to encourage believers to keep in mind that the future, no matter how terrifying it may eventually become, rests in the hands of the sovereign Lord God—and in that assurance to get on with the challenging task of living in God's world for the sake of God's mission.

CHAPTER 1

COMPROMISE OR CONFRONTATION

The world was falling apart. That's how it must have seemed to people who lived through the events that are summarized in Daniel 1.

> In the third year of the reign of Jehoiakim king of Judah, Nebuchadnezzar king of Babylon came to Jerusalem and besieged it. And the Lord delivered Jehoiakim king of Judah into his hand, along with some of the articles from the temple of God. These he carried off to the temple of his god in Babylonia and put in the treasure house of his god. (Dan 1:1–2)

This reads like a straightforward statement of fact, but it leaves a lot unsaid that needs to be filled in a little for the modern reader if we are going to feel the impact of the shattering events that lie behind the book.

CLASH OF EMPIRES (1:1)

It was just over 600 years before Christ. In the part of the world we now call the Middle East (though historians refer to it as the ancient Near East), a sprawling empire was falling apart. Assyria had ruled that part of the world for 150 years, a century and a half of strong, centralized, military rule which had submerged many a small nation in its ruthless conquests. The heartland of the Assyrian Empire was the region we now call northern Iraq and northeast Syria, the very region that at the time of writing is being dominated by the so-called Islamic State (ISIS or ISIL). And Assyria too had a reputation for harsh and uncompromising rule and brutal treatment of those it deemed its enemies.

Among the small nations that had been destroyed was the northern kingdom of Israel with its capital city, Samaria. That kingdom had been smashed and its population scattered to the winds just over a hundred years earlier in 721 BC. The southern kingdom of Judah with its capital city, Jerusalem, had been spared that fate back then, but it had been little more than a subject country within Assyria's Empire for well over a century.

But now Assyria itself was collapsing. The whole region was in turmoil (it seems that things don't change much in that part of the world). Rather like Europe in 1989–90, when the collapse of the Soviet Union led to the resurgence of the many states that had been part of it as they gained their independence, similarly the collapse of Assyria led to an upsurge in nationalism among small states like Judah.

However, there was a new rising power on the map. Babylon, under the energetic leadership of a youthful king, Nebuchadnezzar, was pushing upwards from the southern corner of the Mesopotamian valley. But on the other side of the map, the great western power, Egypt, sensed that the time was right for an attempt to reestablish their former dominance of the region. So in 609 BC, the Egyptian king, Pharaoh Neco, marched with his army up through Palestine with the intention of helping Assyria against this new Babylonian threat.

Now the king in Judah at the time was Josiah. And Josiah was already taking actions to assert Judah's independence from Assyria. So he had no desire to see any delay in the much longed-for collapse of the hated Assyrian Empire. So Josiah marched out with his own army to try to stop Pharaoh Neco coming to the assistance of Assyria. It was a well-intentioned but futile gesture. His hopelessly outnumbered army met the Egyptians at Megiddo (near Mount Carmel) and was defeated. Josiah himself was slain in the battle. Pharaoh Neco captured Josiah's son and heir, Shallum (also called Coniah), and deported him off to Egypt. Neco then installed Jehoiakim on the throne in Jerusalem. That is the king mentioned here in Daniel 1:1. He began his reign in 609 BC effectively as a vassal to Egypt, though that did not last long.

Nebuchadnezzar thwarted Egypt's attempt to strip the dying carcass of the Assyrian Empire. He conclusively defeated Egypt at the battle of Carchemish in 605 BC. As a result of that battle, Babylon became the dominant power in Mesopotamia and the whole of West Asia and remained so for about the next seventy years. You can read the short account of this period of Israel's history in 2 Kings 23:29–35.

So it was the end of an era and the beginning of a new one. Smaller states in the region had to submit to Babylon's authority, and Judah was one of those small states. Shortly after his victory at Carchemish, Nebuchadnezzar came south and threatened Jerusalem. On that occasion he took a small number of captives off to Babylon, probably as hostages to ensure the good behaviour of this new vassal state.

Among these early exiles were Daniel and his three friends, who must have been only young teenagers at the time. Probably they would have been in training for religious or government service in Jerusalem. They would have expected to find employment serving the government of the God of Israel in the city of David. Instead, without warning they found themselves a thousand miles from home, torn away from everything they knew and dumped down in a pagan, gentile, enemy state. All around them were foreign people, a strange language, an alien culture, and worst of all, gods and idols galore. It must have been a horrifying and traumatic experience for those boys. Worse was to come within a few years of the events described in Daniel 1:1–2.

In 597 BC Jehoiakim rebelled against Babylon. As Nebuchadnezzar approached the city bent on retribution, Jehoiakim conveniently died (or was murdered). His son, the next king, Jehoiachin, wisely surrendered to Nebuchadnezzar, which spared the city but not himself. Nebuchadnezzar took Jehoiachin off into exile in Babylon along with a number of the key leadership of the country, the so-called First Deportation (though strictly speaking, in light of the smaller one in 605 BC, it was the second). Among that group of exiles was a young man called Ezekiel, whom God would call to be a prophet five years later.

Nebuchadnezzar installed Zedekiah as king in Jerusalem, expecting him to behave more wisely. Sadly, he did not. Ten years later, against the warnings and advice of Jeremiah, he rebelled yet again. This time Nebuchadnezzar spared nothing and nobody. He besieged Jerusalem, and after eighteen months of great suffering, starvation, and disease, his army broke through the walls in 587 BC and poured into the city, slaughtering as they went. They looted the temple, then burnt it. They destroyed and burnt the City of David, reducing it to rubble and ashes. And then they dragged a large proportion of the people off into exile, including King Zedekiah. Only the poorest people were allowed to remain in the land, including Jeremiah. And in the end even they fled to Egypt. It was the most traumatic event in the whole of Old Testament history, and the awful horror of it is memorialized in the sobbing poetry of Lamentations.

FAITH IN THE MIDST OF A HISTORICAL CRISIS (1:2)

Why had all this happened? Verse 2 gives a breathtakingly blunt answer: "the Lord"—that is, Yahweh, the God of Israel—"delivered Jehoiakim king of Judah into [Nebuchadnezzar's] hand."

God Did It!

Well of course he did, we say. We know that, because we've read the prophets and they kept telling the people of Israel that God was going to punish them through their enemies. We can look back on the story with the benefit of hindsight. The fall of Jerusalem? The exile? God's judgment finally executed after multiple warnings.

But in Judah at the time most of the people had not read the prophets. And even when they had the opportunity to hear prophets like Jeremiah, they habitually ignored them. Or rather, they preferred to listen to other prophets who had a more congenial message. So in the midst of the turmoil of politics and international posturing during that final decade of Judah's life and in the early years of the exile, it must have seemed baffling and inconceivable to many people.

They had a whole raft of questions as they tried to make sense out of current events. How could the God of Israel allow his people to be treated like this? Had Yahweh met his match? Had he grown old and weak? Were the gods of Babylon actually younger and stronger? Would it not be more sensible then to go with the flow and switch to worshipping the gods of Babylon? Or if, as Jeremiah claimed, it really was Yahweh who had done this to his own people, wasn't he being unfair and unjust? (Ezekiel tackled this complaint in Ezek 18). And even if they did deserve the judgment in some way because of their covenant-breaking sin, was the punishment not altogether too severe, way beyond the bounds of what could be endured, let alone accepted? That is the mood of Lamentations.

And, perhaps the hardest question facing those who did accept the word of the prophets (that God had indeed done this), was there now any hope for the future? If God had poured out his judgment on Israel, was there anything left to look forward to? If the covenant had been broken, was it beyond repair? Was this really the end of Israel as the people of Yahweh God?

And what about God's purposes *through* Israel? The Israelites believed that God had made them into a nation in order for them to be the means by which the rest of the nations would come to experience God's blessings. This was built into the promise God had made to Abraham (Gen 12:1–3), and it was the reason why God had built up such a close relationship with Israel. This was the point of the presence of God in his temple and the deeper meaning of all the holy objects which formed part of its furniture. God was the *God of Israel* in order that he could ultimately show he was *God of all the earth*. Many of the psalms sung in the temple celebrated this belief. So what were the people to make of the fact that these very objects associated with the worship of the living God had been taken off by a pagan king and, worse still, been placed in the temple of *his* god (v. 2)?

And that pagan temple was in the land of "Shinar." That is the Hebrew word that the NIV translates "Babylonia" in verse 2 (as noted in the footnotes). It was an unusual name for that region of the world, first used to describe the land where the Tower of Babel had been built (Gen 11:1–9). It was like some ghastly time-warp, as if God had put history in reverse and taken Israel right back before Abraham was even heard of, back to the land which God had called Abraham to *leave*. Something was surely very, very wrong. Everything had gone backwards. History seemed out of control. Had God himself lost control?

It seemed that an enormous chasm had opened up between their faith on the one hand and world events on the other, so that events seemed utterly to contradict their faith. And so they came to the final, crunch question: Is God really still in control? When catastrophe strikes, is God still sovereign? Are we able to accept God's freedom to act as he chooses, even when he does something that seems to contradict his own purposes or, at least, something that runs right against what *we* thought was his will?

It was not hard for Christians to talk about the hand of God in the collapse of European communist dictatorships and the fall of the Berlin Wall in 1989–90. It was not so easy, however, for Christians to understand why God allowed the Iron Curtain to be imposed in the first place by the atheist Soviet Union. It was especially difficult for those who thought the horrific cost of the Second World War was a price worth paying to free Europe from Nazi tyranny—only to see it being replaced by another tyranny that lasted even longer. How could such events be reconciled with the will of God? Where was God when so many Christians suffered under communist dictatorships?

If we believe that God has commissioned Christians to spread the gospel and that it is God's purpose that the church should witness and grow in every nation, how can we reconcile this with the fact that he allows so many countries to close their doors to Christian missionaries and to restrict or ban Christian activities?

When communist China expelled all Christian missionaries in the early 1950s it sent shock waves through the Christian church since

China was one of the largest "mission fields" of that era. I grew up in a missionary home in Belfast, Northern Ireland. Prior, my parents had been missionaries in Brazil for twenty years before I was born as the youngest of four siblings. And I am just old enough to remember the adults getting all upset and talking in hushed tones about the terrible things happening in China back then. If you believe that God wants mission to flourish to the ends of the earth, and if you believe that God is in control of the world, how can you cope when God allows mission to be squashed in the largest nation on earth? Well, looking back now, we can see that the end of *Western* missions in China did not mean the end of *God's mission* in China, nor did it mean the end of the church there. In fact, there are more Christians worshipping God in churches in China every Sunday than in all of Western Europe put together.

We can see all that *now*, but it was a shattering blow at the time. Why does God allow such things?

Today, the most ruthless threat to Christian presence in any region of the world is taking place in the Middle East (in the same region once ruled by Assyria). Christian communities that have lived and preserved their faith there for two thousand years are being brutally killed, or driven into exile, or humiliatingly subjugated. And yet again, we struggle to understand how God can allow such things to happen to his own people. How can we hold on to a faith that affirms the sovereignty of God? How and where can we discern the signs of the kingdom of God in the midst of such appalling suffering and loss?

I have many Arab Christian friends who live in that region. I wrote to one of them to ask exactly those questions. I wondered, in my email, if perhaps in fifty years' time we would be able to look back and see that God was at work even in the midst of the persecution, just as in China. One of my friends wrote back to say this:

> I believe that we as Arab Christians do not need to wait 50 years or so to see that God is at work. What is actually taking

place in the Middle East and North Africa in the midst of the tragedies of the so-called Arab Spring is really beyond belief. Please let me share with you some examples.

There has never been a serious attempt to reach out to Muslims who lived in the strict and fundamentalist areas of Syria. That was almost impossible to do by Syrian Christians due to many religious and political factors. But now, with over one million refugees, most of them coming from those areas, the church in Lebanon has been able to reach out to them with the gospel message. Not long ago I preached in a church in a town not far from the border with Syria where 80 percent of the audience were Muslims and some 30 percent of them have already committed their lives to Jesus Christ. One lady told my wife, "The most amazing thing that happened to us was not escaping the death and destruction in our city in Syria but finding the Messiah Jesus who has changed our minds and hearts."

Of course I am not suggesting for a moment that such opportunities for the gospel make the terrible events good in themselves. Evil is evil, and that is just as true of those who persecute Christians today as it was of those who destroyed Jerusalem in 587 BC. But we believe in the God whose goodness and redemptive purposes ultimately triumph over evil and can even cause that which is intended for evil to serve the cause of the gospel. It is the same faith as Joseph's, who could tell his brothers quite bluntly that what they did (and intended to do) to him was "for evil." But behind it all, God "intended it for good to accomplish what is now being done, the saving of many lives" (Gen 50:20).

The book of Daniel opens, then, with just this sort of contradiction between faith and facts. It goes on to show us the response of a few young men who lived through it, who nevertheless managed not only to survive but to adjust to the new facts and maintain the integrity of their faith. Their God, they were able to affirm, was still in control, even in a world that seemed out of control.

FAITH IN THE MIDST OF A PERSONAL CRISIS (1:3–20)

The international crisis that had engulfed their world also hurled Daniel and his friends into a cultural and personal crisis that tested them severely, even though they were so young at the time. They had to face not merely the fact of *living* in Babylon but also the demand that they enter the service of its political administration. This was due to Nebuchadnezzar's government policy.

> Then the king ordered Ashpenaz, chief of his court officials, to bring into the king's service some of the Israelites from the royal family and the nobility—young men without any physical defect, handsome, showing aptitude for every kind of learning, well informed, quick to understand, and qualified to serve in the king's palace. He was to teach them the language and literature of the Babylonians. The king assigned them a daily amount of food and wine from the king's table. They were to be trained for three years, and after that they were to enter the king's service.
>
> Among those who were chosen were some from Judah: Daniel, Hananiah, Mishael and Azariah. The chief official gave them new names: to Daniel, the name Belteshazzar; to Hananiah, Shadrach; to Mishael, Meshach; and to Azariah, Abednego. (Dan 1:3–7)

Nebuchadnezzar decided to give a cultural re-education to the cream of the populations he had conquered and then employ them in the service of his new and growing state. It may have been rather like the way the British Empire provided English education for an elite among "the natives" in countries like India, so that there could be a class of competent administrators to cope with routine civil affairs under the imperial government. It sounds generous, and doubtless there were some (as in British India) who were grateful for the education and opportunities they obtained. At the same time, of course, it also created distance between the beneficiaries and the rest of the population; it was a subversively privileging tactic that the imperial power could exploit to its own advantage.

Nebuchadnezzar was specific about the kind of people he wanted. They would be physically and intellectually equipped for service. Daniel and his friends had those qualities—qualities that would have destined them for the service of God and the government in Jerusalem but now, by the cruel twist of history, were at the disposal of the king who was soon to destroy Jerusalem.

Nebuchadnezzar's government service diploma course lasted three years and involved four elements:

1. Education in Babylonian Language, Culture, and Learning
2. Maintenance by the State
3. A Career in the Political Administration of the Babylonian Empire
4. The Substitution of Babylonian Names for Their Own Ethnic Names

For young Jewish men brought up in Jerusalem, it called for a huge cultural change and re-orientation. They must have wrestled hard with their consciences as they came to decisions about how to respond. Could they accept these new arrangements? Would they be compromising their faith in Yahweh or even committing idolatry by submitting to such a programme?

Did they have a choice anyway? Well, yes. They could have chosen the path of total refusal, which might have ended in martyrdom. Then they might have gone down in history among the long line of those who have died for their faith and convictions. It wasn't that they lacked the courage for such a course. We know that because later on, in Daniel 3 and 6, we find that all four of them on different occasions were prepared to die if necessary. But instead, we find that they accepted three out of the four requirements. Most sermons I heard on this chapter of Daniel in my youth emphasized the negative refusal, the courageous stand of Daniel and his friends. The preachers and Bible study leaders never commented on the remarkable degree of *acceptance* that they showed. Three times they said "Yes," before they said "No."

They Said "Yes" to a Pagan Education

They were to be taught all "the language and literature of the Babylonians" (Dan 1:4b). That is, they were to have a complete re-education in Babylonian culture and civilization. Now the Mesopotamian civilization was one of the oldest and most advanced of the ancient world. It had made great achievements in literature, mathematics, astronomy, and primitive science. But it was also riddled with all the features of polytheism, that is, a religion with many gods and idols. It was full of magic and occult practices. It was particularly obsessed with astrology and all the superstitions that accompany that ancient pseudo-science. So a Babylonian education was definitely a mixed bag. Much of it could be accepted as positive human achievement, but much of it, from the viewpoint of Jewish monotheism, would have been distasteful to say the least and downright offensive and idolatrous at worst. Babylonian education was based on a religious-cultural worldview that was fundamentally different at many points from the faith of Old Testament Israel.

Yet these young Jewish teenagers not only applied themselves to the study of it but even gained distinctions and got higher final results in their oral examinations than their Babylonian peers! That was in itself an amazing feat. The Babylonian language used a cuneiform script with hundreds of stick-like symbols, far more complex than their own Hebrew alphabetic language. It would also have been spiritually challenging since many of the texts of Babylonian literature would have been religious, full of the gods and rituals of Babylon.

And yet, our text tells us that not only did they work hard in their studies but also that God himself gave them the understanding of all they were learning. That is also remarkable. God helped them to understand things that were actually contradictory to what their faith taught them about God! They needed to know what the Babylonians believed; they didn't need to believe it themselves. There is surely a lesson there that speaks to the challenge of living as believers within secular culture. We need to understand the culture we live in without sharing its belief system.

> To these four young men God gave knowledge and under-
> standing of all kinds of literature and learning. And Daniel could
> understand visions and dreams of all kinds.
>
> At the end of the time set by the king to bring them into his
> service, the chief official presented them to Nebuchadnezzar.
> The king talked with them, and he found none equal to Daniel,
> Hananiah, Mishael and Azariah; so they entered the king's
> service. In every matter of wisdom and understanding about
> which the king questioned them, he found them ten times better
> than all the magicians and enchanters in his whole kingdom.
> (Dan 1:17–20)

The fact that in the following chapters we find them standing firm
in their faith and resisting idolatry must mean that their childhood
grounding in the faith of Israel was strong enough to cope with
Babylon's university course. They pursued their studies objectively
and critically. They could learn all that it had to teach them, but they
didn't have to believe all it assumed. They could master its content
without swallowing its falsehood. And the education they excelled in
gave them access to positions in society and government from which
they were able to have remarkable influence.

There is a line of thinking among some Christians that Christians
ought to have a completely separate educational system. It is said that
the secular, humanist assumptions on which our Western schools and
universities are built don't fit with a biblical view of truth. So we should
either educate our children at home or establish Christian schools and
universities where the whole curriculum would be structured on a
foundation of biblical convictions. I know people who believe this
and act upon it, and I respect their views. I'm sure there is a place for
Christian schools, colleges, and universities, if they truly know what
they are seeking to do. But I am not entirely convinced that it is the
only legitimate way to respond to the increasing secularization (and
paganizing) of the surrounding culture in the West.

It seems to me that what really counts is not to protect young people from the secular paganism of our culture by withdrawing them from all contact with it, but rather to teach them to exercise informed discernment so that from a position of strong faith and biblical knowledge they can interact with it and distinguish what is good from what is evil. *That* is the job of the Christian home and the church (and Christian educational institutions where appropriate), a job in which we sadly often fail. For how can Christians make biblical truth relevant to the needs and questions of our pagan culture unless they understand that culture as well as the gospel? This is what John Stott used to call "double listening," that is, we need to listen to the word of God and also listen to the world around us. We listen to God's word in order to believe it, submit to it, and obey it (or rather to obey God through taking heed to the Scriptures). But we also listen to the world, not in order to submit or conform to it, but in order to understand it so that we can meaningfully communicate and relate the gospel to it.

I have always been grateful that our children spent part of their education for five years in Indian schools, rubbing shoulders with Hindus, Sikhs, and Muslims, and then the next part in a British sixth-form (the two years of high school prior to university), mixing with the usual crop of agnostics, skeptics, and atheists (pupils and staff!) that one finds in a sixth-form. They brought home many a question to hammer out over our evening meal. They had to defend their own beliefs and stand up for their own choices and moral values, but I think they became better aware of the surrounding culture and better equipped to be salt and light in our secular world than if they had had an exclusively "Christian education."

They Said "Yes" to a Political Career

They knew that they were being groomed for government, but whose government? Not merely the government of a pagan nation, with its idolatry and its arrogance, but specifically *Babylon*, a nation which had already been the target of several speeches by Israel's prophets predicting that it was heading for God's judgment. They may well have heard the scroll that Jeremiah sent, predicting complete destruction for Babylon in due course, in Jeremiah 50–51! In particular, they would be serving Nebuchadnezzar, the king who had snatched them from home and who would soon attack Jerusalem again to finally destroy it altogether. How could they possibly betray their homeland and accept a job serving such a king and country?

Yet they did. In fact, they were prepared to regard their service of the government as a way of serving God himself—as they later told Nebuchadnezzar to his face when he was threatening to cremate them alive ("the God we serve . . ." Dan 3:17). Perhaps they drew encouragement from the stories of Joseph who likewise had served a pagan king. Or perhaps they reflected on how Obadiah had held high office under the reign of Ahab and Jezebel in spite of their blatant idolatry, apostasy, and wicked ways (1 Kgs 18:1–14). In other words, they were by no means the first faithful believers who found themselves serving a political government that had no such allegiance to the living God of Israel.

There are Christians who say that Christians should not get involved in politics. They argue that politics is an ambiguous world full of half-truths, corruption, and back-scratching; and if we know that the world in general and our nation in particular stand under God's judgment, what is the point of playing party games on a sinking ship? Again, I believe the Bible cuts across this kind of withdrawal syndrome. God rules the world, and Christians, if they are to be the light of the world, must be more than altar candles shining in church buildings.

I have a sense of gratitude and admiration for Christians who follow God's call to a life in the political arena, in its various forms and branches: legislature, executive, judiciary, or, like Daniel and his friends, in political administration. It is a job where a man's or woman's resources are stretched to the limit with constant demands on mind, body, emotions, and conscience. Rather than questioning or criticizing brothers and sisters in such roles, we should be praying for them and encouraging them in the paths of integrity.

They Said "Yes" to a Change of Name

Names don't mean as much to us as they did to the ancient world. In those cultures (as still in some traditional cultures today), your whole person could be bound up in your name, and certainly names could indicate ethnic and religious identity, as they still do in many parts of the world. So when Nebuchadnezzar insisted that all his new civil servants should have suitable Babylonian names, it was particularly costly for any Jew whose name included the name of his God—Yahweh or El—as these boys' names did. Daniel means "God is judge." Hananiah means "Yahweh is gracious." Mishael means, "Who is like God?" Azariah means "Yahweh is my helper." And it was even worse since the new names included pagan gods, adding further insult and indignity. For example, Abednego probably means, "Servant of Nebo," one of the gods of Babylon. Likewise, the Bel in Daniel's new Babylonian name was another of those Babylonian gods.

I can make this personal. My name, Christopher, includes the name of my Lord and Saviour Jesus Christ. It means "Christ-bearer." I am very glad my parents put Christ in my name and in my life. But suppose that when I went to India, one of the conditions of getting a visa had been that I must change my name from Chris to Krishna, the name of one of the many powerful Hindu gods. Would I have been willing to do that? Even if I had been willing, it would have felt horrible.

So we might have thought that *this* would have been the sticking point for these men. Surely to swop the name of the living God of Israel for the name of a pagan god was impossible for any Israelite believer! Yet once again we find they accepted this change. Perhaps, with the same kind of maturity that Paul called for in relation to idols, they knew that these gods were nothing and their names were nothing; so they could swallow hard and take those pagan names on their lips and on their lapel badges, knowing full well that the living God of Israel was not only still *their* God but the *only* God. Even so, it must have hurt quite a bit to do so.

So we find a remarkable degree of acceptance of the cultural change that had been forced upon them by the action of God in history. Already they were acting in ways which were in line with what Jeremiah later told the exiles in his letter to them (Jer 29), namely that they should settle down in Babylon; that they should live, work, build, and increase there; that they should *pray* for Babylon; and that they should see themselves not just as the victims of deportation but as those whom God had *sent* there.

So they chose to accept a surprising amount of cultural adjustment, even if it was painful and unpleasant. They did not withdraw into a ghetto. They did not refuse to compromise at all and lose their lives. And as a result of that tough but discerning choice, they were able not only to serve Babylon but in some ways to influence it and even to preserve the lives of their fellow Jews at a later stage, as we shall see in later chapters.

They Said "No" to the King's Food

But Daniel resolved not to defile himself with the royal food and wine, and he asked the chief official for permission not to defile himself this way. Now God had caused the official to show favour and compassion to Daniel, but the official told Daniel, "I am afraid of my lord the king, who has assigned your food and drink. Why should he see you looking worse than the other young men of your age? The king would then have my head because of you."

Daniel then said to the guard whom the chief official had appointed over Daniel, Hananiah, Mishael and Azariah, "Please test your servants for ten days: give us nothing but vegetables to eat and water to drink. Then compare our appearance with that of the young men who eat the royal food, and treat your servants in accordance with what you see." So he agreed to this and tested them for ten days.

At the end of the ten days they looked healthier and better nourished than any of the young men who ate the royal food. So the guard took away their choice food and the wine they were to drink and gave them vegetables instead. (Dan 1:8–16)

This is ridiculous! After accepting so much, why take a stand on a matter so trivial as food? When we see how much they *were* prepared to swallow, it's hard to understand why they couldn't swallow royal meat and wine as well. What made these four young lads with doubtless healthy appetites decide to refuse what must have been a pretty tempting royal menu every day for three years?

There have been many attempts to explain the reasons for Daniel's stand on this point. Only two kinds of explanation seem to make sense to me.

1. *The king's food would have been unclean* by Jewish Levitical food laws; or it would have been offered to idols before reaching the palace kitchen and so have been "contaminated." Either way it would have been offensive to strict Jews. This explanation says that Daniel and friends decided to preserve at least one symbolic token of their Jewish identity and monotheistic faith. The food laws of Leviticus were themselves symbolic of Israel's distinctiveness from the rest of the nations (Lev 20:25–26). Daniel and his friends could no longer live in a separate land among their fellow Israelites, but at least they could preserve a separate diet and so make a symbolic gesture, reminding themselves regularly of their true identity and commitment to their God. By refusing the king's food, they were affirming their distinctive way of life as Jewish believers.

A symbolic gesture may be very unimportant in itself, but in some situations it can have a powerful, and potentially dangerous, meaning. Splashing water on someone is a bit of fun at the beach on holiday. But if you do it in the name of God the Father, Son, and Holy Spirit, i.e., as baptism, by that simple symbolic act in some countries you could be endangering their life and your own. Singing songs may seem pretty harmless and ineffective, but the Negro spirituals were a whole category of songs that grew out of the oppression of slavery, many of which kept alive the hope of eventual liberation, often by symbolizing a future reality in poetic imagery for the present. Some Christians wear small lapel badges or brooches with a cross, a fish, or some other Christian symbol as a way of letting their Christian identity be known in an irreligious environment or workplace. They know that since it makes a silent statement about their Christian belief, it commits them to uncompromising standards of behavior. It may also get them into trouble. In recent years in the UK, Christians have lost their jobs for wearing a small cross, allegedly causing offence to people of other faiths.

Sometimes Christian convictions or a Christian conscience need such symbolic expression, even if the actual form of the symbol is of no intrinsic importance in itself. Sometimes the mere *fact* of taking a stand on something, of drawing a line somewhere, can be more important as a witness than the substance of the issue itself. Not everything that Christians have said "No" to is necessarily evil in itself (any more than ritually unclean food was evil in itself). But a principle or a quiet witness may be expressed at the point of refusal or non-participation.

As a student at Cambridge I was in my college's rowing crew. Normally we never trained on a Sunday. But on a few occasions our crew went to a regatta that was held on a Sunday. I declined to participate, saying that I was a Christian and did not want to play sport on Sundays. Naturally, this was not popular with the coach and crew since it involved getting a substitute oarsman to take my place for just one day. (Nobody, however, came along and made a film like *Chariots of Fire* about me!) My own convictions on the nature of Sunday observance have changed somewhat since then, and I am now more concerned about the abuse of Sunday by the forces of greed and profit through unrestrained trading than by physical exercise. So I would probably not take the same stand now, but I am quite sure I was right to do so back then in the context of my own Christian witness and personal conscience. It was a simple statement that, although I loved the sport and would happily sacrifice many things for it, there was something more important in my life than rowing, which in the world of a university college boat club was near enough to blasphemy!

In India the dominant Hindu culture pervades society and Christians often find themselves out of step with practices at work and in the neighbourhood, which involve the recognition of Hindu deities. Sometimes this may be as harmless as distributing sweets or scattering flower petals. It may seem very innocuous, but in Hindu culture such actions can imply honouring the gods. If Christians do not participate, it can give offence and can lead to ostracism or physical abuse. Indian Christians take different attitudes on the question of "where to draw the line" as to whether to participate in such social rituals or not. But wherever that line is drawn, and however insignificant the thing is in itself, Christians need to think through how they can preserve some indication of their distinctive faith in the midst of surrounding culture and religion. Daniel and his friends preserved the distinctiveness of their Jewish diet, if this understanding of their refusal is correct.

But there is another way of interpreting their action.

2. *The food would have symbolized "covenant loyalty" to the king.* This explanation focuses less on what the food would have symbolized from a *Jewish* point of view and more on what it would have symbolized to the *Babylonian* authorities. Those who suggest this way of understanding Daniel's decision point out that *all* food would have been technically unclean in Babylon, for Babylon was an unclean, foreign land. Wine, in any case, was not forbidden by the laws of Leviticus, and vegetables would have been as much dedicated to a god before preparation as meat. Also it seems that their vegetarian diet lasted only while they were being trained and was not a life-long policy, since Daniel tells us of a later period of temporary abstinence from meat which implies that he normally did eat it in later life (Dan 10:2, 3). So the objection may not have been based on the Levitical food laws.

In the ancient world, sharing the food of someone's table was sometimes a way of cementing a covenant bond between people. To eat from the king's table could, therefore, have been seen as declaring total dependence on the king and total loyalty to him. It may have been this implication—the vow of absolute allegiance and obedience to the king—that Daniel and his friends politely refused. This would also explain better the fear that Ashpenaz had for himself and for them if they stood firm on such a refusal. And it fits with a later reference to "eating the king's food." In Daniel 11:26 we are told that some people "who eat from the king's provisions will try to destroy him." That means, they had sworn absolute allegiance to the king (by eating his food), but would later turn traitor and betray him.

These four young Jews had already decided that they could and would serve Nebuchadnezzar and his state. Indeed, they would do so to the very best of their abilities. They would accept all the adjustments that the government required in order to be trained for that role. But they would not give to Nebuchadnezzar or to his state the ultimate loyalty and commitment that they could give only to Yahweh. *Covenant* loyalty was exclusively for God. It could not be shared with a human king, however tempting his menu and wine list.

In other words, Daniel and his friends could make a vital distinction (which so many Christians fail to make) between, on the one hand, recognizing that the king and his government were appointed by God (as Paul says in Rom 13)—put in place by God to serve his purpose for that moment in time—and, on the other hand, giving unquestioning "covenant" loyalty to the king. They would serve the state *under* God. But they would not serve the state *as if it were* God. They would "seek the welfare of the city" where God had put them, but they would not do so with the kind of idolatrous patriotism that silences all critique or questioning. They knew only too well that a man like Nebuchadnezzar might easily inflate his divine *appointment* into divine *status* and make absolute demands that they could not accept (as later happened). So they chose to preserve their independence of conscience, out of loyalty to their higher priority—covenant loyalty to Yahweh the God of Israel. The importance of this insight and the stand they took on the basis of it is fully vindicated later (Dan 3) when royal food became a royal furnace. The decision they made in chapter 1 sustained them when they had a far harder choice to make.

They could not have sung that virtually idolatrous hymn which generations in England have been brought up on:

I vow to thee, my country, all earthly things above,
Entire and whole and perfect, the service of my love;
The love that asks no question . . . .

George Orwell defined nationalism as the "habit of identifying with a single nation or other unit, placing it beyond good and evil, and recognizing no other duty than that of advancing its interests."[1] Or, in popular slogan, "my country right or wrong." That kind of idolatrous patriotism is akin to many other forms of loyalty which can conflict with ultimate loyalty to God himself. We can get sucked into an obsessive, idolatrous loyalty to political parties, to a sports team, to a commercial company, and even, in Christian circles, to a denomination, to one particular theological confession, or to one great and gifted leader who can do no wrong.

We need to watch our loyalties, commitments, and convictions and constantly submit them to critical examination in the light of our one final loyalty to Christ himself as Lord. Have I become over-zealous in a cause which has great value but is not the only Christian priority? Have I become uncritical in my support for a particular public figure or organization—secular or Christian—so that I find myself being defensive and excusing even blatant mistakes or wrongdoing? Is my loyalty to the company I work for a healthy desire for its legitimate and honest success in the marketplace, or an unhealthy blind acceptance of whatever it demands of me, whatever it may do to others, or to principles of truth and honesty? Are my political loyalties and opinions based on prejudice or self-interest rather than a truly biblical view of God's concerns and priorities? Am I allowing my mind to be "conformed to this world" rather than "transformed" into the mind of Christ?

So, Daniel and his friends took their stand courageously but also courteously. It is noticeable that they recognized that their stance on the king's food was going to create a huge problem not just for them but for Ashpenaz, their Babylonian supervisor. But they did not adopt

---

1. George Orwell, "Notes on Nationalism," in *England, Your England and Other Essays* (Secker and Warburg, 1953). His notes were first published in *Polemic* (October 1945).

a belligerent attitude, "We won't eat your king's meat and wine. Get over it. Sort it out yourself." No, they came up with an alternative proposal to help him save face, his job, and possibly his life. Even their act of refusal was clothed in grace and wisdom and commended itself to their boss.

If that was their habitual attitude towards this man (who, we recall, represented the government of the enemy state that had devastated their young lives), then it is not surprising that "God had caused the official to show favour and compassion to Daniel" (Dan 1:9). Even when, as Christians, we have to take a stand on something on conscientious grounds, it can and should be done as courteously as possible and with constructive suggestions. That may not resolve matters as much in our favour as it did for Daniel and his friends, but it is still worth the effort.

And so God vindicated their decision and action. Our chapter puts Daniel and his three friends very much front and centre on the stage of the narrative. But it is noticeable that God is involved in the story three times, and on each occasion the text says that "God gave . . . ." A literal rendering of the Hebrew reads:

- "*God gave* Jehoiakim into the hand of Nebuchadnezzar" (v. 2)—which speaks of God's international sovereignty.
- "*God gave* Daniel favour and mercy before the official in charge" (v. 9)—which speaks of God's personal sovereignty in Daniel's life (similar to Joseph).
- "*God gave* to these four young men knowledge and understanding" (v. 17)—which is surprising, as we noted above, since the object of their knowledge and understanding was the pagan culture and literature of Babylon.

And as a result of this exercise of God's sovereignty, from the battlefield to the classroom, we come to the last verse of the chapter, which reads, "And Daniel remained there until the first year of King Cyrus." (Dan 1:21) This is not just a footnote. It sums up both aspects of the message of this chapter.

On the one hand, it points to the overarching sovereignty of God in the span of history. Cyrus was the king of Persia who overthrew the Babylonian Empire about seventy years after Nebuchadnezzar had established it (which is why Daniel and his friends must have been very young lads when they were taken to Babylon). So, the empire that had destroyed Israel in the first verse of this chapter has itself been destroyed and replaced in the last verse. But Daniel survived, and so did his people, the people of Yahweh, God of Israel.

On the other hand, it points to the personal vindication of the faith and commitment of four individuals in the midst of the turmoil of their day, and the testing choices they had to make all through their lives from a very early age. They proved their covenant loyalty to their God under pressure and threat. God remained sovereign and Daniel remained faithful. So we learn two things:

- God is sovereign and is still in control of the world;
- God alone deserves our total loyalty against all competitors.

These are the two great truths which shine through this chapter and will go on echoing through the rest of the book.

HEAD OF GOLD OR FEET OF CLAY

Chapter 1 began with an international crisis and moved on to a personal crisis. Chapter 2 is the other way round. It starts with a personal problem but ends up on the stage of world history.

NEBUCHADNEZZAR AND HIS DREAM (2:1–13)

In the second year of his reign, Nebuchadnezzar had dreams; his mind was troubled and he could not sleep. So the king summoned the magicians, enchanters, sorcerers and astrologers to tell him what he had dreamed. When they came in and stood before the king, he said to them, "I have had a dream that troubles me and I want to know what it means."

Then the astrologers answered the king, "May the king live forever! Tell your servants the dream, and we will interpret it."

The king replied to the astrologers, "This is what I have firmly decided: If you do not tell me what my dream was and interpret it, I will have you cut into pieces and your houses turned into piles of rubble. But if you tell me the dream and explain it, you will receive from me gifts and rewards and great honour. So tell me the dream and interpret it for me."

Once more they replied, "Let the king tell his servants the dream, and we will interpret it."

Then the king answered, "I am certain that you are trying to gain time, because you realise that this is what I have firmly decided: if you do not tell me the dream, there is only one penalty for you. You have conspired to tell me misleading and wicked things, hoping the situation will change. So then, tell me the dream, and I will know that you can interpret it for me."

The astrologers answered the king, "There is no one on earth who can do what the king asks! No king, however great and mighty, has ever asked such a thing of any magician or enchanter or astrologer. What the king asks is too difficult. No one can reveal it to the king except the gods, and they do not live among humans."

This made the king so angry and furious that he ordered the execution of all the wise men of Babylon. So the decree was issued to put the wise men to death, and men were sent to look for Daniel and his friends to put them to death. (Dan 2:1–13)

The early years of Nebuchadnezzar's reign were very active (and this event comes in his second year, v. 1). He had to fight many campaigns to consolidate his new empire. There were several border revolts and other external threats. Somehow he had to build up his own personal prestige and stature as the new king of a new world power. It seems that all this generated in him an inner insecurity and fear, which manifested itself in troubled dreams.

A bad dream was a bad omen in ancient Babylon, particularly if it was a repeating nightmare, as the text hints. And it was especially bad if you couldn't remember it! The Babylonians had massive dream books, written by experts in interpreting every kind of dream you could imagine, but they were not a great deal of use if you didn't know the dream to start off with! The story doesn't make it entirely clear whether Nebuchadnezzar genuinely could not remember the dream (as is our own common experience) and wanted the magicians to tell him, or whether he could remember it perfectly well and wanted to test the abilities of his personal magic circus.

What is more interesting is the fact that God was involved in the subconscious life of this young pagan king. His advisors admitted that only gods could do what he was asking of them—to tell him what he had dreamt as well as interpret the dream for him. But Daniel later made it clear that the living God could not only reveal and interpret the dream but also that it was the living God who had put it in his head in the first place (Dan 2:23, 28, 45).

The God of Israel, who is sovereign over history and nations, who had up to this point only spoken through the mouths of his own prophets (with a few exceptions like Balaam and his donkey), chooses to reveal his plans for world history not to Daniel and his prayer-fellowship but to a pagan king who did not even acknowledge him (yet). It is remarkable how quick Daniel was to accept this turn of events. The attitudes of many of his contemporaries to all things foreign and pagan were much more hostile. Remember who this particular foreigner, Nebuchadnezzar, was. This was the man who had deported Daniel and his friends, and who, in a few more years, would destroy their city, Jerusalem, burn the Lord's temple, and deport most of the population to Babylon. How could God possibly talk to such a man? If God had revelation to give, should he not use one of his own people? The ways of God must have been as puzzling to the Jews of that era as they can be to us now.

In fact this story is only the first round of a series of encounters between God and Nebuchadnezzar in each of the first four chapters, which ultimately led to his "conversion" when he was willing to acknowledge the higher kingship of the God of heaven (by the end of Dan 4). Here already, God was at work in Nebuchadnezzar's mind through dreams which, once they were faithfully interpreted by Daniel, showed him his own place in history, told him where he had got his power from, offered him a true perspective on the empire he was so energetically building, and warned him of the greater power of God himself over all human empires on the earth. Quite a curriculum of learning, even if he was a king of more than average intelligence.

We need to remind ourselves, with appropriate humility, that the living God has made all human beings in his own image and can communicate with any person without the need of a translator or a contextualizing missionary. Jesus himself told his disciples that, yes, they must testify to him. But before, during, and after their human testimony, it would be the Holy Spirit who would be testifying—not in church, but in and to the world. We need not only to believe that God *can* speak in the hearts and minds of (as yet) unbelievers, but to be more alert to the signs of when he *is* doing so.

DANIEL AND HIS GOD (2:14–23)

> When Arioch, the commander of the king's guard, had gone out to put to death the wise men of Babylon, Daniel spoke to him with wisdom and tact. He asked the king's officer, "Why did the king issue such a harsh decree?" Arioch then explained the matter to Daniel. At this, Daniel went in to the king and asked for time, so that he might interpret the dream for him. (Dan 2:14–16)

As we meet Daniel again, the first thing that strikes us is that his refusal to compromise over the question of royal food in chapter 1 did not mean he had adopted a policy of total non-cooperation with the pagan secular power. He seems only too eager and pleased to help, though presumably the threat of execution concentrated his mind more than a little!

After all, Daniel could easily have taken the attitude, "Interpret your own dream, O hated king. Or kill us if you like, and then we'll be martyrs, but you still won't know what your dream meant." But as we saw in the first chapter, Daniel and his friends had not chosen the path of opting out, of pious separatism, or holy martyrdom. They were now qualified government servants, busy in the conduct of public administration, but they had taken a stand that preserved the distinctiveness and integrity of their faith.

Notice three things in this part of the story.

Daniel's Fellowship of Prayer

> Then Daniel returned to his house and explained the matter to his friends Hananiah, Mishael and Azariah. He urged them to plead for mercy from the God of heaven concerning this mystery,

so that he and his friends might not be executed with the rest of the wise men of Babylon. During the night the mystery was revealed to Daniel in a vision. (Dan 2:17–19a)

Another chorus we used to sing in our Belfast youth group was:

Dare to be a Daniel, dare to stand alone.

It is true that in a later story Daniel did have to face the lions alone (ch. 6), but in these early chapters we find that he and his friends had continued to provide support and fellowship for one another in their careers. Daniel may have been the spokesman and the one to put his neck on the line by going to the king, but he was not a solitary hero. He asked for and got the prayer support he needed.

These four young believers worked together. Together they had sweated through the years of their re-education, together they served the state, together they served God. So together they could support each other in keeping their heads, literally and metaphorically. And when they met to pray together, it was not just to escape from their day's work and have some nice, cosy fellowship. They brought the pressing problem of their public jobs into the presence of God.

I wish all church fellowship and prayer groups did that. So often home groups are mediocre because they float at the level where everybody feels comfortable and never really engage with the hard realities of the lives of the members. We can escape into intellectual Bible study, or into emotional worship, or even fervent prayer. But we can also leave our real lives with our coats in the hall as we arrive.

One of the best home groups I remember was one where we got down to discussing some moral issues that Christians face today. As we did so, one of the younger members, Alf, who worked at a tire dealer's, suddenly started talking about all the fiddles and underhand practices that went on at work. Receipts were tampered with; VAT would be charged but not recorded, and then pocketed; stock would disappear. How could he cope with such things as a junior employee? If he didn't join in the dishonest practices, he would stand out like a sore thumb. Worse, he risked hatred and ostracism by the other staff. On the other hand, when he went to the management (as he did once), he discovered that they knew perfectly well what was going on but chose to ignore it to avoid agitation and rebellion among the workers. So if he reported the fiddles, he would be in trouble with both his mates and with the management and would probably lose his job.

The group suddenly realised that issues of morality and integrity were no longer just a matter for philosophical discussion but were an everyday reality for Alf. Indeed they were putting him under considerable mental pressure and spiritual stress. We were not able to produce neat solutions to his dilemmas, but we were able to pray for wisdom and strength for him. From then on, the group made sure that people's real problems from work became part of our prayer time regularly. We also got the church pastor to arrange a preaching series on Sundays in which he looked carefully at social and moral issues in the public arena from a biblical perspective.

When we lived in India I used to get invited quite often to speak at seminars of Christian lay people in secular and professional life. I would take them head-first into the sharp-edged Old Testament teaching about integrity, justice, honesty—all the strong, ethical heartbeat of Israel's Law and Prophets—and challenge them as the people of God in today's world to see their mission as being called to live differently from the world around.

Then I would ask them to share the tensions and problems of living as Christians in Indian culture and society. It would all come pouring out: the pressure to give or receive bribes (which permeates society from top to bottom), the corruption and dishonest practices, the subtle incentives and not-so-subtle threats, the unscrupulous extortion, the alleged impossibility of being in business at all without participating in the black market on all levels.

On one occasion I asked a group of graduates in various professional jobs what their churches had to say on such matters. I asked what teaching they got from their pastors or what support and prayer they received from the fellowship of other believers in their church that could help them live as Christians in the non-Christian world. I remember vividly the hollow laughter and sheer amazement that the very idea aroused.

"Our pastors don't preach or teach about such things," they said. "Anyway, some of them are no better!" Some of them said that in any case they went to church to *escape* from the wickedness of the world, so they didn't want to hear about it there as well! Whatever the reason, it was clear that there was a gaping chasm between their everyday secular work with all its pressures and problems and their "religious" lives. They were getting no support, no prayer, no wrestling together, and no applied biblical teaching in their churches. No wonder they found it so hard to stand up as Christians and make an effective witness to the light of God's truth in the moral and spiritual darkness of their environment. That was in India. But I wonder if multitudes of Christians in so-called secular professions and work places in the West are any better served by their churches and pastors?

Daniel was able to stand before the king alone because he had knelt before God with his friends.

Daniel's Hymn of Praise

Then Daniel praised the God of heaven and said:

"Praise be to the name of God for ever and ever;
      wisdom and power are his.
He changes times and seasons;
      he deposes kings and raises up others.
He gives wisdom to the wise
      and knowledge to the discerning.
He reveals deep and hidden things;
      he knows what lies in darkness,
      and light dwells with him.
I thank and praise you, God of my ancestors:
      You have given me wisdom and power,

> you have made known to me what we asked of you,
>> you have made known to us the dream of the king."
>> (Dan 2:19b–23)

Not all prayer meetings are as successful as this one, at least directly. Yet all prayer meetings can follow the example of Daniel's praise here, just as they can learn a lot from a different kind of prayer from his lips in Daniel 9. This prayer focuses on God and his ways *before* coming to the personal point at the end.

It is always good to start in prayer where Daniel starts here, by affirming great truths about God. This was also how the early church prayed when they faced an equally life-threatening situation in Acts 4:23–31. Once you have done that, then everything else is put in perspective. Then the truth about God will take priority over our feelings about the situation. It is important for fellowship groups to learn to do this, otherwise they can become very introverted and sink into a kind of spiritual hypochondria; "Just look at all our problems, moan, moan." Or they can become little more than a sort of group therapy for the members, a shot of fellowship in the arm once a week refreshes the parts that the sermons can't reach.

But the point of a prayer fellowship is to learn dependence on *God*, not dependence on the fellowship; so God must constantly be exalted and put first. People must know how to affirm his power and ability for themselves and draw on it when they are on their own again. For even Daniel had to stand alone later when there was no prayer fellowship around him, as far as we can tell; but his prayer life survived and sustained him when he stared death in the face (Dan 6).

In his hymn of praise Daniel affirms two things in particular about God: first, that he controls history (v. 21); second, that he reveals his purposes (v. 22). Both of these truths are repeatedly demonstrated, in stories and in visions, throughout the rest of the book. God acts and God speaks. God is neither impotent nor silent.

Our world doesn't believe that. Even those who like to think they believe in God don't always want this kind of God—the true living God of the Bible. An opinion poll I heard about once asked people if they believed in the God who acts in history. One reply was "No, just the ordinary one." Nebuchadnezzar didn't know it, but by asking to have his dream read, he was asking for an encounter with the God who is very different from "the ordinary God." And he was changed by it, eventually. In our Western churches we see so little dynamic change in people and in situations because we have lost the habit of affirming the greatness of God in any meaningful way.

But Daniel also realized that the God he was affirming was also the God who loved to share himself. Notice how the things he says about God are the same things that he claims God has given him: ". . . wisdom and power are his" (v. 20); "You have given me wisdom and power" (v. 23). Now there is no arrogance in this, no blasphemy. This is simply a statement of fact. Daniel acknowledged that any skill and ability he possessed was his by gift. He admits the same to Nebuchadnezzar in verse 30. It took him a long time to persuade Nebuchadnezzar of the same truth in his own case.

Jesus promised all the resources of the Holy Spirit to his disciples. He promised that we would do the same (indeed greater) works as he did. Wisdom and strength are there for the asking (Jas 1:5, 2 Cor 12:9, 10). But they come from God, not our own intelligence or achievement. And that brings us to our third point.

Daniel's Ability and Its Source

Arioch took Daniel to the king at once and said, "I have found a man among the exiles from Judah who can tell the king what his dream means."

The king asked Daniel (also called Belteshazzar), "Are you able to tell me what I saw in my dream and interpret it?"

Daniel replied, "No wise man, enchanter, magician or diviner can explain to the king the mystery he has asked about, but there is a God in heaven who reveals mysteries. He has shown King Nebuchadnezzar what will happen in days to come. Your dream and the visions that passed through your mind as you were lying in bed are these:" (Dan 2:25–28)

There was a British television commercial for the Automobile Association which portrayed motorists in various states of distress and incompetence when their cars had broken down. The crunch question comes from a passenger, who asks the driver, "Can you fix it?" To which the desolate answer is "No," followed by a cheerful, "But I know a man who can!" Enter the AA man and all is saved.

Daniel's answer to Nebuchadnezzar is on the same classic lines.

Nebuchadnezzar: "Can you tell me what I saw and explain it . . . ?"
Daniel: "No! But I know a God who can!"

Daniel's answer was not, "Sure! Me and my mates down at the Jewish fellowship group have worked it all out easy." But rather, "Nobody can do what you ask. BUT, there is a God in heaven . . . ."

During the 1992 parliamentary election campaign in Britain I tried to do my little bit to help one of the political parties in my local constituency. One evening I went with our constituency candidate, at the invitation of the staff, to a residential home for adults with severe learning difficulties. All kinds of questions were asked and issues raised, and we did our best to answer them patiently and explain the differences between the parties. We realized that for all their learning difficulties, these good people had a grasp of some key political issues and some sharp insights into what was right or wrong.

One young lady, Shirley, had a long list of matters to raise, every one of which concluded with the question, "What can we do about it?"

- There was the lack of a minibus for the institution to use: "What can we do about it?"
- There were no traffic lights on their road: "What can we do about it?"
- There were too few staff: "What can we do about it?"

- She didn't like the word "Disabled" on her bus pass; "What can we do about it?"
- She and her friends got insulted on the streets: "What can we do about it?"

Shirley was most persistent, but it left the candidate and myself feeling more than a little impotent under the onslaught of questions. We could suggest this and advise that, but in the end it was all beyond our power to do anything very much. We didn't have the authority or the ability to "do anything about it." We would try to persuade those who did have such authority, but there was nothing much else we could "do about it." In all honesty, to her question "What can we do about it?" we should have answered, "Nothing." But we could have added, "But we know some people who can—if they choose to."

Among the themes and plots of the book of Daniel, there is this ongoing pressure from God on Nebuchadnezzar to force him to see where *real* power and ability are to be found. The motif of "who is able" comes several times:

- In this chapter Nebuchadnezzar asks if Daniel is able, and Daniel says only God is able.
- In Daniel 3 Nebuchadnezzar asks Shadrach, Meshach, and Abednego if any god will be able to deliver them out of his hand, to which they coolly answer, Yes, their God is able.
- And in Daniel 6 another king, Darius, asks Daniel if his God had been able to save him from the lions. And Daniel answers (more or less)—"Of course!"

Nebuchadnezzar finally had to acknowledge that real power lay not in himself, not even in a golden dream statue of his empire, nor in his magicians, nor in all the splendour of his court, nor in his military machine, nor in his gleaming golden obelisk in chapter 3—but with the God of this young Jewish captive, a God he thought he had defeated and captured but a God who was in reality "the God of heaven" and very much the God of earth as well.

This God, the God of Daniel, is able.

By the end of this chapter Nebuchadnezzar goes so far as to admit this, within the limited context of the remedy for his insomnia. He can see that God is the source of Daniel's ability. But we can see even more clearly that between the truth that "God is able" and the fact that "Daniel was able" (Dan 2:47), lies the life of prayer and the supportive fellowship that upheld Daniel and his friends in their daily working lives.

GOD AND HIS KINGDOM (2:24–49)

So at last, after considerable suspense (as in all good storytelling), we find out what this dream was and what it meant.

> "Your Majesty looked, and there before you stood a large statue—an enormous, dazzling statue, awesome in appearance. The head of the statue was made of pure gold, its chest and arms of silver, its belly and thighs of bronze, its legs of iron, its feet partly of iron and partly of baked clay. While you were watching, a rock was cut out, but not by human hands. It struck the statue on its feet of iron and clay and smashed them. Then the iron, the clay, the bronze, the silver and the gold were all broken to pieces and became like chaff on a threshing floor in the summer. The wind swept them away without leaving a trace. But the rock that struck the statue became a huge mountain and filled the whole earth." (Dan 2:31–35)

Nebuchadnezzar's dream was weird: a great statue, a mixture of shining glory and crazy instability. It was full of inner contradictions by being made partly of costly and useful metals but partly of a stupid and impossible mixture of metal and pottery. And the weakest part was at the place where it most needed to be strongest—at its feet; all that gleaming glory above, but on a fragile, crumbling base below.

And then came the rock, a rock that he somehow knew in his dream had not been quarried by mere mortals. So where had it come from? And as it smashed into the feet of clay, the whole statue collapsed; but it didn't just fall, it crumbled to dust and was blown away in the wind, like the corpse of Dracula at the end of the movie. The rock, however, like some living monster, grew ever bigger till it filled the earth. This is the stuff that science fiction and horror movies are made of.

No wonder Nebuchadnezzar was troubled. What was the dream about?

If the dream was about him, then which part was he supposed to play? Perhaps the statue meant his enemies, and he would be the rock who would smash them all and take over worldwide power. Wonderful!

But supposing the statue were his own empire! Was it really so fragile? Were his people such an impossible mixture of races that they would end up falling apart? And who or what was this smashing, pulverizing rock? Was there some unknown enemy lurking on his borders about to invade and bring his whole empire crashing down to dust? What could it all mean?

Daniel then moves on to interpret the dream for Nebuchadnezzar, no doubt to the king's relief and the readers' as well.

> "This was the dream, and now we will interpret it to the king. Your Majesty, you are the king of kings. The God of heaven has given you dominion and power and might and glory; in your hands he has placed all mankind and the beasts of the field and the birds in the sky. Wherever they live, he has made you ruler over them all. You are that head of gold.
>
> "After you, another kingdom will arise, inferior to yours. Next, a third kingdom, one of bronze, will rule over the whole earth. Finally, there will be a fourth kingdom, strong as iron—for iron breaks and smashes everything—and as iron breaks things to pieces, so it will crush and break all the others. Just as you saw that the feet and toes were partly of baked clay and partly of iron, so this will be a divided kingdom; yet it will have some of

the strength of iron in it, even as you saw iron mixed with clay. As the toes were partly iron and partly clay, so this kingdom will be partly strong and partly brittle. And just as you saw the iron mixed with baked clay, so the people will be a mixture and will not remain united, any more than iron mixes with clay.

"In the time of those kings, the God of heaven will set up a kingdom that will never be destroyed, nor will it be left to another people. It will crush all those kingdoms and bring them to an end, but it will itself endure forever. This is the meaning of the vision of the rock cut out of a mountain, but not by human hands—a rock that broke the iron, the bronze, the clay, the silver and the gold to pieces.

"The great God has shown the king what will take place in the future. The dream is true and its interpretation is trustworthy." (Dan 2:36–45)

Daniel's interpretation is nothing less than a theology of history. It is not, however, a *timetable* for history. People get bogged down trying to identify and date all the parts of his interpretation, which the text does not do, and then miss its real significance.

Daniel starts in the present and then moves on to the future. In the present, he states a simple matter of fact and then gives a theological interpretation of it. "You, O king," he says to Nebuchadnezzar, "are the king of kings."

Now, to us who are used to that phrase as an expression of praise to God, this sounds a bit over the top, maybe even blasphemous. But no, it was a simple fact. Nebuchadnezzar was the great king over a number of smaller states whose kings had been forced into submission to him, Israel's own king being one of them. He was indeed a king over other kings. So Daniel begins at the top of the dream statue and affirms that Nebuchadnezzar himself was the head of gold. No flattery, just current political reality.

But then Daniel adds his theological insight. All this golden glitter, power, and glory belonged to Nebuchadnezzar *only because the God of heaven had given it to him.* Nebuchadnezzar was Top Man of the Top Nation by divine permission and appointment.

Probably Nebuchadnezzar already believed this in a kind of way. Ancient kings tended to attribute their power to their gods since it bolstered their reign by giving it an air of divine approval. So Nebuchadnezzar would not have objected to the view that he was where he was by the gift of the gods of Babylon. But there is no doubt that Daniel himself, when *he* used the expression "the God of heaven," meant by it *Yahweh, his* God, the God of his people, and the only true and living God.

The God of Israel had given supreme power to the king of Babylon! That must have sounded richly ironic, given the position of the two peoples—Israel in captivity and Babylon in power. So the humble government servant declares that it is *his* God who has given the most powerful man in the empire his status as "the head of gold!"

Exactly the same understanding of contemporary history was expressed by Jeremiah. There was a notorious occasion when Jeremiah gate-crashed an international diplomatic conference in Jerusalem, at which all the ambassadors of the small states around Judah had met to plan rebellion against Nebuchadnezzar. Wearing a yoke around his neck as a symbolic gesture, Jeremiah told all those foreign diplomats that Yahweh the God of Israel had given authority to Nebuchadnezzar and the only safe course was for all their countries to submit to him.

> With my great power and outstretched arm I [Yahweh] made the earth and its people and the animals that are on it, and I give it to anyone I please. Now I will give all your countries into the hands of my servant Nebuchadnezzar king of Babylon; I will make even the wild animals subject to him. (Jer 27:5, 6)

"My Servant Nebuchadnezzar!"

The very idea seems outrageous (and it would have been to the people of Judah at the time Jeremiah spoke it). But this was how Jeremiah and Daniel interpreted the events they were living through. It called for a great depth of faith and a broad view of God's sovereignty to do so. Think of the tragic events they were submerged in. Think of the national hatred of a figure like Nebuchadnezzar. Think of the unpopularity of anyone who could stand up and call him Yahweh's servant or a "head of gold." But God's control of history and the mystery of his plans are wider than our prejudices. God had raised up Nebuchadnezzar to accomplish God's purpose at that moment in history, and for that reason Nebuchadnezzar was "Yahweh's servant," whether he knew anything about it or not.

For a generation since the end of the Second World War, we in the West were taught to believe that the world was divided into two. There was the "free world" and there was "the Soviet bloc" (the Third World was invented later). We knew whose side the angels were on. We were told that everything east of the Iron Curtain was "the evil empire." Whose side was God on? The answer seemed so obvious and numerous apocalyptic scenarios in books, comics, and films portrayed the final great battle of Armageddon being fought with the legions of communism all on one side against the forces of (self-) righteousness on the other.

Writing on this side of 1990, after the revolutionary changes which swept through Europe in 1989–90 as the grip of communism fell apart and whole countries gained their independence, it seems hard to believe and to remember all those predictions and "prophetic visions." But if we see the hand of God in that momentous era (as Christians of Central and Eastern Europe certainly do), then we equally have to acknowledge that the *human* trigger was Mikhail Gorbachev, then president of the former Soviet Union. God did not use any of the leaders of the so-called Christian West, though some of them liked to gloatingly claim that "we won the Cold War."

Yet where is Gorbachev now? Not only is he no longer a president, but the state of which he was president no longer exists! There is a divine irony, a sense of humour almost, that the grip of communist tyranny in Europe should be brought down not by the might of its enemies but by the policies of its own foremost head of state. "God moves in a mysterious way." He raises up human leaders, gives them temporary ability and power to set in motion processes and events which achieve God's purpose, and when they have fulfilled that role, he then sets them down and moves on. Nobody is indispensable. That is how it was and would be with Nebuchadnezzar.

Daniel then moves on to give a general outline of the scheme of history to follow, based on the succession of metals. He says these represent a succession of kingdoms to follow Babylon. No identification is given and we need not pause at this point to try to name names. The main points in what Daniel says are the following:

- *The power of the fourth kingdom.* It will be enormously powerful but will have an inherent disunity and instability because of its divided nature.
- *The fall of the statue.* This will be partly because of its own intrinsic fragility and instability. There is here a picture of the ultimate failure of all human power and arrogant claims. In the end all that human beings so proudly build, "tower and temple fall to dust." This picture of a series of governments coming to an end with the fall of the most powerful one could be illustrated from many periods of human history, including our own generation. The twentieth century saw the rise and fall of a "Thousand Year Reich," and a Berlin Wall whose builder announced would last a hundred years, just months before it was demolished. Another prophet put it like this:

  > He brings princes to naught and reduces the rulers
  > of this world to nothing. No sooner are they planted, no
  > sooner are they sown, no sooner do they take root in the
  > ground, than he blows on them and they wither, and a
  > whirlwind sweeps them away like chaff. (Isa 40: 23–24)

- *The arrival of the rock.* The fall of the statue was not just because it had feet of clay, but because it was struck and destroyed by the rock not cut by human hands. The statue crumbles but the rock remains, and in Daniel's interpretation this rock stands for the kingdom of God himself which will ultimately replace all human kingdoms.

Although Daniel describes this rock only briefly, his words are powerfully prophetic of a number of aspects of the kingdom of God as we find it in the Gospels. This is why it makes sense to see the sequence of empires here (and in Daniel's own vision of four beasts in ch. 7) as portraying a symbolic pattern rather than a historical timetable with only one single "meaning" for each item. In the context of the book of Daniel (particularly in view of chs. 10–11), it is most likely that the fourth kingdom referred to the Greek Seleucid domination of Palestine and especially the reign of Antiochus IV Epiphanes in the mid-second century BC. However, from a New Testament perspective it seems that the fourth kingdom was viewed as the Roman Empire, within which the rock of God's kingdom "landed" in the person of Jesus of Nazareth and his proclamation of the kingdom of God.

Notice these points about the rock that foreshadow the kingdom of God in the Gospels:

1. *It comes from outside.* That is, this kingdom is not just one of the series of human kingdoms. It has its origin elsewhere. This is what Jesus meant when he said, "My kingdom is not *of* this world." He did not mean that it was purely spiritual or that it had nothing to do with political power. He meant it had its origin and source not from human power, but from God's power.

2. *It is established in the earth.* It replaces the other kingdoms, but it does not replace the earth itself. The kingdom of God is not just an escape to heaven but the establishing of the rule of God over the earth itself. Creation is restored to its true owner and king.

3. *It is the work of God* and is therefore indestructible. It will bring all human kingdoms to an end, but will itself endure forever.

4. *It will grow and spread.* There will be a *process* of its

establishment until eventually it will fill the whole earth. Jesus made the same point in many of his parables about the kingdom of God (e.g., the mustard seed, yeast in the dough, a net in the sea, etc.) And this, of course, points to the ongoing mission of God through his people in bringing the good news of the kingdom of God in Christ to people of all nations to the ends of the earth.

So Daniel gave this pagan king a theology lesson. His own personal power was a grant from the living God, but it would not last forever. The future held a succession of human kingdoms, but the future ultimately belongs to the kingdom of God. And that is a lesson that needs to be learned repeatedly in every generation.

For Nebuchadnezzar, the dream and its interpretation were meant to bring him face to face with the spiritual realities that lie behind the externals of history. This human king should see his own political power in the light of its transience. Neither he nor his empire were going to last forever. Heads of gold have a precarious future if they rest on feet of clay.

But there is a higher king and a more permanent kingdom. The question was, would Nebuchadnezzar acknowledge them? And to a limited extent, yes, he did.

> Then king Nebuchadnezzar fell prostrate before Daniel and paid him honour and ordered that an offering and incense be presented to him. The king said to Daniel, "Surely your God is the God of gods and the Lord of kings and a revealer of mysteries, for you were able to reveal this mystery." (Dan 2:46, 47)

However, one gets the impression that this was not so much the act of a man sobered by an encounter with the living God whose kingdom was like an invading rock, as the relief of a man who thinks his own power is not immediately threatened. In the next chapter we will see how he reacts to the thought that his kingdom was divided and vulnerable, by setting out to unify it by religion allied with patriotism backed by lethal force. A potent mixture that he was not the first or the last to exploit.

For Daniel and his friends, and for all those in their situation—believers caught in a hostile empire—it was a reassurance that their God was still on the throne. Their lifetime might be lived out under the thumb of a Nebuchadnezzar (to mix metaphors with his golden head), not to mention some of his metallic successors, but in the end the future was secure because it lay with God and the rock of his kingdom. They could live with the metals, knowing the rock was on its way.

And it is this same reassurance that Daniel 2 gives to Christians caught in the pressures of living in the midst of a pagan environment, where so much seems to be weighted in favour of the powers of this world with all their pomp and glory, their evil and corruption.

For what Daniel saw only as a vision for the future is now a present reality at work in the world. The reign of God has begun through the coming of Christ and in his death and resurrection. One day it will be established in all its fullness when Christ returns to claim his kingdom. Then "the earth will be filled with the knowledge of the LORD as the waters cover the sea" (Isa 11:9). Until then "God is working his purpose out as year succeeds to year,"[1] and every act of obedience, every word of witness, and every courageous stand for the truth is worthwhile and vindicated in the light of that future.

It is in this light that we must read the last few verses of this chapter.

> Then the king placed Daniel in a high position and lavished many gifts on him. He made him ruler over the entire province of Babylon and placed him in charge of all its wise men. Moreover, at Daniel's request the king appointed Shadrach, Meshach and Abednego chief ministers over the province of Babylon, while Daniel himself remained at the royal court. (Dan 2:48–49)

---

1. From the hymn by Arthur Campbell Ainger, "God Is Working His Purpose Out as Year Succeeds to Year," (1894).

The point is not merely that Daniel and his friends got a promotion but also that they continued in the political government service of a king whom they now knew to be a head of gold on feet of clay. They went back to work. They turned up at the office next Monday. They did not set up a community of spiritual hope to await the arrival of the rock. Whether or not they were able to continue to meet for their prayer fellowship we cannot tell. But certainly the strength they had derived from it enabled them to face an even tougher test in the future.

So we conclude by noting again the importance of integrating our working lives as Christians with our spiritual fellowship and prayer and holding on to God's call to both. Daniel and his friends probably experienced more revelations and visions from God than any average Christian home group is likely to get in a lifetime (and most fellowship groups would probably be quite happy not to have the kind of experiences and visions that Daniel's friends did). Yet the effect on them was not to stick their heads in clouds of piety nor even to set them up in glossy "prophetic" ministries. They didn't even go off to Bible college to develop their newfound spiritual gifts of prayer and prophetic visions of the future. They simply got on with the job they had trained for. They stuck to their desks. And God used Shadrach, Meshach, and Abednego (Dan 3) and Daniel (Dan 4) to far greater effect in their impact on the king than if they had thundered like Amos or blazed like Elijah. God needs prophets. But God also needs people who understand the prophetic truth and then get on with life in the world God has put them in.

In short, one might say that Daniel and his friends knew what story they were living in. They were, by necessity, living in the story of the statue, serving its head of gold. But they now knew (from the dream, although they would have known it already from their Israelite scriptural understanding of the rule of Yahweh) that they were living in the story of the rock, the eternal kingdom of God that would ultimately replace all earthly kingdoms.

So we need to ask ourselves, not just on Sundays, but throughout the working week and the whole of our lives in this world, "What story are we living in?" We too live within the story of the statue, in the sense that we have to participate in the history of this world with its successive human empires and regimes. But that story, like Nebuchadnezzar's statue, is fragile, broken, and vulnerable. Empires come and go. All empires have feet of clay. Some may last a few centuries, but many do not even survive the century they began in. Britain dominated the late nineteenth to the mid-twentieth century. America became the dominant world power after the Second World War. Will the twenty-first century see Western power eclipsed eventually by China? Or think further back. Spain and Portugal once ruled over phenomenally wealthy empires that controlled the whole of Latin America. Now they are among the poorer members of the family of European nations.

If we live only in and for the world's story then it is doomed to crumble. The statue has feet of clay. It will not last forever.

But we know a different story, the story that is at work even within that story of human empires. It is the story of the rock, the kingdom of God. It is the story, no less, of the whole Bible—the whole counsel of God as Paul called it (Acts 20:27)—the story of God's mission to bring people of every nation, tribe, and language out of all the empires that have strutted the planet into the new creation, redeemed and reconciled through the cross and resurrection of the Lord Jesus Christ. *That* story reaches its climax when "the kingdoms of this world have become the kingdom of our God and of his Messiah" (Rev 11:15).

God calls us to know the story we are in, and to invest in *that* story and its future. For the future ultimately belongs to the kingdom of God, which shall never pass away.

> *So be it, Lord; Thy throne shall never,*
> *Like earth's proud empires, pass away:*
> *Thy kingdom stands, and grows forever,*
> *Till all Thy creatures own Thy sway.*[2]

---

2. John Ellerton, "The Day Thou Gavest, Lord, Is Ended," (1870).

CHAPTER 3

BOW OR BURN

My daughter got a job during one of her student vacations as a kitchen porter in a fair-sized hotel. Kitchen porters do the lowest and least popular of the jobs in the catering department. Thrown in with quite an assortment of local humanity, she actually thrived on the hurly-burly of social chit-chat and arguments in the workplace. "It's really good when people get to know you're a Christian," she once said to me, "because it makes the conversation far more controversial!"

Well, that's fine! But it's one thing to enjoy a heated discussion over the stove in a context where the fact that you have some peculiar beliefs and opinions brightens the day for everybody. It's something very different if those convictions throw you into serious conflict in which your job itself and many other important things in life could be threatened.

It's all very well to take a stand for your faith when you are a young student, perhaps, like Daniel and his friends had been when they first arrived in Babylon. In student days it's almost the done thing to be filled with idealism and radical intentions and opinions, with the added luxury of being free from the responsibilities of family and career. You may risk some popularity for your religious opinions but not much more (although, as we shall consider later, even such youthful freedom is being constrained by a new form of intolerance).

Later in life, the realities of the world of "secular" work and business can squeeze a person's faith and integrity much more severely. How can you survive in the "real world" unless you go along with the ways of the world? It's not so much a matter of bowing to idols as bowing to the inevitable, surely. The world can demand a high price from those who refuse to do things its way. Peter makes exactly this point in 1 Peter 4:3–4.

Here we find Daniel's three friends, who had quietly stood with him in their act of conscientious objection to one feature of their re-education by the Babylonian state, now facing a much more threatening test of loyalty to their faith. This is no longer a matter of meat and wine. This is a matter of life and death.

The least that Daniel had done for Nebuchadnezzar so far was to cure his bad dreams. What he had actually tried to do was to confront him with the God who controls history and the future and make this young Babylonian king face up to his own place in the grand scheme of things within the purposes of God. Nebuchadnezzar was the head of a great empire, but there was a kingdom greater than his. And in the end, it would be God's kingdom that would stand the test of time when the rock of his nightmare had reduced all human empires to dust and rubble.

But Nebuchadnezzar was not ready to face anything like that, yet. It would have put his present status and power at the head of the greatest world empire in question. It would have debunked some of his golden dreams. By the end of Daniel 4 we shall find a very different Nebuchadnezzar singing a very different tune. But for the moment his agenda centred on his own plans.

Freed from the disturbance of his recurring nightmare, he set about solving the problem it represented. If the statue was unstable because of its fragile feet, Nebuchadnezzar decided to strengthen its golden head, himself and his young state. The shattering rock outside human control could be forgotten. If his empire had weaknesses caused by disunity (the feet being an unstable mixture of iron and clay), then he must create a united, harmonious people bound together by ties of political loyalty, religious zeal, and cultural pride. It was this decision, and the policy it led to, that caused problems for Daniel's friends, and doubtless other Jewish believers.

The issue now facing them was one which believers, Jewish and

Christian, have wrestled with all down the ages. What are the limits of patriotism? How is it possible, on the one hand, to obey instructions such as Jeremiah 29:7 and Romans 13:1–7 to seek the good of the country where God has put you, showing loyal submission and good citizenship, and on the other hand, to remain faithful to God's command to worship him alone? Is loyalty to one's own culture and country a good thing? When does it become actually idolatrous, that is, when does it take that place of ultimate importance that should belong only to God? Can we refuse to obey the state authorities and, if so, for what reasons? And can we expect God always to bail us out if we do?

These can be hard enough questions for believers who are ordinary citizens. For those who hold public office, in political life or in civil administration for the government, it can sometimes be a dilemma of literally life and death proportions.

THE CLAIMS OF THE STATE (3:1–7)

> King Nebuchadnezzar made an image of gold, ninety feet high and nine feet wide, and set it up on the plain of Dura in the province of Babylon. He then summoned the satraps, prefects, governors, advisors, treasurers, judges, magistrates and all the other provincial officials to come to the dedication of the image he had set up. So the satraps, prefects, governors, advisors, treasurers, judges, magistrates and all the other provincial officials assembled for the dedication of the image that King Nebuchadnezzar had set up, and they stood before it.
>
> Then the herald loudly proclaimed, "Nations and peoples of every language, this is what you are commanded to do: As soon as you hear the sound of the horn, flute, zither, lyre, harp, pipes and all kinds of music, you must fall down and worship the image of gold that King Nebuchadnezzar has set up. Whoever does not fall down and worship will immediately be thrown into a blazing furnace."

Therefore, as soon as they heard the sound of the horn, flute, zither, lyre, harp and all kinds of music, all the nations and people of every language fell down and worshipped the image of gold that King Nebuchadnezzar had set up. (Dan 3:1–7)

"The image of gold that King Nebuchadnezzar had set up." This phrase echoes throughout Daniel 3. The statue itself is very much center stage in the whole drama. It is unmistakably meant to remind the reader of the head of gold in Nebuchadnezzar's dream statue in the last chapter. We are not told exactly what this golden statue was an image of. Probably it was not any of the gods of Babylon, because they are distinguished from it in verse 12. So it may have been a stylized image of Nebuchadnezzar himself, or of his imperial power. It may have been a huge monument to the Babylonian Empire itself, "The Spirit of Babylon." It was certainly enormous, ninety feet tall and nine feet wide at the base, a gleaming, thrusting shaft of imperial glory and state power.

What was it for? It was not merely a token of Nebuchadnezzar's personal pride, though that was great enough. Rather, it was intended as a symbol of the unity and strength of the empire. We know from Daniel 1 that Babylon ruled over a great mixture of nations and peoples who are referred to in this chapter as "nations and peoples of every language." Nebuchadnezzar's plan was to produce some kind of imperial political unity by imposing a sacred ideology of the state itself—a national religion and culture—for official purposes. He would harness religious zeal and cultural pride (notice the emphasis on all kinds of music), a very powerful combination in any age. There would be no prohibition of the worship of other gods, of course. People could keep and worship the gods of their own nations and cultures, just so long as they gave priority to the official state gods of Babylon. One king, one empire, one official faith—all symbolized in that massive golden statue.

So then he arranged a massive festival of Babylon around the golden statue. It was to be a great unifying spectacular event perhaps lasting many months. It would both enable and enforce the kind of imperial loyalty and devotion that he needed to stabilize and strengthen his relatively young empire. It was an exercise in empire building. Let everybody publicly declare their allegiance to him, the great benefactor and father of the nation. Let all the ethnic groups in his realm keep their own culture and gods, but let them be subordinated to the common cult of the empire. Perhaps he arranged that all the musical traditions of the different groups would take it in turns to display their heritage, so long as it was all done in honour of his golden statue. It could be a great carnival of regional variety, but all for the glory of Babylon. That way he would allow for the expression of regional differences and local pride but harness it all to his desired imperial unity.

National unity, national security, national pride—these were the powerful driving forces behind Nebuchadnezzar's great, gleaming, golden festival. So Nebuchadnezzar's state declared its claim to total allegiance and called on every loyal citizen to acknowledge it.

And they did, as people still do when the drums and music of national pride begin to beat. From the top to the bottom of society they turn out to celebrate. There is intentional humour in the text's repeated lists of officials and of musical instruments. Everybody who was anybody was there. It was the place to be seen. It was noisy, it was festive, it was mesmerising, it was infectious. It was Nebuchadnezzar's Babylon. And such is the seductive power of such great, state-sponsored celebrations that most people were probably there quite willingly, gratefully even.

However, just in case, there was always the "blazing furnace" in the background. Not that it would ever be needed, of course, but state policies need state sanctions, and people should realize that the government is serious. "Bow or burn! Toast the king or toast yourself!" Nobody in their right mind would quarrel, surely.

Such, then, was the claim of Nebuchadnezzar's state. It has a familiar totalitarian flavor, the view that the state itself is the ultimate reality which governs the totality of the lives of its subjects and demands complete loyalty and obedience. It is a claim that has been echoed and repeated many times down through the centuries, right into our own.

Nebuchadnezzar was not the first or the last to link patriotism, religion, and culture for the political benefit of the state itself. In how many countries, ancient and modern, Western and non-Western, have we seen this combination? The state claims total allegiance and justifies it on grounds of necessity, for stability, for ethnic survival, for higher ideals even. And when the state begins to make such claims, it leaves no alternative except the furnace or its many equivalents. Under the Roman Empire, the cult of emperor worship had already taken root by the time of the early New Testament church. Rome had an even bigger problem with ethnic diversity in its far-flung dominions than Babylon ever had. So they called on all peoples, no matter what other gods they worshipped, to burn incense before a bust of the Roman emperor, acknowledging him as divine, and to make the "loyal oath"—"Caesar is Lord." Christians, of course, could not and would not do it. Lips that had confessed "Jesus is Lord" would not then utter "Caesar is Lord." They faced lions and other equivalent sanctions to the "blazing furnace" for their refusal.

The state is a human institution which seems to have a built-in tendency towards idolatry, to claim ultimate authority and demand total allegiance. This tendency flows from our fallen human insecurity. Having rejected God as the source of authority and security, we long for anything that will give life order, stability, security, regularity, and social glue. When a powerful state promises these things, we are prepared to pay a high price to buy such apparent benefits, or at least the promise of them. Or perhaps, more accurately, when the crunch comes, we are not prepared to pay the higher price of not buying them.

Western Christians are rightly grateful for the freedom we currently enjoy from such blatant totalitarianism. We are also acutely conscious still of the high price that was indeed paid to remove just such a virulent tyranny in Europe in the Second World War. But even after that, Christians in Central and Eastern Europe lived for two generations with the shackles of such a state ideology, in which, ironically, states that declared themselves officially atheist claimed the kind of loyalty and obedience that they condemned in theocratic states of the past. As those former communist states of Eastern Europe gained their independence from the Soviet Union, however, more thoughtful Christians among them wondered if they had exchanged the ideology of Marxist materialism for the idolatry of Western capitalist consumerism. Both can be blatantly idolatrous, and neither has any place for the living God.

But there are many other parts of the world where Christians live under regimes that demand loyalty to other gods or totalitarian ideologies, whether they be the remaining communist states in Southeast Asia and China or the increasing number of countries, such as Pakistan and Malaysia, where Islamic governments are reducing or removing the religious and civil rights of adherents of other faiths, even with states with allegedly democratic constitutions. And of course, we are witnessing the tyranny of the religio-political ideology and narrative that has spawned the ISIS-dominated region of the Middle East. Submission or death (or flight) has become the gaunt choice facing millions there.

Even in a country such as India, which is constitutionally secular, the weight of Hinduism is so great in every fiber of public and community life that it can be a very costly thing to preserve a distinctive Christian identity or allegiance in some places. The goals of some Hindu nationalist movements is certainly to achieve the sort of unity of religion, nationality, and culture that Nebuchadnezzar sought. There is, they argue, only one religion for the patriotic Indian. Any other religious allegiance is deemed essentially traitorous. Indian Christians are told that they cannot be true Indians while holding to a "Western religion," in spite of the fact that Christianity is easily one of the oldest religions in India, certainly older than Islam or Sikhism, and arrived there long before the conversion of "the West" (i.e., pagan Europe) to Christianity.

THE COST OF MONOTHEISM (3:8–15)

> At this time some astrologers came forward and denounced the Jews. They said to King Nebuchadnezzar, "May the king live for ever! Your Majesty has issued a decree that everyone who hears the sound of the horn, flute, zither, lyre, harp, pipes and all kinds of music must fall down and worship the image of gold, and that whoever does not fall down and worship will be thrown into a blazing furnace. But there are some Jews whom you have set over the affairs of the province of Babylon—Shadrach, Meshach and Abednego—who pay no attention to you, Your Majesty. They neither serve your gods nor worship the image of gold you have set up."
>
> Furious with rage, Nebuchadnezzar summoned Shadrach, Meshach and Abednego. So these men were brought before the king, and Nebuchadnezzar said to them, "Is it true, Shadrach, Meshach and Abednego, that you do not serve my gods or worship the image of gold I have set up? Now when you hear the sound of the horn, flute, zither, lyre, harp, pipes and all kinds of music, if you are ready to fall down and worship the image I made, very good. But if you do not worship it, you will be thrown immediately into a blazing furnace. Then what god will be able to rescue you from my hand?" (Dan 3:8–15)

The issue came to a crunch for Shadrach, Meshach, and Abednego, though probably not at their own instigation. It doesn't seem like they saw it coming. Three observations about this part of the story come to mind.

Uninvited

First of all, the text seems to suggest that this sudden conflict between them and the state government was *uninvited*. Their whole demeanour and comments when they are brought before the king suggests that they had in fact tried to avoid such a confrontation. Perhaps they had just stayed away from the festival and tried to keep their heads down. At any rate, there is nothing in the text which justifies the Sunday school flannel graph pictures I remember as a child in which we saw a whole plain full of millions of people, all bowed face to the ground like Muslims at prayer, except for these three men proudly and conspicuously standing upright in the middle. It seems far more likely that they did not adopt such a deliberate posture of defiance but simply chose not to participate in the musical concerts. That would fit better with their policy as seen earlier in chapter 1. There we observed their polite refusal to accept one particular detail of their training, against a background of remarkable cultural acceptance and adaptation on other issues. These men were not seeking martyrdom. They were not looking for any opportunity to parade their religious affiliation. They were not posturing to have a confrontation with the authorities. They were simply conscientious government servants getting on with their daily work, serving the empire without worshipping it. So the confrontation happened because they were denounced by others, not because they sought it themselves.

Unexpected

Second, we get the impression that this sudden test of their faithfulness to God was *unexpected*. That is what the story in the book so far would lead us to think. Surely, they must have thought, they had got this issue sorted out right at the beginning of their career in government service. They had declared their conscientious, religious objection to Babylon's "total loyalty" policy (in relation to the meat from the king's table), and it had been accepted. They had not faced any threats or discipline for the stand they had taken back then. They enjoyed a measure of religious toleration. And after that they had got on with the job they were trained for and, as far as we know, they had faced no further serious problem of conscience. Their Babylonian government service had not involved any compromise of their faith commitment to their God. Yet now, suddenly, they are hurled into a conflict with the king himself. Not only was it sudden and unexpected, it was also terrifyingly threatening—one minute a respectable and responsible job in high office, next minute hauled before the king and facing the flames of instant extinction.

Uninvited and unexpected. That is sometimes the way persecution suddenly arrives. Believers can never afford to relax. The tide of human politics can turn amazingly fast, whether for good or ill. The Israelites were comfortable in Egypt until "a new king, to whom Joseph meant nothing, came to power in Egypt" (Exod 1:8), and suddenly their privileged guest status became one of genocidal exploitation. David was a favored court musician one day and dodging javelins the next. Elijah was a public hero on Mount Carmel one day and running for his life from Jezebel the next. The crowds who flocked around Jesus to cheer him into Jerusalem with palm branches on the first day of the week were calling for his death by the end of the same week.

And so it has been through history. States which in one era have welcomed Christian missionaries have sometimes later turned to fierce persecution. America, a land founded by people escaping from religious intolerance, has lately spawned the unimaginably intolerant "Politically Correct" phenomenon. In Britain, laws originally designed to criminalize racial hatred and incitement to violence, and more recent equality legislation, have been used against Christians to penalize them for acting in accordance with their own conscience in relation to society's changing sexual culture and norms. Such intolerance has not taken the form of violence or death threats, but it has in some cases been entirely destructive of people's livelihoods.

We need to remember that we live in a world which, as a whole, is in rebellion against God. So even if we in the West live under substantially benevolent and tolerant political and social arrangements, it may well turn out to be a transient interlude in the great sweep of human history, induced by the relative acceptance of Christianity's worldview and associated values for a few centuries, rather than a permanent state of affairs. For most of history and for most Christians in most of the world, the lives of believers have been lived against the background of threats, intolerance, and varying degrees of persecution. Perhaps we in the West need to recognize our need to be prepared to face such things and to have the humility to learn from sisters and brothers in other parts of the world who have never known any other kind of life.

Returning to our three friends, the way things turn out now vindicates the importance of the stand they took earlier. At that time, in chapter 1, they had stood firm over what may have seemed a small issue. They had refused to enter into the kind of covenant table fellowship with the king that would have symbolized total allegiance and dependence. Way back then, in the early days of their captivity and of Nebuchadnezzar's reign, it may have seemed very remote indeed that Nebuchadnezzar would ever make such an absolute claim. At the time his policy seemed to have been to give relative encouragement to the different ethnic and religious groups in his empire. And in any case, they were from a conquered people, and from a Babylonian point of view their gods were subservient to his. The totalitarian claim of absolute allegiance, and what amounted to worship of the state itself, was not required of them back then, or at least they were able to find an acceptable way to avoid it.

But now that absolute, blasphemous claim was standing ninety feet high in the blue sky and they could not avoid it. And even if they tried to lie low, their refusal was noticed by others and professional jealousy soon did its work, as it later does again in Daniel 6. However, it was their *earlier* decision which strengthened *this* one. In their student days they had set the direction and the limits of their commitment in relation to a relatively small matter. Now that decision was tested by fire when the issue was far greater. "Whoever can be trusted with very little can also be trusted with much" (Luke 16:10).

Tempting

Third, we can reflect on how *tempting* the situation was for them. They were not, after all, being called upon explicitly to *deny* Yahweh their God, at least not in the eyes of the king and his polytheistic contemporaries. It was just a matter of a quick bow to Nebuchadnezzar and his statue. The dilemma posed:

Why insist on your strange monotheism at such a cost? Nobody is asking you to deny your own god—just accept that our god is superior, and salute the national symbols for the common good.

The argument has a very subtle persuasive force. It points up the utter contrast between true monotheism and all forms of polytheism. And in doing so, it also makes very clear the stark difference between biblical faith and religious pluralism.

The seduction of polytheism and pluralism is that they widen every choice and set no limits. Under pluralism you can tolerate anything, except, of course, the person who insists that there is only one true God. Then "tolerance" can lead to fiery furnaces. In India, the vast ocean of Hindu polytheism seems to allow for anything and to pervade everything. Because there is only one final reality, then all religious ways are deemed to lead to it in the end. So everything is tolerated *except* the view that there is only one way. Strictly biblical monotheism, and especially the conviction of the uniqueness of Christ as Saviour, are frowned upon.

It is thus very hard for many ordinary Christians to be truly and consistently monotheistic in practice as well as confession. The temptations and demands of the surrounding polytheism, seemingly harmless and socially expected, are part of everyday life. It is very hard to distinguish between what is "cultural" and what is "religious," since they are so closely intertwined and mutually reinforcing. Christians who take a stand for their monotheism and refuse to take part in activities such as dedications to Hindu deities in the work place or neighbourhood collections for Hindu festivals can find themselves facing ostracism, dismissal, violence to themselves or their homes, discrimination against their children, and even death threats. Loyalty to Christ alone can be costly, personally and socially. It is far easier to keep your monotheism in your heart and keep society happy with passing nods to the gods when required.

Doubtless that was how Nebuchadnezzar tried to reason with his three government officers. We can imagine that there might have been the man-to-man approach.

Let's not make a big fuss over this, gentlemen. Why be so narrow-minded and dogmatic? After all, I am your king. In fact, I am the one whom you claim was actually appointed by your own god! Did Daniel not tell you that I am the head of gold, appointed (so he believes) by your god? So surely even your god would expect you to demonstrate your loyalty to me and my statue, would he not? Be reasonable with me and I'll be reasonable with you. Why waste your lives for a futile gesture of religious intolerance?

But they would not give in, and prepared themselves to face the cost of the central, revealed truth of their faith: "The LORD is God in heaven above and on the earth beneath. There is no other" (Deut 4:35, 39).

THE COURAGE OF FAITH (3:16–18)

> Shadrach, Meshach and Abednego replied to him, "King Nebuchadnezzar, we do not need to defend ourselves before you in this matter. If we are thrown into the blazing furnace, the God we serve is able to save us from it, and he will deliver us from Your Majesty's hand. But even if he does not, we want you to know, Your Majesty, that we will not serve your gods or worship the image of gold you have set up." (Dan 3:16–18)

These are staggeringly impressive verses. The reply of the three friends to Nebuchadnezzar is calm, dignified, and confident, full of trust in God and yet not presumptuous before him.

The first thing to note is how they coolly deflate the king's arrogance. Look at the contrast between what he says at the end of verse 15 and the way they answer in verse 16.

"What *god* can deliver you from *my* hand?" he asks, as if to say, "I, Nebuchadnezzar, am better than the average god." It was a not too subtly disguised claim to divinity. Or at least it was an assertion that, as far as the present issue was concerned, his actual royal power mattered far more than any religious faith. His status, gleaming in gold and blazing in fire, far outweighed what any mere god could do for them.

Part of Nebuchadnezzar's problem, as Daniel 4 shows clearly, was that he was quite happy for the gods to rule in heaven just so long as it was clear who ruled on earth. With his fiery furnace round the corner, it must have seemed a perfectly reasonable assumption to make. Anyhow, that is how he addresses these three mere government servants. What madness to imagine that their absurdly narrow religious scruples would be any match for his absolute royal power!

But Shadrach, Meshach, and Abednego simply reply, "Nebuchadnezzar . . . ." They use his simple name. (The word "king" in the Hebrew comes later in the narrative, not in their immediate speech: "[they] said to the king, Nebuchadnezzar . . . .") No titles, no honourifics, no optimistic "O king, live forever!" They address him as a man, nothing more. He might have a ninety foot statue beside him, but in the underwear beneath all his robes and gold plate, and in spite of all his absurd claims, he was just plain Nebuchadnezzar. He was their king, yes; but he was simply a man with a name, like themselves.

Next, they refuse to grovel or to try to excuse or explain themselves. Their record speaks for itself. "We do not need to defend ourselves before you in this matter." They had served the king competently and with integrity for years, and their religious affiliation had never stood in the way of that before. Their work was a matter of public record, and their efficient service of the king had never been threatened by their covenant commitment to the God of Israel.

Then they go on to an even more courageous bit of mimicry. They turn the king's threats head over heels, echoing the precise structure of the king's ultimate threat with an ultimate refusal.

> "*If* you are ready to fall down," he had said, "very good . . . *but if not*, then . . ." (v. 15).
>
> "*If* you throw us in the fire," they replied, "then . . . *but if not* . . ." (v. 17).

It was cool. It was courageous. But really it was nothing more than the facts as they saw them. "You do what you like, Nebuchadnezzar. Either way, we can't meet your demands."

But alongside this coolness, there was also a remarkable confidence in God, expressed in classic terms in verse 17. Every phrase counts.

- "*The God...*" Who was that? Yahweh, the God of Israel, the God of all their history, Yahweh of the exodus, Yahweh of Sinai, Yahweh of the conquest. These Jewish believers, with their first-class degrees in the literature, philosophy, arts, and science of Babylon, had not forgotten their childhood faith. They were still part of that covenant people of Yahweh, and they knew who their God was.

- "*[whom] we serve...*" They say this as they stand in front of their political lord and master—the supreme embodiment of the state itself. "Yes, Nebuchadnezzar, we are your servants, and good ones too. But in serving you we actually serve our God, the God who appointed you." They did not quite say, as another more famous Jew said when he too stood before a hostile political power on trial for his life, "You would have no power over me if it were not given to you from above" (John 19:11), but that was certainly what they meant.

- "*... is able to deliver us from [the fire]...*" Of course he is! Who made fire in the first place? The same God who made the sea and then rescued Israel from it. The omnipotence of Yahweh, and especially his power to save, were a proven part of every Israelite's creed. As we have already seen in chapter 2, there is a sub-plot running through Daniel as to who really "is able." Where does the real executive ability in world affairs reside? Politicians and government servants don't always know the answer to that question, but these three did.

- "*... and he will deliver us from Your Majesty's hand.*" As we say in Northern Ireland, where I come from, "Catch yourself on, Nebuchadnezzar. If it's a fight you're wanting, then you and your swanky image are no match for our God." It is the simplicity of their reply that is so impressive. We have to fill it out to get its full flavour, but its original simplicity is majestic. There's no argument at all, no pleading, no protest. Just a quiet confidence in God's ability to save.

- Verse 18, however, is even more arresting: "*But even if he does not . . . .*"[1] These are the crucial words in their reply to the king. They should not be taken as a sudden collapse into doubt and uncertainty. It's not a loss of faith or "preparing for the worst, just in case." Rather, it is a continuing affirmation of complete faith in God while still leaving God his freedom to do as God pleases. That was the nature of Israelite faith in the power *and* the sovereign wisdom of Yahweh. They fully expected a miracle, but they would serve God without one. They declared total faith in God's ability, along with the total acceptance of God's freedom.

This is a combination which is not easy to hold together in practical everyday life, let alone in life-threatening tests of faith. It sounds rather contrary to some kinds of popular teaching today on the sure-fire certainty of faith. Certainly it doesn't fit easily with the insurance policy kind of faith—"Name it and claim it." We are told that any need we may have which requires a miracle from God should be ours if we claim it by faith. In so-called Prosperity Gospel teaching, that faith should be embodied in a "seed" or "pledge," usually in the form of some financial or material gift to the preacher himself. Then, once you make your seed-faith claim, you can be certain that God will do whatever you ask.

---

1. There is a possibility that the words "but if not" refer to the assertion that their God is able to save them. That is, they were saying, "Even if he is not able to save us, we will not serve you or your gods." However, although the exegetical arguments are complex, I think the understanding reflected in the NIV (and most English versions) is correct and defensible: "But even if he does not." The NEB nuances it as follows, "If there is a god who is able to save us from the blazing furnace, it is our God whom we serve, and he will save us from your power, O king; but if not, be it known to your majesty that we will neither serve your god nor worship the golden image . . . ."

A more subtle form of that teaching is sometimes applied to the healing ministry. I remember when I was a young assistant pastor, our church believed in and practiced a ministry of prayer for healing for people in all kinds of physical, mental, and spiritual illness. It was a blessing to many, and God did answer prayers. But I remember that there were some people who told us, "Never say, 'If it be your will,' when praying for something or someone, especially when praying for healing. God is able, God has promised, and God always will. Just have faith."

Well, verse 17 alone could lead us to think that way, if it were not for verse 18 immediately following. The three friends were saying, "Of course our God is able to save us from the fire. But God is still God, he is sovereign in wisdom as well as power, and he may choose not to. But even if God does not deliver us from that furnace, we still give to him alone our total trust and commitment, and we will not serve your gods" (not that they would have been in any fit state to do so, but this was not the moment for logical precision).

I remember an African student who arrived one day in the fellowship meeting that we went to on a Sunday evening when we lived in Pune, India. She had come as a student to one of the universities in Pune. What a testimony she had! God had provided everything!

- She was not really qualified to have received admission to the university, but she believed it was where God wanted her to go, so she claimed it . . . and got it.
- She had no money for the university fees, but she claimed it . . . and got it.
- She had no ticket for her flight, but she claimed it . . . and got it.
- She needed a visa, coming from an African country. She claimed it . . . and got it.

And so it went on, one thing after another for which she had trusted God and God had delivered every time. It was stirring stuff and we all rejoiced with her and praised God.

I don't think I am a cynical person, and I did not for a moment doubt her word or sincerity. But I couldn't help wondering how her faith would cope with the first time God says "No" to her. For he undoubtedly will (or has already, I expect). Will she go on trusting God when she "claims" something and doesn't get it?

It is a great relief to me to know that God's wisdom is greater than mine and that I can trust him to say "No" if my requests are way off beam. God can do miracles for any of us, but I am glad God is not bound to our every notion of what we think would be a good idea. Even our sincerest requests may need to be overridden by God's wise refusal.

More seriously, the Bible shows clearly and often that God can rescue some people but allow others to suffer or die, without explanation. And there is no hint that the first group had any more or any less faith than others. Have you ever wondered how John, the brother of James, felt when God sent an angel to rescue Peter from prison, but his own brother James had been executed by Herod only shortly before (Acts 12)? Did James have no faith while Peter had lots? The text doesn't even mention Peter's faith; if anything he was pretty surprised. Did the church (and especially his own brother John) not pray for James just as they did for Peter? One presumes so, but God said "No." A sword for James, an angel for Peter. Why save Peter and let James die? Only God knows the answer.

And even that most famous chapter which describes the heroes of faith and what God accomplished through them, Hebrews 11, reminds us that all was not glory and miracles. Hebrews 11:33–35a reads like an amplification of Daniel 3:17. In fact it clearly alludes to two of the stories in Daniel:

> [Those] who through faith conquered kingdoms, administered justice, and gained what was promised; who shut the mouths of lions, quenched the fury of the flames, and escaped the edge of the sword; whose weakness was turned to strength; and who became powerful in battle and routed foreign armies. Women received back their dead, raised to life again.

But then Hebrews 11:35b–38 reads much more like Daniel 3:18.

> There were others who were tortured, refusing to be released, so that they might gain an even better resurrection. Some faced jeers and flogging, and even chains and imprisonment. They were put to death by stoning; they were sawed in two; they were killed by the sword. They went about in sheepskins and goatskins, destitute, persecuted and ill-treated—the world was not worthy of them. They wandered in deserts and mountains, living in caves and in holes in the ground.

Now the enormous encouragement of taking those verses in Hebrews 11 closely together is that, whether you end up among the "some" who experienced all the miracles, or among the "others" who were killed, "these were *all* commended for their faith" (Heb 11:39). They are *all* included in that great crowd of witnesses (Heb 12:1). In other words, when someone we know (or ourselves, for that matter) seems to be left in the lurch in spite of prayer and whatever other ministry is done for them, when a friend is not healed, when the miracle doesn't happen, when the persecution or suffering just goes on, we should not jump to the conclusion that they did not have faith, or enough faith. To think or say that is usually untrue and pastorally disastrous. God knows and God sees—whether he acts in immediate deliverance or not.

Coming back to our three friends, what was the real foundation of their ability to live with the "but if not?" It lies in the way they use the word "serve" twice—positively and negatively.

> The God we serve . . . we will not serve your gods.

What they were saying, in effect, was this:

> We serve our God not just because he is stronger than your gods, though he is.
> We serve our God not just because he can work miracles for us, though he can.

We serve Yahweh our God ultimately because he is in fact the only God around to be served. He alone is God. He alone is Lord. He alone is worthy to be served, worshipped and obeyed.

So you see, it is not a choice between serving *our* God or serving *your* gods. That is a choice open only to a polytheist who thinks there are plenty of gods out there for the choosing; just take your pick and serve somebody.

No, it is merely a choice between *serving or not serving* the *only* true and living God. And we choose to serve him, whatever he chooses to do regarding us.

Now that is the mark of real faith. It is the determination to go on serving and trusting God in the face of any "If not . . . ." It is to say, with Job, "Though he slay me, yet will I hope in him" (Job 13:15).

It might mean being able to say,

- Lord, I believe that you are able to protect me and my family from all danger, illness, accident, or death. And I pray that you will. But even if not, I will not bow down and serve the gods of bitterness and resentment.
- Lord, I believe you are able to preserve my reputation and my job if I take a stand for what I believe to be right and just, following my conscience not just orders. And I pray that you will. But even if not, even if I lose all of that, I will not bow down and serve the god of cowardice and go the way of the world.
- Lord, I believe you are able to open the door into that job, that ministry, that country, that opportunity that seems so right to me. And I pray that you will. But even if not, and if I seem to be walking in the dark, I will not bow down and serve the gods of despair and anxiety.
- Lord, I believe that you are able to provide all the funding that is needed for this ministry that we are doing in your name to be successful and bear fruit. And I pray that you will. But even if not, I will not bow down and serve the gods of manipulated

success and sacrifice my integrity by producing statistics and stories that I know are exaggerated or untruthful.

• Lord, I believe you are able to help me find a life partner and enjoy all your normal gifts of marriage and family. And I pray that you will. But even if not, I will not bow down and serve the gods of self-pity.

Do not be afraid of the "But even if not . . . ." It is not doubt or unbelief. It is the humble acceptance of God's sovereign freedom to do with us as he will and to put us to the ultimate test of faithfulness if he chooses. Then, as the disciples did, we should pray for the grace to count it an honour to suffer for his name.

We need to affirm with equal passion both the gloriously objective and biblical truth of verse 17 and the searching, demanding personal (and equally biblical) commitment of verse 18.

THE CONFUSED NEBUCHADNEZZAR (3:19–30)

Then Nebuchadnezzar was furious with Shadrach, Meshach and Abednego, and his attitude towards them changed. He ordered the furnace heated seven times hotter than usual and commanded some of the strongest soldiers in his army to tie up Shadrach, Meshach and Abednego and throw them into the blazing furnace. So these men, wearing their robes, trousers, turbans and other clothes, were bound and thrown into the blazing furnace. The king's command was so urgent and the furnace so hot that the flames of the fire killed the soldiers who took up Shadrach, Meshach and Abednego, and these three men, firmly tied, fell into the blazing furnace.

Then King Nebuchadnezzar leaped to his feet in amazement and asked his advisers, "Weren't there three men that we tied up and threw into the fire?"

They replied, "Certainly, Your Majesty."

He said, "Look! I see four men walking around in the fire,

unbound and unharmed, and the fourth looks like a son of the gods."

Nebuchadnezzar then approached the opening of the blazing furnace and shouted, "Shadrach, Meshach and Abednego, servants of the Most High God, come out! Come here!"

So Shadrach, Meshach and Abednego came out of the fire, and the satraps, prefects, governors and royal advisers crowded around them. They saw that the fire had not harmed their bodies, nor was a hair of their heads singed; their robes were not scorched, and there was no smell of fire on them.

Then Nebuchadnezzar said, "Praise be to the God of Shadrach, Meshach and Abednego, who has sent his angel and rescued his servants! They trusted in him and defied the king's command and were willing to give up their lives rather than serve or worship any god except their own God. Therefore I decree that the people of any nation or language who say anything against the God of Shadrach, Meshach and Abednego be cut into pieces and their houses be turned into piles of rubble, for no other god can save in this way."

Then the king promoted Shadrach, Meshach and Abednego in the province of Babylon. (Dan 3:19–30)

The Fourth Man in the Flames!

It is somewhat pointless to argue about his identity. It may seem easy for us, from our perspective, to say it must have been the preincarnate Christ. The important thing in the story is that, from Nebuchadnezzar's point of view, it was one "like a son of the gods," that is, a divine person, someone or something beyond all human comprehension or power, somebody from outside his experience or his control. In verse 28 he simply says that the God of Shadrach, Meshach, and Abednego had sent his angel to rescue his servants.

For Nebuchadnezzar, then, it was a shattering confrontation with the "rock" of his worst nightmare. Who was this? What was this external power beyond all his puny efforts and threats? It was God of course, engaging in yet another episode of dealing with this man, a process which will come to a climax in the next chapter.

It was obviously a highly emotional experience. Nebuchadnezzar, in the course of this chapter and within a few verses, is filled first with fury, then with fear, and finally falls into flattery. The closing verses of the chapter are hardly yet a conversion, more like a confusion! The king is confounded. This is a disturbing encounter with the kingdom of God, a kingdom that so dramatically set limits to the power of his own. Only this time it was not in a private dream but in publicly witnessed reality that neither he nor all his court could deny.

And for the three friends? And for all who would read the story later, whether Jews or Christians down through the centuries? It was spectacular proof of the truth of Isaiah 43:2, "When you walk through the fire, you will not be burned." You're never alone in the flames, whether you walk out alive or not. This is a truth that has brought comfort and courage to all persecuted believers. For of course, for every Shadrach, Meshach, and Abednego who enjoyed the truth of verse 17 in experiencing miraculous deliverance from danger or death, there have been many, many more who have had to live with the experience of verse 18 and yet have gone on affirming their faith, even unto martyrdom.

HEAVEN RULES . . . ON EARTH

I once read that in a poll to discover the most hated figures in America (the things people have polls for!), among the top ten came . . . televangelists. At one level, I find that healthy and encouraging. It shows that people are not entirely taken in by the prostitution of the gospel and the gross self-exaltation of human media manipulators. There are few manifestations of modern Western Christianity that I find more distasteful or further removed from the teachings, example, and lifestyle of Jesus of Nazareth than the posturing and self-exalting images of such preachers. So there is a kind of relief in hearing that so many other people find them repulsive as well. But, on the other hand, of course, there is a deep sadness that the name of Christ should be so smeared with the unpopularity of these false prophets and millionaire pedlars of false promises.

The conflicted reactions to televangelists gets even more muddled when, as has happened several times in recent years, some of them fall off their pedestals and are caught with more than their metaphorical pants down—shamed by either sexual or financial scandals. Sometimes, we may sense the hand of the God who is able to humble "those who walk in pride" (Dan 4:37). But it is also hard not to feel a twinge of relief, or something not far from gloating, when such mega figures are reduced to size and exposed as ordinary sinners like the rest of us. But as soon as I catch myself with such feelings, the sobering thought immediately comes to mind—as it should for all of us who know our own hearts—that "there, but for the grace of God, go I." Gloating, like pride itself, tends to go before a fall. Pride and self-congratulation can be a serious temptation for Christians, whether in pastoral and preaching ministry or in public life.

For Christians in the world of the secular workplace, coping with pride can be difficult, whether the pride of others or the pride that easily infects oneself. Suppose we have to work within an authority structure which is oppressive and unpopular. Everybody hates the boss! How do we feel if that arrogant boss is sacked or demoted? Do we join in the gloating and cheers? Or suppose we find ourselves going from success to success in our career. How then do we sort out godly ambitions from mere thirst for power and position or greed for financial rewards?

Daniel 4 is a colourful and very penetrating study of pride and humility from various angles. And it is in a form that we instinctively pay attention to—a testimony! Here we have Nebuchadnezzar's own written testimony to whoever has ears to hear. He would have been a big attraction at some big Christian conferences and rallies!

This is an interesting shift in perspective in the book. In chapters 1–3 the main focus is on Daniel and his three friends. But the three friends are not in chapter 2, and Daniel is not in chapter 3. One character, however, features in all four chapters—Nebuchadnezzar, king of Babylon. And there has been a progressive sharpening of his awareness of the God who is dealing with him, from merely being impressed with the competence of some young Israelite students to being so astounded at the power of their God that he won't hear a word said against him. Now, in chapter 4 we come to the climax and final curtain on Nebuchadnezzar, narrated by Nebuchadnezzar himself. He is not just the subject but also the speaker, which adds to the rhetorical power of the whole chapter.

> King Nebuchadnezzar,
> To the nations and peoples of every language, who live in all the earth:
> May you prosper greatly!
> It is my pleasure to tell you about the miraculous signs and wonders that the Most High God has performed for me. (Dan 4:1–2)

Like a good preacher, Nebuchadnezzar states the main point of his testimony at the beginning (v. 3), summarizes it again at the end (v. 34), and repeats it three times in the middle (vv. 17, 25, 32). It is simply this, that the Most High God is king, and not just king in heaven: He rules among the kingdoms of men on earth. In short, "Heaven rules" (v. 26). This is the lesson that Nebuchadnezzar finally learns by the end of this amazing story.

The chapter is like a drama with three main actors.

NEBUCHADNEZZAR THE BUILDER (4:1–8, 29–30)

I, Nebuchadnezzar, was at home in my palace, contented and prosperous . . . .

Twelve months later, as the king was walking on the roof of the royal palace of Babylon, he said, "Is not this the great Babylon I have built as the royal residence, by my mighty power and for the glory of my majesty?" (Dan 4:4, 29–30)

Nebuchadnezzar was a builder in many different ways:

- *He built an empire.* Out of the tatters of Assyria and in competition with Egypt he built an empire that lasted some seventy years.
- *He built a culture*, known as the Neo-Babylonian culture to historians. It is perhaps reflected in the great music festival of Daniel 3.
- *He built an educated, multi-racial government administration*, as we saw in Daniel 1.
- *He built a city—Babylon.* He glorified and beautified it, so that it was not for nothing that the famous "Hanging Gardens of Babylon" are among the Seven Wonders of the ancient world.

Altogether, it was a remarkable and creditable achievement. Humanly speaking, Nebuchadnezzar had plenty to be pleased about and proud of; his boasting had its basis in fact. Even theologically speaking, we recall that it was God who had raised him up and given him authority, power, and wide dominion with all the wealth and opportunities that go along with such a position (Dan 2:37, 38; 5:18). And he had used all of those things well, to great advantage. Of course, we also know from Daniel 3 that there was a nasty side to Nebuchadnezzar. Apparently he was not averse to cremating a few dissidents, but we need not exaggerate that out of proportion. It was fairly standard practice in his day (and until relatively recently in world history). By the standards of his own age, Nebuchadnezzar was a competent, efficient, and constructive ruler.

However, as so often, the Bible sees beyond and behind the external splendour to the reality as God knows it. The Bible, speaking for God, looks inside Nebuchadnezzar's heart and sees the pride that filled it. And it looks underneath the glory of Babylon and sees the social evil that it was built on.

Nebuchadnezzar's pride, you see, was not just your ordinary, everyday kind of pride. He still had the delusions of divinity that we saw earlier in chapter 3. He was still refusing to acknowledge what God had been trying to teach him for years. In fact, it was Jeremiah who had declared it publicly in an international diplomatic conference that took place in Jerusalem only four years after Nebuchadnezzar came to power (Jer 27:1–11, and cf. 28:1). Almost certainly Nebuchadnezzar heard about what Jeremiah said that day; his intelligence service was very good. On that occasion Jeremiah made it plain that all Nebuchadnezzar's power and authority were strictly *ex officio* as the "servant of Yahweh" (Jer 27:5–7). It was the God of Israel, the God of Daniel, Shadrach, Meshach, and Abednego to whom Nebuchadnezzar owed his throne and the resources that went with it.

Instead, Nebuchadnezzar was turning the gift of God to his own glory. Already, in chapter 3 we have seen in him a model of state arrogance and idolatrous totalitarianism—the classic pride of great civilizations and collective "grand designs." Here in Daniel 4 we see a portrayal of human pride at the personal level.

There is something of a Nebuchadnezzar in most of us. Many people, of course, suffer from a low self-image (not Nebuchadnezzar's biggest problem!). Lack of self-worth can be a terribly crippling thing, but it is probably still true to say that pride is the more common, and much more serious, problem. Not for nothing is it included among the classic "cardinal sins." It is even possible, according to some Christian psychologists, that preoccupation with a low self-image may in itself conceal a form of pride, or at least ego-centredness. I remember a rather arrogant man once being described as a person who is fighting a low self-image—and winning!

David Myers and Malcolm Jeeves are two Christian psychologists who present the findings of various pieces of research that reveal the pervasiveness of the self-serving bias in human nature. They describe the "self-centred filter" through which people explain their experiences. We all tend to take credit when our plans succeed but try to find ways to blame others, or adverse circumstances, when we fail. We are very cynical about this as the habitual stance of politicians, but apparently it is a universal tendency. They also point out that in published surveys of how people rate themselves over a range of skills and aptitudes, most of us believe we are better than average in every sphere researched. And that of course is statistically impossible, since the very concept of "average" requires that approximately the same number of people fall below it as above it. They comment on the difficulties we all have in accepting we have made a mistake, combined with energetic attempts to justify or defend ourselves.

> Human nature is governed by a totalitarian ego that continually revises the past in order to preserve a positive self-evaluation. Because of our mind's powers of reconstruction, we can be sure, argues Mike Yaconelli, that "Every moving illustration, every gripping story, every testimony, didn't happen (at least, it didn't happen like the storyteller said it happened)." Every anecdotal recollection told by a Christian superstar is a reconstruction. It's a point worth remembering in times when we are

feeling disenchanted by the comparative ordinariness of our everyday lives.[1]

Myers and Jeeves go on to point out the serious consequences of pride, in terms that this chapter of Daniel fully confirms.

> The Bible does warn us against self-righteous pride—pride that alienates us from God and leads us to disdain one another. Such pride is at the heart of racism, sexism, nationalism, and all the deadly chauvinisms that lead one group of people to see themselves as more moral, deserving, or able than another. The flip side of being proud of our individual and group achievements, and taking credit for them, is blaming the poor for their poverty and the oppressed for their oppression.[2]

We are all building something. It may be our own personal little empire, or just our own little nest. It may be our career, our project, or our business. It may even be our "ministry," if we are in so-called full-time Christian work. Sadly the Nebuchadnezzar complex can infect work we believe (or claim) we are doing for God. If God could use Nebuchadnezzar, it is equally true that there are "Nebuchadnezzars" around who "use God" for their own advantage.

In fact, the more God gives to us—the greater our natural and spiritual gifts, the more resources God puts at our disposal to build with—all the greater is the temptation to play little Nebuchadnezzars. I am grateful for the person who said to me, at an early stage of my ordained ministry (at a point when I was beginning to get praise and admiration for being able to do some things moderately well), "Remember, Chris, the more gifted you are, the more dangerous you are." A true and sobering observation.

It is tragic that the world of Christian ministry and mission is littered with bloated egos and wonderful gifts being prostituted to

---

1. David G. Myers and Malcolm A. Jeeves, *Psychology Through the Eyes of Faith* (Leicester: Apollos, 1991), 131–32.
2. Ibid., 135.

the idols of pride. People may not say it in so many words, but the echo of Nebuchadnezzar lies just beneath the surface.

Is not this a great institution that I have built up?

Is not this a great movement that I have launched?

Is this not a great mission that I have helped to found.

Is this not a great business that (with God's help, of course) I have helped to prosper?

Is this not a great church that I built from scratch as a young pastor to the megachurch it is today?

It disturbs me that so many Christian foundations, funds, colleges and schools, ministries and missions are built on their founder's own name (usually with "International," or "Incorporated" spliced on the end for even more effect). It distressed Martin Luther very much that people were calling churches by his name. He never wanted there to be a "Lutheran" church, when Christ was its only Lord. Even the apostle Paul rebuked the Corinthians for the misuse of human names as labels for factionalism and pride. For a number of years, the branch of the Langham Partnership that is based in the USA chose to use the name John Stott Ministries, after the founder. It was a decision, taken at a board meeting when he was not present, that John Stott himself never liked (though he was willing to accept it for the reason the board gave—that it enabled many Americans to understand and support the Langham ministries more readily). And shortly before he died, he requested the board not to perpetuate that beyond his death but to revert to the name Langham Partnership USA—a request they honoured. John Stott had no desire for his own name to be glorified in the ministries he had initiated for the good of the church and the glory of Christ.

And yet, of course, I have to be scrupulously honest here. The temptation to pride (or at least a subtle pleasure) in one's own achievements, even when done for and offered to the Lord, cannot be avoided. Or at least, I have not found a way of eliminating it. I have to admit that, while I certainly pray that the books I write will be a blessing to God's people, a means of grace and growth, and that they will bring glory to Christ, I am certainly pleased to see my name on the cover of them. When I speak at Christian conferences, of course I want (and constantly pray) to preach and teach for God's glory, but it would be dishonest to deny that I enjoy seeing my name on the programs. When people say kind things in praise and appreciation for some presentation, preaching, or lecture I have given, it warms my heart. How could it not? I am as human and susceptible to praise and self-congratulation as any other sinner.

So what to do? I find two simple things helpfully counterbalance the temptation to ungodly pride. One is to remember a favorite saying of John Stott himself. He used to say, "Flattery is like cigarette smoke. It does you no harm if you don't inhale." I think there might be some pedantic and politically correct criticism of that saying, but it makes a good point. When people praise you, don't let it sink into your inner thoughts and breed the cancer of pride. Don't inhale it! It obviously worked for John Stott. He must have received more praise and flattery than most other people, and yet he remained (and was universally recognized to be) one of the most humble, Christ-like believers you could ever meet.

The other counter-strategy is to develop the habit, as soon as words of praise come along (spoken or written), of the upward look. For me, this goes along with a mental gesture with my hands, passing it up to God. "Here, Lord," I say (inaudibly of course, if someone is speaking words of praise to me at the time), "you take this. It won't do me any good if I keep it. It's to your credit anyway." I find that habit turns the temptation to pride into an opportunity for gratitude, which is an altogether more healthy frame of mind. Then I can be thankful to God that he has given me the ability to give others something that blesses them—and in thanking God, neutralize any sinful self-satisfaction.

Not one of us, then, is immune to the temptations of pride or of scheming and building for our own advantage, success, or reputation. Only as this universal tendency is honestly recognized, confessed, and kept open before God can we hope to walk in humility with God and others. Otherwise, like Nebuchadnezzar, we may find that God may have to intervene in less pleasant ways to humble us and bring us back to sanity. And this story shows that he can indeed do that.

So, in the next act of this drama, we find that God, in his final move to bring Nebuchadnezzar to his senses, resorts to two familiar tools: a well-tested method, dreams; and a well-trusted messenger, Daniel. As in Daniel 2, Nebuchadnezzar is disturbed by a weird and threatening nightmare, which shattered his complacent ease. Notice the sudden change.

> I, Nebuchadnezzar, was at home in my palace, contented and prosperous. I had a dream that made me afraid. As I was lying in my bed, the images and visions that passed through my mind terrified me. So I commanded that all the wise men of Babylon be brought before me to interpret the dream for me. When the magicians, enchanters, astrologers and diviners came, I told them the dream, but they could not interpret it for me. Finally, Daniel came into my presence and I told him the dream. (He is called Belteshazzar, after the name of my god, and the spirit of the holy gods is in him.) (Dan 4:4–8)

All the wise men of Babylon troop on stage to do their stuff but, not unexpectedly, prove as incompetent as they were the last time Nebuchadnezzar had bad dreams (though at least this time he told them what the dream was, but it didn't help). So they make their exit even more promptly, and Daniel comes on stage to hushed whispers of expectancy from the audience.

DANIEL THE CHALLENGER (4:9–27)

Nebuchadnezzar loses no time in telling Daniel his dream.

> Belteshazzar, chief of the magicians, I know that the spirit of the holy gods is in you, and no mystery is too difficult for you. Here is my dream; interpret it for me. These are the visions

I saw while lying in my bed: I looked, and there before me stood a tree in the middle of the land. Its height was enormous. The tree grew large and strong and its top touched the sky; it was visible to the ends of the earth. Its leaves were beautiful, its fruit abundant, and on it was food for all. Under it the wild animals found shelter, and the birds of the air lived in its branches; from it every creature was fed.

In the visions I saw while lying in my bed, I looked, and there before me was a holy one, a messenger, coming down from heaven. He called in a loud voice: "Cut down the tree and trim off its branches; strip off its leaves and scatter its fruit. Let the animals flee from under it and the birds from its branches. But let the stump and its roots, bound with iron and bronze, remain in the ground, in the grass of the field.

"Let him be drenched with the dew of heaven, and let him live with the animals among the plants of the earth. Let his mind be changed from that of a man and let him be given the mind of an animal, till seven times pass by for him.

"The decision is announced by messengers, the holy ones declare the verdict, so that the living may know that the Most High is sovereign over kingdoms on earth and gives them to anyone he wishes and sets over them the lowliest of people."

This is the dream that I, King Nebuchadnezzar, had. Now, Belteshazzar, tell me what it means, for none of the wise men in my kingdom can interpret it for me. But you can, because the spirit of the holy gods is in you. (Dan 4:9–18)

There are two striking features of Daniel's response to the king's dream.

His Pastoral Concern

It seems that the bond established between Daniel and Nebuchadnezzar as a result of the last bout of royal insomnia in Daniel 2 had lasted throughout his reign. Once again, we should marvel at the fact that Daniel so freely, so willingly, so competently served the man who had destroyed his homeland, devastated his city, and deported his people. We could hardly have a more practical example of "Love your enemies" in Old Testament dress. Daniel was only resident in Babylon by force. He had not asked to be sent there. He was, at best, a conscript missionary. He could have sunk down into a life of permanent bitterness and a disgruntled, antagonistic attitude towards his Babylonian employers and neighbors. But he did not do that. And because he had not made himself unpopular with all those around him, he was now able to speak a word from God to this troubled, pagan king.

I also think Daniel's life was an example of Jesus' command to "pray for those who persecute you." I have no proof, of course, but I think it is highly likely that Daniel, since he was among the first batch of exiles, would have heard the reading of the letter that Jeremiah sent to the exiles in Babylon, way back before the final destruction of Jerusalem, telling them to *pray for Babylon*! That in itself must have been a shocking piece of advice. The exiles wondered if they could even pray *in* Babylon (they certainly felt they couldn't sing their songs there: Ps 137:1–4), let alone pray *for* Babylon. But Jeremiah told them that such was their continuing mission: the Abrahamic mission of being the means of blessing among the nations.

> This is what the LORD Almighty, the God of Israel, says to all those I carried into exile from Jerusalem to Babylon: ". . . seek the peace and prosperity of the city to which I have carried you into exile. Pray to the LORD for it, because if it prospers, you too will prosper." (Jer 29:4, 7)

We know that Daniel was a man of prayer, with the habit of praying three times daily (Dan 6:10). I wonder if Nebuchadnezzar was top of his prayer list? For Daniel, serving the king was actually a means of serving the God who had appointed the king, and that was a perspective forged and preserved by regular prayer. Prayer sets our thinking straight and fosters the kind of maturity which we see in

Daniel here. He had grown beyond a desire for revenge, or a simple racial or religious hatred. It is hard to go on hating somebody you're praying for every day.

Rather, as Daniel listened to Nebuchadnezzar tell his dream, he could once again discern the voice of God speaking to his pagan political boss.

But put yourself in Daniel's shoes for a moment and think what you are hearing. There you are, standing, listening to a dream in which a huge tree gets chopped down, somebody gets driven out to eat grass with the cattle, a voice pronounces divine judgment upon him . . . and suddenly you realise that *it all applies to the man who is telling you his dream*—the king himself.

Nebuchadnezzar is for the chop!

Wouldn't you have inwardly cheered? Wouldn't you have thought, "Yes! And about time too!" Wouldn't you have silently been saying, "Thank you God for letting me live long enough to see your vengeance on my enemy, on this beast of a man who raped and pillaged your holy city and burnt your temple?" Such reactions would be perfectly understandable. But they were not Daniel's.

> Then Daniel (also called Belteshazzar) was greatly perplexed
> for a time, and his thoughts terrified him. So the king said,
> "Belteshazzar, do not let the dream or its meaning alarm you."
> Belteshazzar answered, "My lord, if only the dream applied
> to your enemies and its meaning to your adversaries!" (Dan 4:19)

Daniel was dismayed. He couldn't speak. He couldn't bear to tell the king. He could only express a forlorn wish (what the king was probably secretly hoping to hear), that the dream applied to Nebuchadnezzar's enemies. But Daniel knew it did not. It was for Nebuchadnezzar, and it must be faithfully interpreted. But he explained the dream reluctantly, pastorally. Daniel had gone beyond malice and vengeance and could take no pleasure in the destruction of the wicked. That seems to me to be the mark of a person who is becoming more and more like the God he spends time in prayer with (Ezek 33:11).

If it is a test of our maturity how we deal with pride in ourselves, it is equally so when we have to handle pride, or its downfall, in others. The instinct for revenge is very strong. We long to see the arrogant and prosperous brought down a peg or three. But how do we react when they are? Then the true motives of our hearts are exposed. Then it will be seen whether we reflect a self-righteous rejoicing in another human being's frailty or a Christ-like sorrow over those who even betray and deny him.

His Prophetic Courage

It took courage for Daniel to interpret the dream faithfully, to say to the most powerful man on the world, as far as he was concerned: "You are that tree . . ." (v. 22); to tell this monarch of all he surveyed that he would soon be sharing food with the beasts of the field; to tell this "head of gold," who was always accustomed to looking down from the top of his statue to the lesser mortals below, that he must look up and acknowledge a higher king than himself; to direct his attention to the reign of the Most High God before it was too late. Another New Testament command about "speaking the truth in love" (Eph 4:15) finds its Old Testament illustration here also.

But even more courage was needed for what Daniel said next. He had given his straight interpretation of the dream and the words that were part of it. But now he risks a word of his own.

"Therefore, Your Majesty, be pleased to accept my advice . . . ." (v. 27)

Now Nebuchadnezzar hadn't asked for any advice. All he had asked for was the interpretation of the dream, and that must have been unwelcome enough. He needed a stiff drink, not superfluous advice. But Daniel courageously keeps speaking. It shows, I think, that Daniel had confidence in the king's respect for him, respect which matched Daniel's own pastoral concern and personal respect for the king. And the word Daniel spoke took all the authentic strength of a prophet to deliver. Now that was probably not familiar ground for Daniel.

He was no professional prophet. He was a government servant, and government servants are not notorious for hazarding risky opinions to their overlords. Opinions can get you into trouble, especially if they aren't asked for. "If I'd wanted your opinion, I'd have asked for it," is the usual response in such circumstances. But Daniel keeps calm and carries on.

Daniel put his finger on the sore spot of Babylon's imperial glory, its social costs in terms of human oppression and exploitation. Daniel could see firsthand what the prophet Habakkuk had condemned when, speaking about Babylon, he had delivered words of divine rebuke and judgment:

> Woe to him who piles up stolen goods
> > and makes himself wealthy by extortion! . . .
> Woe to him who builds his house by unjust gain,
> > setting his nest on high
> > to escape the clutches of ruin! . . .
> Woe to him who builds a city with bloodshed
> > and establishes a town by injustice! (Hab 2:6, 9, 12)

That was exactly what Nebuchadnezzar was doing. So Daniel had the courage to call the king both to personal repentance and to social reform in ringing, razor sharp words that an Amos would have been proud of:

> Therefore, Your Majesty, be pleased to accept my advice: Renounce your sins by doing what is right, and your wickedness by being kind to the oppressed. It may be that then your prosperity will continue. (Dan 4:27)

This makes it very clear that Nebuchadnezzar's sin, in the eyes of God, was not merely personal pride and arrogant delusions of grandeur, but actual, practical injustice and oppression in the social realm. So the word of God to him was not merely "Confess your sins and change your attitude." No, Nebuchadnezzar had to have a radical change of heart and then prove it by a change in official state policy. He had to replace exploitation with justice and kindness. He had to *do* something to relieve the poverty and oppression that was the dark side of the majesty of Babylon.

There is a sharp irony in the words Nebuchadnezzar says in verse 30. "Is not this the great Babylon *I* have built . . . ?" *He had built?* Nebuchadnezzar probably never handled a brick in his life. *He* had not built Babylon. It had been built by the sweat of the nameless thousands of oppressed slaves, immigrants, and other poor sections of the nation, the kind of teeming multitudes whose labours have built every vaunting civilization of the fallen human race in history.

But the God of Daniel saw, heard, and was concerned, just as he had heard the outcry coming up from Sodom and Gomorrah (Gen 18:20, 21; Ezek 16:49), just as he had heard the groaning of his own people in Egypt (Exod 2:23, 24). Daniel also, his ear attuned to the mind of his God, felt the heartbeat of the God whose commitment to the poor and oppressed was part of his spiritual heritage, history, and worship.

> [The LORD] upholds the cause of the oppressed
>> and gives food to the hungry.
> The LORD sets prisoners free,
>> the LORD gives sight to the blind,
> the LORD lifts up those who are bowed down,
>> the LORD loves the righteous.
> The LORD watches over the foreigner
>> and sustains the fatherless and the widow,
>> but he frustrates the ways of the wicked.
> The LORD reigns forever,
>> your God, O Zion, for all generations.
> Praise the LORD. (Ps 146:7–10)

So now, the LORD God knows what is going on in Babylon and holds the king accountable for it. And he speaks a word into the situation that is as sharp as any prophet spoke to an Israelite king, though a lot shorter!

We should not miss the tremendous drama of this moment in

Daniel's life. Here was a mere government servant, albeit a respected one with a title he would probably have preferred to do without ("Chief of the Magicians," v. 9), standing before the supreme head of state, challenging him in the name of God on the whole social and economic direction of his state policy. People have lost their heads for far less than that. John the Baptist lost his for criticizing a petty king over his marriage! And Daniel not only challenges, he calls the head of state to repent, with the explicit threat that if he does not, he will face humiliation. His words may have been padded out a bit with the official political politeness—"Be pleased to accept my advice" and all that—but they packed a lethal punch. Daniel faced the king with the social wickedness of his government and called on him to grasp the nettle of reform, or eat the nettles of his punishment.

By the end of this story, one of the things which Nebuchadnezzar finally admits about the God he has encountered is his justice: "everything [God] does is right and all his ways are just" (Dan 4:37), which may be a way of saying that Nebuchadnezzar now knows what *he* must do to follow up his submission to God. He must reflect the character of God of heaven in the affairs of his own earthly kingdom. *But who put that idea in his head in the first place?* Daniel, years before. Daniel, who not only had the courage to speak the truth to the king but *who was also in a position to speak it*. In other words, Daniel was only able to speak this word of challenge and rebuke, which ultimately led to the king's conversion, because he had spent a lifetime of faithful service in the secular administration of this alien country. How does that sound to us who are used to instant results? A lifetime's secular job and then a moment's opportunity to speak the challenging prophetic word to the key person at the right time.

When you think back to Daniel 1 and the decisions that Daniel and his three friends took in their youth, you can see how much depended on these decisions later. Their decision to say "No" on the (probable) issue of total allegiance to the state led them into the fiery furnace, only to prove there the power of their God. But their decision to say "Yes" to the programme of training and the administrative career meant that Daniel was in the right place at the right time when the prophetic word needed to be spoken right into the ear of the political power.

If Daniel had not said "Yes" at the beginning of his career, he would not have been in a position to speak at all. If he had not said "No," he would not have had the critical distance to deliver the kind of challenging word that he did. If he and his friends had opted out of public secular life altogether, they could have had no impact or witness in relation to it. If they had been co-opted in as mere stooges of the government, they would have had no prophetic leverage to say anything that cut across official policy. They were in the world, but they had not sold their souls to the world. So this later chapter vindicates their discernment in chapter 1 as to the need to say both "Yes" and "No" to the world in different respects, in order to preserve meaningful engagement alongside critical distinctiveness. It is not an easy or obvious boundary to discern, but a lot depends on that practical discernment and acting on it.

I believe there is a word of tremendous encouragement here to Christians who work in the secular world. As someone who has lived the coward's life of a Christian environment, first in ordained pastoral ministry in the Church of England, then as a missionary in India but living and working in a Christian college there, then in a community of people training for cross-cultural mission, and now within an agency seeking to strengthen the ministry of God's Word in majority world churches and seminaries, I have a very profound respect for Christians who stick it out in all kinds of secular jobs, and especially those who are in public or political service of any kind. You are the real "salt of the earth" in the sense that Jesus meant. You are those who stand against corruption and shine as lights in the midst of "a warped and crooked generation" (Phil 2:15, a verse that probably reflects Daniel 12:3). You are Daniels *in situ*.

Yet so often the church gives the impression that what really counts is "the ministry" or "missionary work," when in fact it is the presence and faithful work and witness of the hosts of Christian so-called lay people that matters far, far more in relation to the world around us. This is why I generally prefer speaking at conferences of Christians in secular professions and jobs than at clergy or theological student gatherings. There is a sense of reality. There is an awareness of the sharp and rough edges of life. There is a wrestling with agonizing dilemmas. There is also a healthy refusal to let the tame theologian get away with any vague answers that don't engage with the real issues.

And my word to such groups is always to get them to grasp that ministry and mission in God's world are far too important to be left to ministers and missionaries. Daniel had a mission but it took him a lifetime of hard work in a government office to fulfil it. He earned the respect of the king and the right to speak, and when the moment came he had the courage to speak it in the name of God. So wherever God has put you and whatever your daily grind, see it as the place where you may be called to be the spark plug where the power of God's word jumps explosively across the gap into the secular world.

GOD THE HUMBLER (4:28–37)

God gave Nebuchadnezzar twelve months, a whole year to act on the implications of his dream and its courageous interpretation by Daniel; a year to do something in response to the advice and the warning he had been given. But he ignored it all. In verses 29 and 30 we find him quite unchanged.

> Twelve months later, as the king was walking on the roof of the royal palace of Babylon, he said, "Is not this the great Babylon I have built as the royal residence, by my mighty power and for the glory of my majesty?" (Dan 4:29–30)

At last God moves to his final act to humble this man and bring him to his senses. Nebuchadnezzar had delusions of being more than human, so, with a kind of poetic justice, God sent him delusions of being less than human! The delusion of thinking oneself to be a particular animal and behaving as such is a known form of mental illness.

Even as the words were on his lips, a voice came from heaven, "This is what is decreed for you, King Nebuchadnezzar: Your royal authority has been taken from you. You will be driven away from people and will live with the wild animals; you will eat grass like the ox. Seven times will pass by for you until you acknowledge that the Most High is sovereign over the kingdoms of the earth and gives them to anyone he wishes."

Immediately what had been said about Nebuchadnezzar was fulfilled. He was driven away from people and ate grass like the ox. His body was drenched with the dew of heaven until his hair grew like the feathers of an eagle and his nails like the claws of a bird. (Dan 4:31–33)

The fact of the twelve-month delay in carrying out the threat of the dream shows God's own reluctance. God took no pleasure in reducing a human being, made in God's own image, to the level of a brute beast. God wants humility, not humiliation. But, if necessary, he will humiliate the proud into genuine humility if there is no other way. Not only is he able to humble "those who walk in pride" (v. 37), but it is something he characteristically and typically does (see Prov 3:34 and its application in Jas 4:1–10).

The humiliation lasted only as long as it took Nebuchadnezzar to learn his lesson. "Seven times" is a deliberately vague phrase; it need not mean seven years. So what was it he needed to learn? Answer: the three-times-repeated truth, which forms the theme of this whole chapter, that the Most High God rules over the kingdoms of men. Nebuchadnezzar, head of a human kingdom, was up against the kingdom of God, and it was an uncomfortable experience to say the least.

Nebuchadnezzar would certainly have accepted that the Most High God ruled in heaven. No problem about that; that's what a god is for. Let him rule in heaven all he likes—so long as he stays there. But the point he could not take was that the God of heaven rules *on earth*. The reign of God is "earthed" among the kingdoms of men.

This point was bowled at him in his first dream in the shape of the rock which toppled all human empires and grew to fill the whole earth. Daniel told him then that this portrayed the rule of God which was indestructible. But Nebuchadnezzar had not taken the point, yet. He would not accept that heaven rules on earth. So he had felt free to build his city and empire on injustice and oppression. When human beings act without any sense of a higher authority, with no sense of accountability to God, then both individually and as a society we are capable of terrible cruelty to one another. Individual pride and state pride get out of control when they are unchecked by any submission to a transcendent authority.

This is one reason why the *real* Jesus was and is so uncomfortable to many. Jesus challenged the people of his day to recognize that the reign of God was among them. In his teaching and parables he showed that it was a kingdom that turned the world's values upside down. It cut across the political drift of his nation. It cut across the economic values that led to wealth for some, and debt and poverty for others. It cut across personal attitudes and behavior that excluded and marginalized whole categories of people. The only way to cope with such a kingdom was to submit, repent, accept it, and live a radically changed life—or to resist it and be destroyed.

It is also why when the church of today tries to make people acknowledge the presence of the kingdom of God by holding them morally accountable for public policies and their social consequences, it becomes unpopular. No government cheerfully accepts criticism, least of all from "interfering clergy." Let the clergy stay in their pulpits and stick to spiritual matters. Let God stay in heaven and keep it warm till we all get there. This is how the state and its political servants would prefer things to stay. That way, we can get on with preserving the unjust *status quo*, unchecked by uncomfortable notions of a living God who might call us to account.

Finally, however, Nebuchadnezzar saw the truth that God had been trying to teach him for years.

At the end of that time, I, Nebuchadnezzar, raised my eyes towards heaven, and my sanity was restored. Then I praised the Most High; I honoured and glorified him who lives for ever.

> His dominion is an eternal dominion;
>> his kingdom endures from generation to generation.
>
> (Dan 4:34)

It is interesting how an attack of humility also led to sanity! Pride, especially the kind of pride that tries to get away with ignoring God and his demands, is really a kind of madness. To live in God's world and behave as if we have the right to own it, and treat others as we like without reference to him, is mad! Even to try to live our everyday life and work as if God was only for Sundays is asking for trouble. God refuses to be sidelined like that, and we need to walk in humility before him, willing to say, as Nebuchadnezzar now virtually said though not quite in these words, "Your kingdom come, your will be done, *on earth as in heaven*."

For it is still true that "those who walk in pride [God] is able to humble" (v. 37). But God would infinitely prefer that we humble ourselves first.

CHAPTER 5

THE WRITING ON THE WALL

If you are a businessman and you've been failing to meet your targets, you may find yourself "weighed in the balance and found wanting." If the situation gets worse, you could be told that "your days are numbered." It could even be that "the writing is on the wall" for your company. All three proverbs of failure and impending doom are derived from Daniel 5. It is a very dark chapter indeed, all the more so coming after chapter 4 with its ringing testimony and happy ending.

THE BLASPHEMY OF BELSHAZZAR (5:1–9)

King Belshazzar gave a great banquet for a thousand of his nobles and drank wine with them. While Belshazzar was drinking his wine, he gave orders to bring in the gold and silver goblets that Nebuchadnezzar his father had taken from the temple in Jerusalem, so that the king and his nobles, his wives and his concubines might drink from them. So they brought in the gold goblets that had been taken from the temple of God in Jerusalem, and the king and his nobles, his wives and his concubines drank from them. As they drank the wine, they praised the gods of gold and silver, of bronze, iron, wood and stone. (Dan 5:1–4)

There is no doubt that the author of the book wants us to see a deliberately pointed contrast between Nebuchadnezzar and Belshazzar in at least two respects:

- Nebuchadnezzar was a builder (as we saw in the last chapter). Belshazzar was a waster. Here we find him drunk and incapacitated at the very time when his whole kingdom was under threat. Historically, Belshazzar was only the deputy ruler on behalf of Nabonidus, who was the successor to Nebuchadnezzar. Nabonidus was absent from Babylon at this moment, but the fact that he was the real king explains why Belshazzar could only offer the job of "third highest ruler in the kingdom" as a prize to the successful handwriting-on-wall expert (Dan 5:7). Belshazzar himself occupied the second highest seat, but it is clear that the Babylonian Empire was being mismanaged and in terminal collapse.

• Nebuchadnezzar had some religious respect for the holy things of other nations. He had taken the captured vessels of the temple in Jerusalem and at least put them in another temple, a sacred place for sacred objects (Dan 1:2). Belshazzar treated these same objects with intentional mockery and profanity.

What makes his action so offensive? These temple vessels were highly symbolic and emotive objects. Like the temple itself, they were associated with the presence and the holiness of the God of Israel. The temple was the earthly dwelling place of God's name, and thus of his person, in the midst of his people. So the capture of the precious objects inside it symbolized not only the humiliation and defeat of Israel but also must have been seen as proof of the inferiority of their God. Yahweh was a beaten and captured deity, and his sacred bits and pieces were stashed away in a pagan shrine. The sense of outrage and shame must have been as great as or greater than the appalling capture of the ark of the covenant by the Philistines many centuries earlier in the time of Eli (1 Sam 4).

The temple vessels are mentioned with greater detail in several other places as well as at the beginning of the book of Daniel (2 Kgs 25:13–15, 2 Chron 36:18). But it is clear that although their capture was a great national shame, the very fact that they were still *there*, somewhere, was a symbol of hope. In the early days of the exile there was an argument over them between Hananiah, a false prophet, who predicted that they would soon be back in Jerusalem, and Jeremiah, who replied that although he would like to believe that too, it simply wouldn't happen, not for a long, long time (Jer 28). Jeremiah was right; and Hananiah, who said the vessels would be back within two years, was dead in two months.

So we need to understand that Belshazzar's blasphemy was not just that he showed some minor disrespect for a few sacred objects of another people's religion, like the thoughtlessness of a tourist who forgets to remove his shoes in the holy place of some foreign religion. Or even the stupid act of some British teenagers who stripped their clothes off at the summit of the sacred Mount Kinabalu, in Sabah, Malaysia, in June 2015. This was rather a calculated and intentional mockery of what those vessels represented, namely the God of Israel; the God of that wretched ethnic minority who were still derisively labelled "the exiles of Judah" (Dan 5:13, 6:13); the God who, in Belshazzar's eyes, was defeated more than a generation ago and who was certainly powerless to do anything about a spot of teasing and taunting by his reveling young party set.

Belshazzar's blasphemy went further still. The text suggests that he had to be drunk to go this far. For it was not merely that he used the sacred vessels for ordinary drinking at his party. That would be offensive in itself, rather like taking a church's communion silver plates and goblets and using them at a cheese and wine party. He did more than that. He and his cheering chums used these sacred goblets—goblets that had been used in the service of the only living God—to pour out drink offerings to *other gods*, lifeless gods, mere objects (Dan 5:4)! In shock value this would be like using a church's communion table and vessels for occult, satanic rituals. The blatant sacrilege and idolatry in such action would draw gasps of disbelief from any Jewish listeners to the story. How could God tolerate such offence to his holiness? Well, he didn't for long, since the next word is "Suddenly . . . ."

But before we move on to God's intervention, we should pause and think a bit more about what we really mean by blasphemy in our day. Is it still a real thing? Does it happen? Does it matter?

Belshazzar's blasphemy consisted of taking what belonged to the true and living God and using it for his own corrupt and decadent purposes in a context of contempt for God's assumed powerlessness. He could use the name of Yahweh and the things of Yahweh for fun, pleasure, or spite, believing that Yahweh was outdated, irrelevant, and impotent. I think, when you look at it like that, blasphemy in the form of attitudes and actions like that is by no means dead in our world. It is more than merely bad language. It involves using what belongs to God in a way that debases the thing so used by exploiting it for spite, profit, amusement, political advantage, or military ends.

There is a blasphemy law in the UK, but it currently applies only to something which mocks or insults the Christian religion. There are those who argue that such a one-sided law should either be extended to include the religious sensibilities of all faiths in the land, including Muslims, Jews, Hindus, etc., or else be abolished altogether. I must say that I tend to agree with this view. I do not think *Christ himself* needs the "protection" of our human laws. But on the other hand if the law is intended to protect all citizens, of whatever faith, from unreasonable and gratuitous offence and distress caused by deliberate mockery of what their religion holds dear, then it ought to apply to people of other faiths too.

However, there are more serious forms of blasphemy in our society which, like idolatry, are often unrecognized because we take them almost for granted.

The Media

I think it is blasphemous, though I would put it at the less serious end of my scale, that the name of Christ, the cross itself, and other precious factors of the biblical faith are so easily used in the media as expletives or as a source of comedy. I remember watching a very talented British comedian, whom I normally enjoy immensely, using communion wine and wafer as props for a skit that combined the priesthood and sexual innuendo. I am not, I think, squeamish in my sense of humour. Certainly I do not think that we should never laugh at religion or sex—humans do some pretty laughable things in both departments. But I found the act uncomfortably close to blasphemy, using objects some people hold sacred purely to create a lewd joke.

The almost mindless use of divine names and Christian symbols in the media may not be deliberate mockery of what they stand for, but it is certainly based on the assumption that there is no reality behind words like God, Jesus, Christ, hell, etc., certainly nothing that matters. So perhaps the fact that such constant media misuse reflects and amplifies the cheapening and irrelevance of the Christian message in society in general makes it a more serious matter that my personal "blasphemy scale" suggests.

Patriotism and Militarism

I love my country and I believe that the human kaleidoscope of nations and ethnic diversity is a creation gift of God for us to enjoy. So I am certain there is a wholesome and positive affection for one's own country, provided it does not sink into hatred and contempt for the countries of others. However, it is clear that there is another kind of patriotism which is undeniably idolatrous and blasphemous, as we already observed in chapter 3.

I think it is more seriously blasphemous when the church uses the name of God and Christ to "bless" weapons of war and destruction or sanctifies acts of war by claiming that "God is on our side." That was the great claim, of course, made by both Germany and Britain (as well as by Russia and America) during the First World War. It was a use and abuse of the Christian faith that has had detrimental effects in the whole following century, as Philip Jenkins has chronicled so formidably in his book *The Great and Holy War: How World War I Changed Religion For Ever*.[1]

But long before that book exposed the relentless use of Christianity in support of national war aims, I have always been uncomfortable

---

1. Philip Jenkins, *The Great and Holy War: How World War I Changed Religion For Ever* (New York: HarperOne, 2014).

with the linking of church and military. In England, for example, many churches have military emblems such as regimental flags in prominent places. What is the message such a location for the symbols of war conveys? And while, as I said, I do not question healthy patriotism and love for one's own country, I am equally uncomfortable with the habit of some churches of placing the national flag in prominent places in or on church buildings or of parading the national flag into church along with the Bible, the communion elements, the choir, and the preacher. What kind of association is assumed in the minds (and hearts) of those who gather to worship the living God with the exclusive loyalty that the Bible calls for, when symbols of the presence of God (particularly the Lord's Table) are set alongside the symbols of statehood? Is the state being placed in proper subjection to God, or is God being used to bolster the claims of the state? What message was I supposed to read from an ornament I found in a church bookstore: a small wooden cross wrapped in the Stars and Stripes of the USA? At the very least I find such things confusing and potentially syncretistic, and at worst they verge on the blasphemous, if they are using the most precious objects and costly symbols of the sacrificial, redemptive work of our Lord and Saviour as an expression of national pride or a tool of corporate profit.

Consumerism

I think it is blasphemous that Christmas and the name of Christ (nativity scenes, grottos, and all) have been hijacked by the idolatry of mammon. However, I see that as only one part of the wider blasphemy by which our society has sacrificed virtually all its principals on the altar of consumerism. We now live with a philosophy of "The Market" which is given quasi-religious commitment and under which we are being turned into "customers" in every walk of life. Moral values such as compassion, and social values such as education, are all subject to the rigor of market competition. The sick are no longer patients; they are customers whom hospitals must compete to win. The young are no longer pupils and students; they are customers whom schools and universities must compete to attract. Even rail passengers are always customers now, perhaps with more justification, though they never ride on trains any more but on "services."

Will charities start calling their projects and beneficiaries "customers"? Perhaps some already do. Will worshippers become customers of the church? In the West we have certainly turned church into a consumerist market. You can buy whatever kind of worship experience you like—megachurch or missional church, or you can have it drive-in, or online in the comfort of your own home.

In a world where mammon is god, the name of the living God himself can be enlisted to serve mammon, as the charlatans of the church in every age have proved, from Tetzel selling his indulgences for buying forgiveness in the sixteenth century to televangelists selling salvation, healing, and prosperity today.

The fate that overtook Belshazzar is not one we would wish on anyone, no matter what their blasphemy. But it is a solemn object lesson in the truth that "God is not mocked," and that his judgment is certain—whether it leads to repentance as in the case of Nebuchadnezzar in Daniel 4 or simply destruction, as here.

> Suddenly the fingers of a human hand appeared and wrote on the plaster of the wall, near the lampstand in the royal palace. The king watched the hand as it wrote. His face turned pale and he was so frightened that his legs became weak and his knees were knocking.
>
> The king summoned the enchanters, astrologers and diviners. Then he said to these wise men of Babylon, "Whoever reads this writing and tells me what it means will be clothed in purple and have a gold chain placed around his neck, and he will be made the third highest ruler in the kingdom."
>
> Then all the king's wise men came in, but they could not read the writing or tell the king what it meant. So King Belshazzar became even more terrified and his face grew more pale. His nobles were baffled. (Dan 5:5–9)

THE PROPHECY OF DANIEL (5:10–28)

At least Nebuchadnezzar was allowed to have his nightmares in the privacy of his bedroom. Belshazzar is confronted with the in-breaking word of God in public. The finger of God that scattered plagues on Pharaoh (Exod 8:19), that carved the Ten Commandments (Exod 31:18; Deut 9:10), that would later drive out demons (Luke 11:20) takes visible form and writes mysteriously on the wall. The king is transformed from sacrilegious revelry to shaking panic and collapse.

Once again we are treated to the comic spectacle of the parade of the magicians, and once again they don't disappoint us. They are as useless as ever. "All the king's horses and all the king's men couldn't put the king's knees together again!" Incompetence, of course, has never been a disqualification for high political office.

Enter the queen.

> The queen, hearing the voices of the king and his nobles, came into the banquet hall. "May the king live for ever!" she said. "Don't be alarmed! Don't look so pale! There is a man in your kingdom who has the spirit of the holy gods in him. In the time of your father he was found to have insight and intelligence and wisdom like that of the gods. Your father, King Nebuchadnezzar, appointed him chief of the magicians, enchanters, astrologers and diviners. He did this because Daniel, whom the king called Belteshazzar, was found to have a keen mind and knowledge and understanding, and also the ability to interpret dreams, explain riddles and solve difficult problems. Call for Daniel, and he will tell you what the writing means."

> So Daniel was brought before the king, and the king said to him, "Are you Daniel, one of the exiles my father the king brought from Judah? I have heard that the spirit of the gods is in you and that you have insight, intelligence and outstanding wisdom. The wise men and enchanters were brought before me to read this writing and tell me what it means, but they could not explain it.

Now I have heard that you are able to give interpretations and to solve difficult problems. If you can read this writing and tell me what it means, you will be clothed in purple and have a gold chain placed around your neck, and you will be made the third highest ruler in the kingdom." (Dan 5:10–16)

Enter Daniel.

The preliminary speeches introducing Daniel to the action, by the queen and Belshazzar himself, are more fulsome than ever. If we did not know that the king was in a state of drunken terror, his words of praise would sound almost deliberately sarcastic. The real irony is that he is now begging for help from one of the very people whose God he had been insulting only moments before.

By this time, following the sequence and chronology of the stories so far, Daniel must have been an elderly man, probably in his eighties. He had been brought to Babylon before the fall of Jerusalem in 587 BC and he is now just about to witness the fall of Babylon in 539 BC. Yet here he is, still in government service, as he had been for over fifty years, still available to a drunken crown prince, still as courageous as ever. Brushing aside the offers of material and political reward, which he no longer needed, he delivers a searing word of divine judgment on the drunken, drivelling royal before him, before he even deigns to read and interpret the writing on the wall as requested.

There is a striking contrast between Daniel's stance here and the way he handled Nebuchadnezzar's problem in Daniel 4. There, as we saw, his approach had a pastoral warmth, a reluctant but truthful interpretation of the dream followed by urgent advice to repent and change in the hope of avoiding the falling blow of judgment. Here he delivers a more characteristically prophetic message, a direct word of outraged, divine justice and holiness to a man who was deliberately mocking God, climaxing in a final word of inescapable doom.

"Your Majesty, the Most High God gave your father Nebuchadnezzar sovereignty and greatness and glory and splendor. Because of the high position he gave him, all the nations and peoples of every language dreaded and feared him. Those the king wanted to put to death, he put to death; those he wanted to spare, he spared; those he wanted to promote, he promoted; and those he wanted to humble, he humbled. But when his heart became arrogant and hardened with pride, he was deposed from his royal throne and stripped of his glory. He was driven away from people and given the mind of an animal; he lived with the wild donkeys and ate grass like the ox; and his body was drenched with the dew of heaven, until he acknowledged that the most High God is sovereign over all kingdoms of earth and sets over them anyone he wishes.

"But you, Belshazzar, his son, have not humbled yourself, though you knew all this. Instead, you have set yourself up against the Lord of heaven. You had the goblets from his temple brought to you, and you and your nobles, your wives and your concubines drank wine from them. You praised the gods of silver and gold, of bronze, iron, wood and stone, which cannot see or hear or understand. But you did not honour the God who holds in his hand your life and all your ways. Therefore he sent the hand that wrote the inscription." (Dan 5:18–24)

There are two aspects of Daniel's speech to Belshazzar.

The Lesson He Would Not Learn

Daniel recounts what had happened to Nebuchadnezzar. The events were still very clear in his mind even though it had happened several years earlier. Nebuchadnezzar was not Belshazzar's actual father; there had been a couple of short reigns between Nebuchadnezzar's death and the reign of Nabonidus for whom Belshazzar was now deputising as crown prince. But "your father Nebuchadnezzar" was a standard way of referring to the illustrious ancestor.

Daniel also repeats the theological truth on which his whole relationship to Nebuchadnezzar had been built. It was God himself who had raised up the Babylonian king and given him human sovereignty over the whole ancient Near East, as the head of gold on his dream statue. His power and glory were God's gift. But because he refused to acknowledge the fact, those very gifts became his downfall. And so, as we saw in Daniel 4, it took a searing and humiliating mental illness to make Nebuchadnezzar acknowledge the real identity and sovereignty of God. All this Daniel spells out, probably to the great impatience of the drunken crowd, still staring goggle-eyed at the writing on the wall. They didn't want a history lesson about the last government. They wanted to know the meaning of what the moving finger had written.

Then comes the fatal blow: *"Though you knew all this . . ."* (v. 22). Belshazzar had fully known all the facts about his famous ancestor's glorious reign and the ignominious period of madness. He would also have known, perhaps he had even read, Nebuchadnezzar's proclamation with its testimony to the living reality of the Most High God whose kingdom rules over all human kings (and princes). Belshazzar would have known the ominous warning at the end of that testimony that "those who walk in pride, [God] is able to humble" (Dan 4:37). He knew all this. He knew the truth. But it all made no difference. He still went ahead with his arrogant mockery of the living God who had so humbled his predecessor.

The sin of Belshazzar, in other words, was sin against the light, sin against the truth, sin against what he knew, sin against the grace of having had an example and a lesson that should have been an effective warning. And such deliberate, open-eyed sin is the most serious kind. In its extreme form it becomes what Jesus called "sin against the Holy Spirit." This is when a person, having seen and known the power of God at work, refuses to acknowledge the hand of God and instead attributes it to Satan or evil. The kind of moral and spiritual perversion necessary to reach that state makes it impossible for the person to recognize the evil, repent of it, and thus be forgiven. As far as evil is concerned, they have hardened their mind and heart into a state of non-recognition and non-repentance. That is why Jesus said that such sin will not be forgiven. For where there is no repentance there is no forgiveness. It is a very serious and dangerous thing to go on doing what you *know* to be wrong while justifying it as being perfectly in the right. It is a serious thing to witness the work of God and ignore or deny it. If it becomes a habit, it can be terminally fatal.

The God He Would Not Honour

Far from learning the lesson that Nebuchadnezzar had learnt (the hard way), Belshazzar "set [himself] up against the Lord of heaven" (v. 23). In the light of chapter 4, the very idea of doing such a thing seems foolhardy. And Daniel can point to the evidence for his accusation. He was not talking just about inner pride or mental attitudes. The goblets that had been used to pour libations to lifeless gods, in mockery of the living God to whom they belonged, were still rolling and dripping on the tables. If Nebuchadnezzar had been judged for mere words that passed his lips, how much more did Belshazzar deserve for such deliberate and practical blasphemy?

Nebuchadnezzar had finally been prepared to admit that he owed everything to God, but Belshazzar would not even credit God with his next breath. "You did not honour the God who holds in his hand your life and all your ways" (v. 23). One pictures Belshazzar slumped in his chair, still clutching in his hand some figurine of an idol, unaware that he himself is held in the very hand of the God he has mocked. "It is a dreadful thing," said the author of Hebrews, speaking about deliberate sinning that is contemptuous of God's grace, "to fall into the hands of the living God" (Heb 10:31). Perhaps he had Belshazzar in mind.

Belshazzar is a model of what the human race in general tends to do. One of the original marks of our fallenness is our refusal to honour God. Knowing the truth about God, we choose to deny it. And the more we go on doing so, the more we come to believe our own lies, until we reach the point where the truth itself is regarded as falsehood while our own lies are paraded as absolute truths. Our Western culture has been systematically doing this for nearly two centuries now. We have banished God from what we choose to call "the real world" and have given our credence instead to all manner of myths; social, economic, scientific, political, and now also religious, in the form of New Age gods of wood and stone, i.e., the natural world itself.

Paul's comments on this great reversal are strikingly relevant.

> For although [people] knew God, they neither glorified him as God nor gave thanks to him, but their thinking became futile and their foolish hearts were darkened. Although they claimed to be wise, they became fools and exchanged the glory of the immortal God for images made to look like a mortal human being and birds and animals and reptiles. (Rom 1:21–23)

As Christians living in such a world, we have to be prepared to face up to its blasphemy. That means more than having to tolerate bad language in the workplace. The kind of implicit blasphemies of the world around us, as we saw above, are much more serious than habits of speech. For our society as a whole, having refused to honour God, bows down to a host of other idols. It is a hard tide to stand against. If things are going well, then the Christian will be the butt of questions and taunts about the irrelevance of his old-fashioned belief in God. If disaster strikes, he may well find himself bearing the brunt of accusations against God for allowing such things to happen. It is typically human to take credit for success and to blame God for disaster. It is also typical of some atheists to blame the God they don't believe exists for things he should not have allowed to happen if he did exist.

But we cannot get away with only pointing the finger at the fallen world. Do we as Christians learn from the lessons we know full well or give due honour to the God who holds our lives and all our ways in his hands? "Though you knew all this" (Dan 5:22) is a terrifying phrase. The finger of God has given us the commandments, and the word of God has given us many illustrations of the danger of ignoring them.

- Though we know full well (ever since David and Bathsheba) the dangerous consequences of adultery, more and more Christian marriages are hurt and often shattered by it.

- Though we know (ever since Achan and from the warnings of Christ himself) of the horrid sin of covetousness, we still flirt with the gods of consumerism and greed along with the rest of our society while so many in our world live in poverty and hunger.
- Though we know how much importance God gives to truth and integrity, we still pollute our churches with gossip, broken confidences, bickering, and false accusations.
- Though we know that dishonest weights and measures literally stink in God's nostrils (as an "abomination"), we still compromise with dodgy deals and justify questionable and unfair practices on the grounds that "business is business."

I sometimes shiver to think of some apocalyptic video recording of *all that we know* from the Bible, history, and experience played on a split screen alongside *all that we do or don't do* in spite of what we know. "But you . . . have not humbled yourself, though you knew all this . . . you did not honour [God]." May God save us from ever having to hear such a judgment.

And so at last to the interpretation of three enigmatic words.

This is the inscription that was written:

MENE, MENE, TEKEL, PARSIN

Here is what these words mean:

> *Mene*: God has numbered the days of your reign and brought it to an end.
> *Tekel*: You have been weighed on the scales and found wanting.
> *Peres*: Your kingdom is divided and given to the Medes and Persians. (Dan 5:25–28)

The three words on the wall literally meant a mina, a shekel, and a half, which were three descending values of coin, but in Daniel's alternative reading of the roots of the words they meant numbered, weighed, and divided. And that was God's verdict on Belshazzar and his kingdom. The honour and office conferred on Daniel (v. 29), in all its drunken hollowness, lasted scarcely a few hours.

> That very night Belshazzar, king of the Babylonians, was slain, and Darius the Mede took over the kingdom, at the age of sixty-two. (Dan 5:30)

THE MYSTERY OF PROVIDENCE (5:29–31)

Daniel 4 and 5 leave us with an unanswered question regarding the dealings of God in human history. They have certainly answered the question of who rules: God does, and all human authority is subject to him. Both chapters have reinforced that fundamental biblical affirmation. But the question can still be asked as to why Nebuchadnezzar and Belshazzar were treated so very differently. Why humble the one into repentance, grace, and restoration, but humiliate the other with merely a few hours' notice of his doom and destruction?

The text gives us no real answer, except for the distinguishing facts of Nebuchadnezzar's repentance and Belshazzar's deliberate rejection of the knowledge he had. Yet outwardly, humanly, as far as matters of public observance went, they were both state authorities, both were secular rulers, both were autocrats, both were proud.

So consider the role of Daniel in relation to them both. He was a public servant of both governments and also considered that he was serving the God of heaven by serving both. Furthermore, he was called to be faithful to the demands of the word of God as it was revealed to him in relation to both of these Babylonian rulers. To Nebuchadnezzar he had to give a warning and a challenge to respond, in the hope that he could avert judgment, a word which enabled Nebuchadnezzar to find restoration, after judgment. To Belshazzar, however, Daniel had to give an unequivocal word of irreversible doom. No warning. No appeal. Presumably the time of patience and possible repentance was long past.

How did Daniel know the difference? How did he know what the word of God was in each situation? I suspect that once again it had something to do with his thrice-daily prayer life in the midst of his busy administrative duties. I wonder if, in fact, it was out of that prayer life, combined with his public office, that the sharp edge of Daniel's true mission was forged. As we said before, Daniel was not a prophet in the true sense. He was a political administrator. Yet he was called on these occasions to deliver the word of God, plainly stated to the point of extreme discomfort, right into the very heart of government.

Now we know from Daniel 7 onwards that Daniel received more insights into God's dealings in history and the spiritual meaning of the contemporary affairs of his day than any of us are likely to "enjoy." But even if we never have visions like Daniel's (which is a relief as far as I'm concerned!) we *can* emulate both his life of persistent prayer and his bold faith in affirming the superiority of the reign of God over all human authorities.

At any time the secular state, within and under which we have to live and work and carry on our Christian mission, may become a Nebuchadnezzar or a Belshazzar. Our task is to get on with the job God has given us to do but to be ready at any time with the word of witness, with pastoral warning or prophetic protest, undergirded by constant prayer. And we must be prepared to be treated to extremes. Belshazzar's response (civic honours and high praise) is unlikely to be much repeated. The lion's den of Daniel 6 seems more probable in today's world, or, most often of all in our wearily cynical society, we are likely simply to be paralysed by waves of hostile, suffocating apathy.

CHAPTER 6

FACING THE LIONS

My wife says she never saw me really angry till we went to India! I am normally a fairly placid person, not given to great extremes of emotion at the upper or lower ends of the scale. Anger and I are not often found in each other's company, for any length of time at least. But it was there, in a Christian institution, that I experienced for the first time in my life the nastiness of being misunderstood. I mean seriously misunderstood, and not just because of my Northern Irish accent! The circumstances no longer matter now, and indeed I can scarcely remember them, but it was one of those issues in a community where administrative breakdowns are compounded with personal shortcomings and animosities, and then inflated by pride and the fear of losing face. Things were said and done which lacked integrity in themselves and did injustice to some other people, particularly students. I was drawn into it unavoidably because of some official responsibilities I held in the institution. Then I found that my motives were being judged and misinterpreted. I heard about things being said about me in senior meetings at which I was not present. My family also were a target of criticism. Things were even said about my daughter. I felt stung and hurt. It came at a very pressurized time of exams and marking at the hottest time of year, so I was feeling pretty exhausted and sorry for myself as well. So I went through a time of serious anger, some of which got expressed and some carefully concealed. It was a time of feeling the pressure of being a victim, of being "got at," of proverbial stabbings in the back. It was not, in short, very nice.

And if that is the worst such experience of personal animosity that I go through in my life, I shall, of course, be a very fortunate man. For although it was nasty, it was at least moderated by the Christian environment, and it didn't last very long. Some wise and mature Indian students helped to pull me out of my anger and self-pity into a better frame of mind. But it gave me some tiny insight into the kind of pressures that Christians live under in the pagan, secular world when they are subjected to the hatred and spite of others. The proverb about being thrown into "a den of lions" is not at all an exaggerated metaphor for what some believers face in our world.

One of the most powerful sermons I have heard or read on Daniel 6 was by the late Archbishop of Kenya, David Gitari. His outspoken condemnation of social and political injustice in his country made him a target of government attacks. He not only received death threats, but on one occasion he was attacked along with his family in his own home by thugs sent to kill him. Like Daniel he had only just preached on, he was delivered from death. Other Christians, however, including a fellow bishop, have died for their convictions.

So Daniel 6 has a very sharp relevance to all Christians who are put under pressure by authorities, especially in those parts of the world where to stand up for the living God can be a matter of life or death. There are many thousands of our sisters and brothers around the world who face this kind of pressure and danger as a "normal" part of life.

Where do we find Daniel in this final story in the first half of the book?

Daniel had survived the collapse of the Babylonian Empire and had now risen to the higher ranks of government administration in the Persian Empire that replaced it. As they say (in Britain anyway), governments come and governments go, but civil servants go on forever. By this time Daniel would have been a very old man, yet once again we find him subjected to a severe test of his faithfulness to God, a test even more searching than anything he had faced as a young student in Nebuchadnezzar's academy in chapter 1.

That Daniel faced this challenge to his faith in old age is a sobering lesson. There never comes a time in life when we can sit back and think that our faithfulness to God is so well established that it will never be challenged or tested again. I have always been impressed with the wisdom of Joshua who, when he himself was an old man, addressed the assembly of those who had shared in the conquest with him many years earlier. They would have been the older generation like Joshua himself. Yet he challenged them to "choose for yourselves *this day* whom you will serve" (Josh 24:15; cf. 23:1, 2). Yesterday's covenant loyalty was not enough. Today calls for a fresh choice. When did you last actually *choose* to serve God, in any situation where there was a real alternative?

So what was the choice that faced Daniel? First of all, our narrator sets the scene by reminding us of the integrity of our main character.

DANIEL'S EXCELLENCE (6:1–4)

> It pleased Darius to appoint 120 satraps to rule throughout the kingdom, with three administrators over them, one of whom was Daniel. The satraps were made accountable to them so that the king might not suffer loss. Now Daniel so distinguished himself among the administrators and the satraps by his exceptional qualities that the king planned to set him over the whole kingdom. At this, the administrators and the satraps tried to find grounds for charges against Daniel in his conduct of government affairs, but they were unable to do so. They could find no corruption in him, because he was trustworthy and neither corrupt nor negligent. (Dan 6:1–4)

Daniel had not got where he was by luck or by belonging to a privileged elite by birth (quite the reverse—he had overcome the disadvantages of his racial and social background). Nor was he there by royal favoritism. The opening verses of this chapter intentionally leave us in no doubt that Daniel's high position was thoroughly deserved and appropriate to his high qualities as a person. Two things stand out.

1. *His personal ability.* Daniel was outstanding. This simple fact is expressed in the phrase "his exceptional qualities." The text says he had "an excellent spirit." He himself, and all that he did, were

noticeably distinguished by a superior quality. He was a man of great natural gifts which were being thoroughly used through consistently applied hard work. The qualities which had brought him to the notice of King Nebuchadnezzar in his youth had not been the brief, bright flare of a young academic egghead who could mug it all up for exams but who would then fizzle out under the pressures of real life in the rough world of politics. Daniel was top quality in every way.

2. *His personal integrity.* This is the vital other side of the story. Sometimes people of great ability lack integrity and so their gifts are used corruptly. The financial world has been shaken in recent years by the almost incredible frauds that have been perpetrated by extremely clever people, people whose enormous expertise has been bent to facilitate greed and theft on a grand scale. In the political world we regularly read stories of corruption in public servants who use their office to line their own pockets. Doubtless the administration of a bureaucracy as vast as Persia's provided men in Daniel's position with plenty of scope for similar scams in the ancient world. They could get rich quick through a whole range of corrupt and exploitative practices.

But Daniel was trustworthy. He could be trusted by those below him, the common people he served. He could not be bribed by higher officials to work against their interests. And he could be trusted by those above him, particularly the king himself. The king knew that Daniel would not be bribed by any court conspirators or corrupt officials who might be plotting against him. So even his enemies could find no sniff of corruption.

However, it was not just that Daniel was not corrupt. He was "neither corrupt nor negligent." There are some people who are pretty harmless, but only because they are too lazy to be anything else. We all know the kind of officials in public offices who are infuriating, not because they are doing *wrong*, but because they are doing *nothing*. Seats are kept warm and paper shuffles around desks, but nothing moves in the real world. Daniel was not one of those. Things got done. He was "not negligent." So for both reasons—his ability and his integrity—the king knew that with Daniel in charge, he would not suffer loss. Here was a man who could be trusted to get the job done. Here was a man who would protect the interests of the state. Neither the king nor the country would come to harm with Daniel in charge of affairs.

From the perspective of the story in Daniel 6, the point of dwelling on these characteristics of Daniel himself is clear. It is to underline the fact that the persecution and testing that suddenly came his way were entirely unjust. There is a Job-like quality about Daniel in this story. In the book of Job we are invited to contemplate a man who was as righteous as we could imagine but who suffered the worst calamities we could imagine because of things he knew nothing about and had no control over. Here in Daniel 6 we see a man who is the perfect model of excellence and integrity in his profession who nevertheless suffers unjust hatred and attack.

In fact, the irony of the story is that Daniel was put under such pressure by the very state he was serving so well. As he later points out, courteously but powerfully (in view of where he said it from), he was not only innocent in the sight of God, but he had never done the state any wrong either (v. 22). *No wrong?* That was a massive understatement! Daniel had done the state more good through his honest and efficient administration than all his enemies put together. And yet he suffered.

And even more remarkably, *after* his brush with the lions, Daniel went on serving the state. He did not hand in his resignation in a fit of righteous indignation. Just as he modelled in advance the saying of Jesus about loving our enemies, so he is an example of what Peter encouraged Christians of his day to do. Even if you suffer for doing good, he said, endure it patiently, *and go on doing good*. Daniel is a perfect illustration of the teaching of Peter in the following texts.

> Submit yourselves for the Lord's sake to every human authority. . . . For it is God's will that by doing good you should silence the ignorant talk of foolish people. (1 Pet 2:13, 15)

Who is going to harm you if you are eager to do good? But even if you should suffer for what is right, you are blessed. "Do not fear what they fear; do not be frightened." But in your hearts revere Christ as Lord. Always be prepared to give an answer to everyone who asks you to give the reason for the hope that you have. But do this with gentleness and respect, keeping a clear conscience, so that those who speak maliciously against your good behaviour in Christ may be ashamed of their slander. For it is better, if it is God's will, to suffer for doing good than for doing evil. (1 Pet 3:13–17)

However, if you suffer as a Christian, do not be ashamed, but praise God that you bear that name . . . .

So then, those who suffer according to God's will should commit themselves to their faithful Creator and continue to do good. (1 Pet 4:16, 19)

There is another point worth noting here. All Daniel's ability and integrity had been put at the disposal of this secular, pagan, political authority. His daily work was his opportunity and mode of serving both his government and his God. Apart from his daily prayer, we know nothing about Daniel's personal or religious life. We don't know if he was involved in any kind of social or religious good causes. We don't know if he was a prominent lay leader in his local synagogue. We don't know if he went around telling Babylonians the "gospel" story of what God had done for Israel and summoning them to believe in the one true God. What we *are* told is that in his daily secular job he was the very best. Even apart from the rest of the story and its major point, that is worth taking to heart.

It is a very sad thing if Christians have the idea that a secular job is just a means of keeping the body fed and clothed and therefore feel at liberty to invest just enough of their ability and effort to keep the job. Then they reckon they can save their best talents and time for "God's work." Such a dichotomy fails to see the whole of life as "God's work." By contrast, Paul urged even slaves who were believers to work hard and honestly for their masters—even non-Christian masters—on the basis that in doing so they were in reality serving the Lord Christ.

> Slaves, obey your earthly masters in everything; and do it, not only when their eye is on you and to curry their favour, but with sincerity of heart and reverence for the Lord. Whatever you do, work at it with all your heart, as working for the Lord, not for human masters, since you know that you will receive an inheritance from the Lord as a reward. It is the Lord Christ you are serving. (Col 3:22–24)

All Nations Christian College, where I was a teacher and then principal for thirteen years, is in the business of training and equipping people for a wide variety of callings in cross-cultural Christian mission. When people applied to come there as students, we would ask for at least three letters of reference—one from a personal friend, one from a church minister or Christian leader, and one from a secular employer (most All Nations students have already been working in some secular professional capacity). Before interviewing candidates, I always looked with greatest interest at the third reference. You can expect that a person's Christian friends and pastor will say nice things about them, but I wanted to know what impression they had made in the *non-Christian* workplace. Had they been reliable, honest, hard working? Did they relate well to colleagues? Were they known for doing a good job? Because if there were questions over the quality of their work in secular life, what guarantee was there that they would be any different in the pressures of Christian work? What used to warm my heart most was when the secular employer's reference said something to the effect that, although the employer respected their employee's decision and sense of vocation (even if they didn't understand it), they really wished that he or she were *not* leaving because they would be such a loss to the company. If this candidate was really going to be missed from their secular job, I thought, then I knew we'd got somebody worth having!

The example of Daniel's excellence, therefore, challenges us to think hard about our daily lives as Christians in the world. On the one hand it warns us not to be surprised (as Peter and James wrote) if we experience unfairness and injustice in the way we are treated. On the other hand it searches our motives and integrity in the way we actually do our work in the secular sphere.

DANIEL'S ENEMIES (6:4–9)

> At this, the administrators and the satraps tried to find grounds for charges against Daniel in his conduct of government affairs, but they were unable to do so. They could find no corruption in him, because he was trustworthy and neither corrupt nor negligent. Finally these men said, "We will never find any basis for charges against this man Daniel unless it has something to do with the law of his God." (Dan 6:4–5)

It is very common in life that those who are good and competent arouse the dislike of those who are neither. It's just one of the many perversities of human nature. The nursery tale of The Ugly Duckling (like many nursery tales and rhymes) illustrates a truth of experience. Nobody likes somebody who is different from the comfortable crowd, who is not "one of us," especially if the difference is over a matter of morality or anything that threatens to show up what is really going on. So this account of how such a competent man as Daniel had such nasty enemies is a mirror of the real life experience of many people. What they thought and did is only too plausible.

Their Hatred

What made them hate Daniel so much? The text gives some hints at the reasons behind their malicious thinking and tactics.

1. *Jealousy.* They heard about Daniel's promotion (Dan 6:3). There was a leak from the royal cabinet: somebody who had the confidence of the king's counsel told his colleagues about the king's intention

to promote Daniel to the top job as head of the whole government administration. So an acute epidemic of professional jealousy sets in. Political life is, of course, an incubator for this kind of jealousy. We know how much we groan with cynicism as we watch many modern politicians jostling for the limelight, the best photo opportunity, the catchiest soundbite, the plummiest jobs. Sentimental lipservice is paid to the ideals of public service and false modesty is knee-deep, but the reality for many is a ratrace for power and influence, and/or the benefits in terms of wealth or prestige that may follow.

But Christians and Christian institutions are not at all immune to the ravages of professional jealousy. Churches and denominations sometimes have their "career structure," their hierarchy (the very word is out of tune with a biblical view of ministry). And in some parts of the world ecclesiastical positions are fought over (sometimes literally) with all kinds of nasty and corrupt practices, simply because of the access to money and power that such positions give.

2. *Racism.* Daniel's enemies decided to attack him in relation to his religion ("the law of his God"), but of course that was not merely a matter of private belief. It was his ethnic identity as well. Their racist attitude is betrayed by the way they describe Daniel to the king in verse 13. He is, they sneer, "one of the exiles from Judah." Now this incident takes place more than fifty years after the Israelites had been forcibly brought to the region by the military power of Babylon. People from Judah had settled down in Babylon now for two generations. Many, like Daniel, were thoroughly integrated into the country's social and political system, after a comprehensive academic and cultural re-education (as we saw in Dan 1). And now Babylon had been replaced by Persia. Yet these hostile officials still refer to him in terms probably as derogatory as calling second and third generation black British citizens "immigrants." Daniel 6 is not just a spiritual tale of courage in the face of danger. It carries an unmistakable whiff of anti-Semitism and thus unmasks the twisted face of racism.

If it is hard to tolerate someone else getting promotion, it is even harder if that person comes from a despised ethnic group or social class or regional background or is just the wrong gender. Then personal jealousy is linked to group pride, and all our human instinct to protect the in-group from the outsider surges up. Racism is a very horrid and destructive cancer in society, and this story shows where it can lead.

3. *Spite.* Jesus once said that people love darkness because their deeds are evil, so they hate the light. Goodness is not popular, unless it coincides with the self-interest of others. Since people of integrity pose a constant threat of exposure to those who are evil, they are often in danger. Those who are corrupt will seek to eliminate the threat of those who are "too good for their own good" in order to protect their own vested interests. These officials probably realized that if Daniel was promoted to the top of the civil administration, then it would be difficult for them to carry on their own corrupt practices. They could be exposed and dismissed. So their reaction is to do their utmost to drag Daniel down to their own level, to get *him* dismissed on a charge of corruption before he can expose their corruption. They knew all about "negative campaigning," about muck-raking. They tried all the tactics of political crucifixion. However, finally they had to admit defeat. Nothing would stick to Daniel. His record was so clean that any charges would be so lacking in credibility that it would make his accusers look foolish.

"Do not be surprised," warns the New Testament. We live in a world which is in rebellion against God. So it will show all the marks of that rebellion when faced with anyone who stands for the values of God's kingdom—truth, honesty, integrity, goodness, and even plain competence. Such things are not welcome in our world.

Their Methods

1. *They Exploited His Strength.* Since they could find no chink in Daniel's armour, they decided to trap him in the armour itself. Having failed to find a weakness, they decided to engineer his downfall by using his own strength against him. They asked what it was that was most distinctive about Daniel. What mattered most to him? They realized that above and behind all his excellent work record was the

fact of his loyalty to his God. Now there was no conflict in practice between this loyalty to God and his obvious loyalty and service to the state, but if they could set up a situation in which they would *force* a conflict, then his strength of religious conviction would bring about his own downfall. It was brilliant.

In fact, it was diabolically clever. For the tactics of Satan are often like this. In the early days of a Christian's life, Satan can "enjoy" tripping us up through our weaknesses—old habits, ingrained personality traits, attitudes and prejudices that haven't been converted yet, simple ignorance of the Bible's teaching, or lack of good advice and guidance on how to live as a Christian. But as a Christian grows up, by teaching, experience, and God's grace, these weaknesses are tackled. New, Christ-like qualities begin to take their place. Now of course it is never true that we shed all our weaknesses. It would be daft as well as ignorant to imagine that. But, by the grace of God and the fruit of his Spirit, our weaknesses are turned into strengths.

And at that point Satan changes tactics. If he cannot pull us down by obvious and easy temptations and sins, he will use the very things we thought were our strengths or our gifts to trap us into situations where we end up flat on our face again in sin and defeat.

For example, being a Christian strengthens a young person's sense of responsibility towards parents, since that is a clear part of biblical and Christian duty. So let that newly reinforced commitment to respect and obedience grow and develop till it becomes a definite, conscious virtue. This young Christian has a new desire to honour and be kind to his or her parents, something that the parents may welcome, if they are not hostile to their child's Christian faith. But then, let the strength of that commitment to their parents be thrown into conflict with loyalty to the call of Christ himself. Then how will they cope with the conflict of loyalties?

An Indian woman among my students at All Nations found this an intolerable tension in her young life as a newly converted Christian in a Hindu home. She wanted to obey her parents in all things (that was an Indian cultural duty too, and her Christian faith only strengthened it). But she could not yield to their severe and prolonged pressure to give up her loyalty to Jesus as her only God and Lord and worship the Hindu deities with them. With God's help, she stood firm. But as she explained, what made the temptation so sharp was that, if she had given in to their demands and worshipped their gods, she would not have seemed to be doing anything wrong or immoral. Quite the reverse, she would have seemed to be fulfilling the duties of an obedient daughter. That's what her parents expected and didn't the Bible teach it too? For her, the teaching of Jesus himself, that discipleship to him could cause "a sword" within families, was a painful reality.

It is also a sad fact that many Christian pastors fall into sexual temptations that arise out of the very nature of their work. According to a survey years ago in *Christianity Today*, 12 percent of those who responded to a questionnaire distributed to a thousand pastors admitted having had illicit sexual intercourse in the course of their pastoral work. Eighteen percent admitted to more general sexual involvement. I am sure it is very unlikely that these men and women became pastors with any intention or desire to do that kind of thing. Most, if not all of them, probably never imagined at the start of their pastoral ministry that they would ever become entangled in this way. Yet they fell, tripped up by the very thing that was their gift and strength: a pastoral heart and a caring spirit—but careless eyes. The thing they thought was a strength turned out to hide a vulnerable weakness.

The lesson is: Don't guard only your weak points. Watch your strong points as well. Satan knows how to attack both.

2. *They Violated the Constitution.*

So these administrators and the satraps went as a group to the king and said: "May King Darius live for ever! The royal administrators, prefects, satraps, advisers and governors have all agreed that the king should issue an edict and enforce the decree that anyone who prays to any god or human being during the

next thirty days, except to you, Your Majesty, shall be thrown
into the lions' den. Now, Your Majesty, issue the decree and put
it in writing so that it cannot be altered—in accordance with
the laws of the Medes and Persians, which cannot be repealed."
So King Darius put the decree in writing. (Dan 6:6–9)

The proposal they put to the king was very flattering. It had to
be, because it was only by dazzling him with flattery that they were
able to divert attention from the fact that their proposal was quite
unconstitutional.

For the fact was that the Persian Empire granted a significant
measure of religious freedom to subject peoples. One of the first acts
of Cyrus the Persian when he defeated Babylon and took over its
whole empire was to issue an edict liberating captive peoples and their
gods (Dan 1:21; 6:28; Ezra 1:1–11). It was this edict which gave the
exiles of Judah (along with other peoples that had been captured by
Babylon) the freedom to return from exile to Jerusalem and to rebuild
the temple to Yahweh, their God. The part of Cyrus's edict relevant
to the Jews is recorded in Ezra 1:1–4. Full details of his policies are
recorded on a stone cylinder, known as the Cyrus Cylinder, which
you can see in the British Museum.

Cyrus's idea, which became official colonial policy of the Persian
Empire, was the opposite of Assyrian and Babylonian policy before
him. They had taken the view that the best way to keep nations
subject to the imperial power was to disrupt them, to disperse and
deport populations, and especially to capture their gods by bringing
their idols to the capital city. Yahweh had no idol, so, as we saw at
the beginning of the book of Daniel, Nebuchadnezzar brought other
sacred vessels from the Jerusalem temple instead. Cyrus seems to have
considered that such a policy was a recipe for constant discontent
and rebellion. Why keep all the gods cooped up in your capital city
where they would get angry with you when you could release them
all back to their homes? Build nice temples for them, and then your
subject peoples would be grateful to you, pray to their gods for you,

and you'd have a peaceful, contented empire. That seems to have been Cyrus's thinking.

The official policy of the Persian Empire, therefore, was to grant relative religious freedom to its subject peoples, within the limits of overall loyalty to the Persian state itself. In this respect it was a more liberal regime than before. Constitutionally, therefore, there was no reason why, in Daniel's case or for any of the Jews, the requirements of "the law of his God" should have come into conflict with "the laws of the Medes and Persians." But his enemies succeeded in gaining what amounted to a temporary suspension of the constitution in order to engineer precisely such a conflict. They knew that if they forced Daniel to choose between the law of his God and the law of the state, he would choose his God. But they could only force such a choice by changing the law of the state. So they went to Darius to do just that. But they concealed their negative intention (to destroy Daniel) under a charade of positive flattery (to honour the king). Doubtless they threw in some other supporting arguments, like these perhaps:

- "We need to encourage harmony and unity among all the races of our empire so our proposal will be good for race relations." (I remember seeing a large poster in Bombay airport [before the city was renamed Mumbai], that proclaimed: "Whether Hindu, Muslim, Christian, Sikh or Jain, we are Indians first and Indians last.")
- "It's all right for people to follow their own religion privately, but everyone must acknowledge that loyalty to the king and the state comes first."
- "There's really only one patriotic religion and everybody should acknowledge that for a specified period, and then they can revert to their own religions afterwards."

And the king bought it. Fooled by the flattery, he rubber-stamped the new bill so that it became law, without further consultation or reflection. The rest of the story makes it clear that he later regretted his hasty decision. However, the deed was done. The constitution was effectively suspended by a law which was itself unconstitutional, and it gave the enemies of Daniel enough time to bring him down under a cloak of legality.

We need to be on our guard as Christians and as citizens with regard to the constitutional framework of our countries. Constitutions matter, for they frame the values and conditions under which social and political life will be conducted—and we know from the Bible that God cares about such things. It has been said that the book of Deuteronomy is somewhat like a constitution for Old Testament Israel. So, if we believe that all human authority is delegated authority, entrusted by God; and if we believe that basic human rights and constitutional freedoms reflect God's moral will and are for the good of all people; and if, in other words, our biblical faith tells us something about our humanity and not just about our Christianity, then we of all people must stand up for constitutional rights and freedoms.

We are all aware of how human rights in general are violated in many parts of the world. We know about the struggles that Christians face in many countries where the law itself discriminates against them. However, even if we live in a so-called secular democracy, we need to watch out for the subtle ways in which the enemies of the Christian faith will undermine or remove the precious freedom to worship and witness.

In India in the 1970s a number of states in the Indian union passed "Freedom of Religion" bills. Contrary to the impression given by the title, the meaning of these acts was that people were free to have their own religion, but *not* to convert anyone from another religion to their own, or indeed to choose to convert to another religion voluntarily, without a very long and complicated legal process. In a few states these laws have survived and are used harshly against Christians. This is in spite of the fact that they have been shown to be contrary to Article 25 of the Fundamental Rights section of the Indian constitution, which guarantees the "the right freely to

profess, practice *and propagate* religion."[1] Indeed, there are powerful
movements of Hindu nationalism in India which would prefer India
to have a constitution more like the one that used to govern Nepal,
which prohibited conversion from one religion to another—thus
making Christian evangelism among Hindus illegal.

> Article 19 Right to Religion (1) Every person shall have the free-
> dom to profess and practise his own religion as handed down to
> him from ancient times having due regard to traditional practices;
> provided that no person shall be entitled to convert another
> person from one religion to another.[2]

Prison sentences of three to six years used to be imposed for vio-
lation of this law, and many Christians there experienced such spells
in prison. Nepal has since gone in a different direction and granted
freedom of religion under which the Christian church has grown
phenomenally in the last quarter century. Meanwhile, a much more
pro-Hindu government has come to power in India.

Surely nothing like that will ever happen in our Western liberal democracies, we might think. We should not be complacent.
Nobody would suggest banning Christianity or anything so crude.
But we might be told that any form of evangelism, especially among
communities of other faiths, is detrimental to racial or community
harmony, and therefore it should be declared illegal. Or it may even
be equated with "hate speech" and prosecuted as such. Already, certainly in the UK, equality laws are being used to prevent Christians
exercising rights of conscience in moral areas where their conscience
conflicts with the culture's understanding and legislation of sexuality,
particularly in relation to same-sex marriage. People are not exactly
thrown in a den of lions, but the loss of employment or career can be
devastating to whole families.

Those of us who do live in democratic societies need to be on

---

1. "Subject to public order, morality and health and to the other provisions of this
Part, all persons are equally entitled to freedom of conscience and the right freely to profess,
practise and propagate religion." Article 25 (1) of "The Constitution of India 1949."

2. Cited from the "Constitution of Nepal," 1990.

our guard to defend constitutional freedoms by all legitimate means. There is nothing "unchristian" about doing so. But at the same time we need to be prepared for whatever biblical response might be called for if laws are passed by the state that prohibit us from some part of our Christian duty in obedience to Christ. Among other things, such a reality would force us to listen and learn from the great majority of Christians around the world who do in fact live and witness in the midst of such restrictions, particularly those living in states with powerful Muslim-controlled legal systems, such as in the Middle East and North Africa, Pakistan, Malaysia, etc.

Such a reality would force us to learn again from Daniel, a man whose loyalty to the state is now thrown into conflict with his loyalty to God. It is worth noting, in view of what we have just been discussing, that the test for Daniel had to do with something being *forbidden*, not something being *required* (as in the case of Shadrach, Meschach, and Abednego in Dan 3). In some ways, if the state orders you to do something that you know God forbids, it is a simple matter (though costly!) to refuse. But if the state merely tells you to stop doing something, it is rather easy to go along with it, especially if, as is the case with evangelism, we weren't doing it very much anyway!

Who would have noticed if Daniel had just stopped praying for a month? Could he not have stopped the outward physical actions of prayer and just gone on praying silently and secretly? But to do that would have been to give in to precisely the idolatry that the state was demanding. If the state begins to make claims that amount to divine status, then even prayer becomes a political act, because in prayer, especially public, visible prayer, you are affirming the reality of a higher authority than the state. You are appealing *beyond* Caesar. You are denying the claims of the state to have ultimate power and authority over you. Prayer is a political statement.

This is why, in the New Testament, instructions to Christians to submit to political authorities is linked to the command to *pray* for them (1 Tim 2:1–2). Prayer puts political authorities in perspective. If you pray for kings and governments, then you are automatically seeing them in their proper, subordinate place—under the rule and control of the God you are praying to. For that reason, I think there is no contradiction between both praying *for* those in authority and in some circumstances praying *against* them. That is to say, we should pray for our political rulers, as the Bible commands, that they would govern well, with justice, integrity, and compassion, and that they might personally come to faith in Christ and be saved. But at the same time, where we know that they are engaged in corrupt or unethical practices, or when they are passing legislation that is contrary to biblical, ethical values (legislation, for example that unfairly penalizes the already poor while favouring the already wealthy), or when the state perpetrates excessive and unwarranted violence either internally or in questionable external wars, or when the state perpetuates practices that irreparably damage God's creation and threaten the earth's climate, at such times we can and should *pray against* such policies, and where appropriate speak out against them too, as the biblical prophets certainly did. There is no contradiction between *praying* for the state (and indeed submitting to the state as Paul says in Rom 13) and *critiquing* the state. On the contrary, the more we pray for the political realm, the sharper will become our ability to evaluate what goes on there by God's own standards revealed in Scripture.

I believe that Daniel was probably praying for Darius, just as I think he had been praying for Nebuchadnezzar and Babylon, according to the instructions of God through Jeremiah (Jer 29:7). And this is why he refused to stop praying, even when the same Darius ordered him to. Daniel's prayer life kept him in touch with a higher authority than Darius, and no edict would change that, not even "the laws of the Medes and Persians."

DANIEL'S VALUES (6:10)

> Now when Daniel learned that the decree had been published, he went home to his upstairs room where the windows opened

towards Jerusalem. Three times a day he got down on his knees and prayed, giving thanks to his God, just as he had done before. (Dan 6:10)

Daniel's lifetime of disciplined, regular, habitual prayer probably meant that it would have been more difficult to stop praying than to carry on. Some features of his prayer life are mentioned almost incidentally, yet in such a way as to show us that it was not something bizarre or abnormal:

- He prayed three times a day.
- He got down on his knees.
- He gave thanks to God.
- He asked God for help (vv. 10, 11).

All simple things that any of us could imitate.

It shows the desperation of his enemies and the evil depths of their determination to get him out of the way, that they had him arrested and charged for such activity. Not only was it no threat to the king (Daniel's loyalty to the state could not be questioned), but in fact, if the king only knew, it was probably to the king's benefit since almost certainly part of Daniel's prayer was *for* the king. The prayer of God's people is for the good of the world, not just the church. And that adds to the tragic irony of the trap Darius fell into. He was tricked into preventing someone doing something which was actually for his own benefit!

But what about those windows in the room where Daniel prayed, the windows that were "opened towards Jerusalem?" It is hardly accidental that those windows are mentioned here, just as it is hardly accidental that Daniel chose to pray in this room with west-facing windows. Was it simply superstition or nostalgia? Was he just mentally escaping to his homeland?

I remember when I was a young student in Cambridge, how I suffered the heartache of separation from my girlfriend, Elizabeth (now my wife and better known as Liz). As it happened, the window of my room faced roughly northwest and I used to gaze out of it, especially at sunset, thinking of all the miles between me and her across the sea in Belfast, Northern Ireland. I would dream that I could beam across those 500 miles in an instant to see her (then beam back and finish the essay I should have been concentrating on!). Somehow it seems unlikely that Daniel, now in his eighties, was gazing out the window in that kind of reverie.

There were probably two reasons why Daniel chose to pray in a posture facing towards Jerusalem. The first reason was his deep knowledge of the Scriptures (cf. Dan 9:2). The record of Solomon's prayer at the dedication of the temple in 1 Kings refers repeatedly to people praying "towards" the city, or the temple, or the land. And towards the end, that prayer anticipates precisely the situation Daniel and his friends were in.

> If [your people] turn back to you with all their heart and soul
> in the land of their enemies who took them captive, and pray
> to you toward the land you gave their ancestors, toward the city
> you have chosen and the temple I have built for your Name; then
> from heaven, your dwelling place, hear their prayer and their plea,
> and uphold their cause. (1 Kgs 8:48–49)

We know from Daniel 9 that this was exactly the burden of Daniel's heart. So, in praying towards Jerusalem at windows opened in that direction, he was simply doing what his Scriptures said. Daniel was a man of the Bible as well as a man of prayer.

But a second, deeper reason is that this action reveals the whole orientation and inspiration of Daniel's life. Here he was, living and working for all his adult life in Babylon, the city of Nebuchadnezzar and then his Persian successors. But all the time he was looking, praying, meditating, *turning*, towards Jerusalem, Zion, the city of God. Daniel drew from that source the identity, character, and values of his own life.

Jerusalem, to the people of Israel, was not merely an attractive hilltop city. It was not merely the capital city of the Southern Kingdom of Judah. In fact, it was not really a very impressive city at all, as world cities go, even in those days. Nothing in Jerusalem ever made it onto the list of the Seven Wonders of the World.

But it was the place where Yahweh, God of Israel, had made his name to dwell. The presence of Yahweh was there in the temple, the law of Yahweh was known and proclaimed there, the worship of Yahweh was going on there (at least it had been until Nebuchadnezzar destroyed the city and temple). So, although it often failed in reality (as the prophets show us so clearly), it was supposed to be the place where the righteousness and justice of the God of Israel were modeled. It was the place celebrated in the Psalms as Zion, the heartbeat of the kingdom of God.

Jerusalem was the place to which, in prophetic vision, the nations would come to learn about the true God and his ways (Isa 2:1–5). Jerusalem was the focal point of the messianic hope and of God's future reign. God would one day rule from Zion. Jerusalem, even Jerusalem in ruins (as it was through most of Daniel's life, although by the time of Dan 6 it was being resettled), symbolized all that great heritage of history and hope. Jerusalem, though physically flattened, reminded Daniel of the kingdom of his God, past, present, and future.

To pray "towards Jerusalem," then, was to align himself in the direction of the God of Israel and to embrace that God's purposes and values. It was like taking a daily compass bearing for his life, enabling him to set everything else in its true perspective in relation to the reality and the requirements of Yahweh his God.

For Daniel, then, the key to the future and all the purposes of God, the meaning of life, and the source of his ultimate values, lay *not in the city Nebuchadnezzar had built, but in the city Nebuchadnezzar had destroyed.*

Daniel lived in the midst of the dazzling imperial and urban culture of the most powerful world empire of his time. The Persian Empire stretched from the borders of India to the borders of Greece. He rubbed shoulders with the great, the wealthy, and the powerful. He walked the corridors of earthly power and glory. He could stand in the presence of the emperor. Yet every day, three times a day, he got down on his knees and thought about God and Jerusalem. He kept his orientation right.

Prayer reminded Daniel of his true values. Prayer "towards Jerusalem" re-aligned his busy political life in the direction of God's will and God's commands. Prayer was the means by which Daniel was able to be a faithful and honest servant of one of the kingdoms of this world and yet, at the same time, serve the kingdom of God. Daniel was living in Zion, not when he got to heaven, but in the midst of the ambiguous, complex, and potentially bestial (see Dan 7) world of human power politics.

So when I think of those open windows, I don't see them as an escape hatch but as an entry shaft. That is, they were not so much *to let Daniel's prayers out* as *to let the God of Jerusalem in*. Daniel's prayer life was not escapism *out of* the daily grind of political administration. Rather, his daily prayer was his means of bringing the power and presence of Israel's God *into* his immediate work. Daniel was God's salt and light in the secular world in which he moved. His saltiness was preserved and his lamp kept polished by his daily contact with their source, God himself. The light that shone through those windows gave his life the power to shine in a dark world.

Whatever our personal pattern of devotional life, it is worth asking the question: How does my life of prayer relate to the everyday real world of secular life and work? Is it a moment of blessed relief and escape from surrounding pressures? Or is it the means of drawing the presence of God—with all God's values and priorities—into that world? This applies not only to our private prayers but also to our participation in Sunday worship and our times of fellowship, prayer, or Bible study with other Christians. Are they evasive or invasive? Escapist or transformative? Let's make sure the windows of our prayers are "opened toward Jerusalem," that we daily re-orientate our lives in the direction of God's name, God's will, God's mission, God's direction, and God's standards. Like Daniel, who once again serves as a model of obedience to one of Jesus's commands, let us "seek first his kingdom and his righteousness."

DANIEL'S VINDICATION (6:11–28)

The rest of the story of this chapter is the familiar bit! Certainly it's the bit that goes down best with the Sunday school children.

> Then these men went as a group and found Daniel praying and asking God for help. So they went to the king and spoke to him about his royal decree: "Did you not publish a decree that during the next thirty days anyone who prays to any god or human being except to you, Your Majesty, would be thrown into the lions' den?"
>
> The king answered, "The decree stands—in accordance with the laws of the Medes and Persians, which cannot be repealed."
>
> Then they said to the king, "Daniel, who is one of the exiles from Judah, pays no attention to you, Your Majesty, or to the decree you put in writing. He still prays three times a day." When the king heard this, he was greatly distressed; he was determined to rescue Daniel and made every effort until sundown to save him.
>
> Then the men went as a group to the king and said to him, "Remember, Your Majesty, that according to the law of the Medes and Persians no decree or edict that the king issues can be changed."
>
> So the king gave the order, and they brought Daniel and threw him into the lions' den. The king said to Daniel, "May your God, whom you serve continually, rescue you!" (Dan 6:11–16)

The art of the Hebrew storyteller brilliantly brings out the shocked dismay of the king when he realized how cunningly he had been trapped. There was a great emphasis on "law and order" in Persia. Not for nothing has the expression "the laws of the Medes and Persians" become proverbial for hard and fast rules. Now the king finds himself forced to trample on basic human rights in order to maintain a law which itself violated constitutional freedoms, all because he had allowed himself to be deceived by flattery. Flattery, like bribery, blinds the eye of those who need the clearest vision. And Darius was neither the first nor the last politician to end up in a blind alley, faced with a dilemma that had been brought about by his own self-interest and pride. Nor is he the only one to be trapped into sacrificing the innocent but vulnerable, to placate the wicked but influential. Such injustice is the stock in trade of politics locally, nationally and internationally, to this day.

There is a similarity here with Pontius Pilate. Like Darius, Pilate also found himself cornered into denying justice to a man he knew was innocent, in order, in his case, to maintain a peace which was based on oppression and violence. Like Daniel, Jesus accepted the human authority of the pagan ruler, knowing that real power lies elsewhere. Pilate functioned with a delegated authority under the actual kingdom of God.

There are also echoes of Daniel 6 in the story of the resurrection. Early Christian art often portrayed the story of Daniel's deliverance from the den of lions as a prefiguring of the resurrection. As we read the narrative, it is not hard to see why.

> A stone was brought and placed over the mouth of the den, and the king sealed it with his own signet ring and with the rings of his nobles, so that Daniel's situation might not be changed. Then the king returned to his palace and spent the night without eating and without any entertainment being brought to him. And he could not sleep.
>
> At first light of dawn, the king got up and hurried to the lions' den. When he came near the den, he called to Daniel in an anguished voice, "Daniel, servant of the living God, has your God, whom you serve continually, been able to rescue you from the lions?"
>
> Daniel answered, "May the king live forever! My God sent his angel, and he shut the mouths of the lions. They have not hurt me, because I was found innocent in his sight. Nor have I ever done any wrong before you, Your Majesty."
>
> The king was overjoyed and gave orders to lift Daniel out of the den. And when Daniel was lifted from the den, no wound was found on him, because he had trusted in his God. (Dan 6:17–23)

Notice the stone placed over the "tomb" and the official seal to prevent any tampering with it. Notice the early morning rush to the tomb, followed by the overwhelming discovery of miraculous life in the place of certain and inescapable death. Above all, notice that Daniel is fully vindicated, just as the resurrection was the vindication of Jesus and all he claimed and taught. Daniel's faithfulness and integrity had been tested to the final extreme, and they had been upheld by an unmistakable divine verdict. Daniel had been faced with a choice between his principles and his personal safety (to put it mildly!), and his principles had been vindicated.

There is one significant point of difference, however. Jesus went to the cross, knowing full well the horror and agony it held, but also knowing that God would not abandon him to the grave but that he would be raised again. He shared that confidence on several occasions with his disciples. But in Daniel's case we cannot know whether Daniel could have known in advance that the lions would suffer an acute attack of lockjaw. That the lions were unable to bite him may well have been as surprising for him as it doubtless was for the lions. Like his three friends a long time earlier Daniel trusted in God's ability to deliver him but was prepared to pay the final cost of his loyalty to God and leave his ultimate vindication in God's hands. And that points to another difference: Daniel was delivered *from* death and vindicated. Jesus was delivered *through and after* death, and thereby vindicated.

But the real vindication at the end of this story is not merely Daniel's but of Daniel's God. The testimony of Darius echoes the words of Nebuchadnezzar, both when he was amazed by God's deliverance of Shadrach, Meshach, and Abednego from the furnace and also when he himself was restored to sanity (Dan 3:28–29 and 4:34–37).

> Then King Darius wrote to all the nations and peoples of every language in all the earth:
> "May you prosper greatly!
> "I issue a decree that in every part of my kingdom people must fear and reverence the God of Daniel.

"For he is the living God
    and he endures forever;
his kingdom will not be destroyed,
    his dominion will never end.
He rescues and he saves;
    he performs signs and wonders
    in the heavens and on the earth.
He has rescued Daniel
    from the power of the lions." (Dan 6:25–27)

The irony of this proclamation is that here was a man who had allowed himself and his state to be set up as the ultimate kingdom to which all his subjects must bow and pray, yet now he orders everybody in *his* kingdom to acknowledge a higher kingdom than his own. And that, of course, is the point of the whole story in Daniel 6.

That is also the final reality to which the whole book points. The second half of the book will go on to reinforce the point through visions portraying the ultimate triumph of God and the people of God through one like a "son of man," over the bestial arrogance and destructiveness of human kingdoms (Dan 7). Multitudes of Jews and Christians through the ages and today have faced lions—literally and metaphorically. Many have been delivered and vindicated. Many have not, in this life.

But the God of Daniel is still the king of heaven and of earth. His kingdom still rules the kingdoms of this world. He *can* deliver, and he often does. But he calls his people to faithfulness and integrity in our everyday lives, whatever the cost. He calls us to build our lives on the values of the kingdom of God not "when we all get to heaven," but in the here and now.

If we are also called to the extreme test of martyrdom for doing so, as so many in our present world are going through, let us pray that we may have, with them, the grace of God to meet it with the courage and conviction of Daniel, confident in that final vindication which is guaranteed in the resurrection of Christ himself.

BEASTS, THRONES, SAINTS AND . . . A MAN

This chapter functions like a hinge or pivot between the two halves of the book of Daniel. Looking back, its opening date throws us back to a period earlier than chapter 6 and connects with the dream in chapter 2. Looking forward, chapter 7 introduces us to a different side of the Daniel we met in chapters 1–2 and 4–6. Those chapters relate stories *about* Daniel. The later chapters are presented as testimony *by* Daniel of his various visions, prayers, and conversations with heavenly messengers. However, the fundamental message is the same throughout the book: the sovereignty of the God of Israel in the midst of the world of human nations and empires. In chapters 1–6 we encounter the sovereignty of God in the context of human stories. In chapters 7–12 we encounter the sovereignty of God in the context of heavenly visions.

The chapter falls into two clear halves. First of all, Daniel reports the disturbing content of a vision he had in the closing years of the Babylonian Empire (vv. 1–14). Then he reports how, still within the vision, one of the characters in it explains to him the meaning of the vision (vv. 15–27)—which did nothing to lessen his disturbed frame of mind (v. 28). So we shall look at both halves, and then draw together some connecting themes.

THE DOUBLE VISION (7:1–14)

> In the first year of Belshazzar king of Babylon, Daniel had a dream, and visions passed through his mind as he was lying in bed. He wrote down the substance of his dream. (Dan 7:1)

The date is significant. Belshazzar, as we know from the ending of chapter 5, was the last ruler in Babylon before it was captured by Cyrus of Persia. For the exiles of Judah, most of them the second generation since the fall of Jerusalem in 587 BC, and some of them very elderly, like Daniel, it must have been a time of mixed hope and anxiety. If Babylon was coming to the end of its dominance (as Jeremiah had said; see Dan 9:2), what would come next? Would they be restored to their homeland, as God had promised? And if so, what lay ahead then? Would the great visions of Isaiah 40–55 be fulfilled in a glorious age of renewed security and prosperity in their land?

Undoubtedly the future held great hope, and God would not (and will not) ultimately default on those promises. But the historical reality for the people of Israel in the coming centuries was to be much more ambiguous. They would return to the land, but not return to glorious independence. The end of exile in Babylon would not mean the end of suffering at the hands of hostile powers. Other empires would follow, some of which would be much larger than Babylon and more oppressive too. So there would be severely testing times ahead for the people of God.

Daniel, a man close to the heart of the imperial government of Babylon, doubtless had profound insight at a purely human and political level into the likely international outcomes if Babylon fell. He is not likely to have been lounging on a bed of illusions and false optimism. On the contrary, it may have been a well-warranted fear for the longer-term future that prepared his mind for the visions that he now begins to recount.

Four Beasts and Eleven Horns (vv. 1–8)

Daniel said: "In my vision at night I looked, and there before me were the four winds of heaven churning up the great sea. Four great beasts, each different from the others, came up out of the sea.

"The first was like a lion, and it had the wings of an eagle. I watched until its wings were torn off and it was lifted from the ground so that it stood on two feet like a human being, and the mind of a human was given to it.

"And there before me was a second beast, which looked like a bear. It was raised up on one of its sides, and it had three ribs in its mouth between its teeth. It was told, 'Get up and eat your fill of flesh!'

"After that, I looked, and there before me was another beast, one that looked like a leopard. And on its back it had four wings like those of a bird. This beast had four heads, and it was given authority to rule.

"After that, in my vision at night I looked, and there before me was a fourth beast—terrifying and frightening and very powerful. It had large iron teeth; it crushed and devoured its victims and trampled underfoot whatever was left. It was different from all the former beasts, and it had ten horns.

"While I was thinking about the horns, there before me was another horn, a little one, which came up among them; and three of the first horns were uprooted before it. This horn had eyes like the eyes of a human being and a mouth that spoke boastfully. (Dan 7:2–8)

Daniel's mind had gone back to the king's dream in chapter 2. That was the curious incident in the night that had first brought Daniel and Nebuchadnezzar together almost fifty years ago. Perhaps Daniel was now reflecting on that statue with its four metallic empires succeeding one another: the golden head (Babylon's Nebuchadnezzar himself), and then the silver, bronze, and iron mixed with clay. The Babylonian Empire was clearly drifting to its own extinction, what was to follow? The pattern of four repeats itself.

First of all, Daniel's dream takes him to the sea, being churned up by the four winds of heaven at the same time—a frightening enough image in itself. The sea in Israelite thinking was a dangerous place to be, and it came to symbolize chaos and uncontrollable evil. That is why it was theologically so important to affirm, as the Old Testament does, that Yahweh the God of Israel not only created and owns the sea (as all the rest of creation) but controls it, subdues it, and limits it.

Then, out of this raging sea, four enormous beasts arise, one after the other. The first three are recognizable animals: lion, bear, and leopard. All of them are beasts of prey, dangerous to humans. But in the vision, they all have strange additional features (such as wings and extra heads), which makes them even more frightening and dangerous. And each of these first three are given something: a human mind, permission to devour, and authority to rule.

Then comes a fourth beast, which is so much more horrific and destructive that Daniel cannot identify it with any known animal. It is a terrifying monster, sporting iron teeth, and of such enormous size that it could devour and trample everything in its path. It would be at home in the computer-generated graphics of modern monster movies, a figure of seemingly indestructible, destructive power and cruelty.

In addition to its iron teeth and trampling feet, this awesome beast has ten horns—symbols of violent, aggressive power in all directions. Daniel, in his dream, is fascinated by those horns but suddenly sees one more, much smaller than the other ten but apparently even more powerful. Just by its forceful arrival it displaces three other horns. And then, as happens in dreams, this little horn takes on human features, including the capacity to speak. And what speech Daniel hears from this little horn! Out pours its bragging and boasting that carries on, even as the scene changes (v. 11).

Thrones and a Son of Man (vv. 9–14)

> "As I looked,
> "thrones were set in place,
>   and the Ancient of Days took his seat.
> His clothing was as white as snow;
>   the hair of his head was white like wool.
> His throne was flaming with fire,
>   and its wheels were all ablaze.

A river of fire was flowing,
>   coming out from before him.
Thousands upon thousands attended him;
>   ten thousand times ten thousand stood before him.
The court was seated,
>   and the books were opened.

"Then I continued to watch because of the boastful words the horn was speaking. I kept looking until the beast was slain and its body destroyed and thrown into the blazing fire. (The other beasts had been stripped of their authority, but were allowed to live for a period of time.)

"In my vision at night I looked, and there before me was one like a son of man, coming with the clouds of heaven. He approached the Ancient of Days and was led into his presence. He was given authority, glory and sovereign power; all nations and peoples of every language worshipped him. His dominion is an everlasting dominion that will not pass away, and his kingdom is one that will never be destroyed. (Dan 7:9–14)

There is a sudden change of scene, something else that is typical of dreams and visions. But it seems that it is not a complete substitution. It feels more like what we can now do with split-screen technology. For Daniel says that, even as his attention focuses on the throne of the Ancient of Days, he can still see and hear what is going on with that fourth beast and its little horn. There are, as it were, upper and lower segments of the screen of his vision.

This is important. It is not that one picture replaces or merely follows after the other. *They are both going on at the same time.* Daniel is seeing two realities but they are not totally separate and independent. Rather, one is happening somehow "above" or "behind" the other. There is (below) the world of rampaging of the beasts; there is (above) the world of the heavenly court. Both are real and both are "present" together in the vision. It is ultimately one whole integrated reality, but Daniel is seeing it from two perspectives.

So what is going on in the "top half" of Daniel's split-screen vision? He sees thrones. Thrones speak of kingship and sovereign authority. The plural form probably simply intensifies that truth. This is the seat of effective government and executive power.

He sees the Ancient of Days. We put the words in upper case because we know they refer to God, but the words simply mean "a very old person." And age, of course, in that culture, was a mark of great wisdom and authority. The whiteness of his clothing and hair speaks of radiant purity (as at the transfiguration of Jesus). Fire is consistently the symbol of God's holiness and presence (as at Mt. Sinai). The millions of attendants around the throne also speak of the instant executive power of the one on the throne; any whisper of his will finds a messenger or agent for any task, anywhere, anytime.

But this is also a court scene, so it is a place of judgment and decisions about rights and wrongs—and how important is that, in the context of the rampaging beasts below? And the books are opened so that the court can see the full record of all that is done on earth and evaluate it according to God's own standards and bring the story to the just and good resolution that only God can accomplish. The fate of the world will be decided not by the boastful claims and power of the beasts but by the will and purpose of God and his ultimate judgment on all that takes place in his world.

So, as Daniel's gaze reverts to the lower screen (vv. 11–12), Daniel sees, doubtless to his great relief, that although three of the beasts continue for a while under the authority of the one on the throne, the fourth beast with its boasting horn is finally slain and totally destroyed by fire. Neither the beasts nor their horns will win the day. Their judgment is sure.

Back to the upper screen, Daniel is in the world of the thrones again (vv. 13–14) and witnesses a scene that is very surprising. With the cacophony of the beasts still going on below, and in the midst of the blindingly white and fiery radiance of God's throne above, Daniel suddenly sees "one like a son of man." That expression means simply a human being. It is not (in this context) any kind of title or role, but simply a description comparable to "like a lion . . . like a bear . . . like a leopard." This figure is simply, "like a man." In the midst of a world of beasts ravaging the earth, Daniel sees a man arriving in the presence of God in his heavenly court. And then this mysterious human being is given the right to rule in a way that sounds divine. He comes with the clouds of heaven—a very God-like ambience. He receives not only "authority, glory and sovereign power" (which human kings also received by God's permission), but also *worship*. This is a heavenly man indeed. Yet still . . . a man.

What a mysterious climax to a mysterious sequence of scenes: from beasts rising from the sea, to God seated in his fiery white throne, to . . . a man. Yet that man receives an everlasting kingdom that is described in language that clearly echoes the rock of the kingdom of God in Nebuchadnezzar's dream statue (Dan 2:44).

We can pick out several things about this part of Daniel's vision, even before we get to the interpretation in the second part of the chapter, since the contrast with the beasts is clearly stark and deliberate.

First, this is clearly an investiture, rather than an invasion. The beasts came up out of the sea to trample and devour on the earth. But this human person comes with the clouds of heaven and is led purposively into the presence of the Ancient of Days. He is not (at this point) doing battle with the beasts; he is simply being invested with divine power and authority.

Second, the beasts are given authority to do what they do, but only "for a period of time," then they are destroyed. But this man is given authority, glory, and sovereign power that is "everlasting," that "will not pass away," and "will never be destroyed." Bestial rule is terrible but temporary. This man's rule will be heavenly and eternal.

Third, they are beasts and he is human. So the chaotic and rebellious reign of beasts is ended by the reign of the human—restoring creation to what God intended. Granted, of course, that the beasts in the vision are morphed into mythical monsters. Nevertheless, three of them have the appearance of known animals. But God created human beings in God's own image in order to have dominion over the rest of the animal creation. The rule of this "son of man" in Daniel's vision seems, therefore, like a deliberate echo of Psalm 8:4–8 where the same phrase, "son of man," clearly means humanity in general. Its point is that God gave to humanity the responsibility of ruling over creation. But that rule should reflect God's own rule, namely, the rule of love, compassion, provision, and justice. Fallen humanity, however, corrupts dominion into domination and ends up creating power structures like the empires of Daniel's vision, which are "bestial." The investiture of this "son of man" restores the rightful rule of humanity, which, in the true image of God, will be "humane."

THE DOUBLE MEANING (7:15–28)

In the stories of chapters 2 and 4, Daniel is the one who can interpret Nebuchadnezzar's dreams, so we might have expected him to wake up, call his friends, and tell them both his dream and its meaning. But that's not how it works in the second half of the book. He needs someone to interpret for him, and that explanation takes place within the vision itself, leaving him pretty troubled when he "wakes up."

> "I, Daniel, was troubled in spirit, and the visions that passed through my mind disturbed me. I approached one of those standing there and asked him the meaning of all this.
>
> "So he told me and gave me the interpretation of these things: 'The four great beasts are four kings that will rise from the earth. But the holy people of the Most High will receive the kingdom and will possess it forever—yes, for ever and ever.'" (Dan 7:15–18)

First of all, Daniel gets a summary explanation of the two "split screens" of his vision. The four beasts represent four earthly kingdoms (something Daniel had probably already guessed on the basis of his memory of the four metals of Nebuchadnezzar's statue) while the "one like a son of man" represents the saints—"the holy people of the Most High." This second point means that any interpretation of the identity of this son of man has to include a corporate element. This is reinforced again in verses 26–27, as we shall see in a moment. This single human person in Daniel's vision is a *representative* figure (just as the single visionary beasts represented whole empires). His identity is combined with the identity and destiny of the people of God.

The Violence of God's Enemies (vv. 19–25)

As I said, even in his own dream Daniel had probably identified the first three beasts as carrying the same symbolism as the first three parts of Nebuchadnezzar's dream statue. These were successive kingdoms stretching into the future. And the first one, the lion with eagle's wings, was clearly Nebuchadnezzar's Babylon. The curious way the lion in the dream is able to stand up on two feet like a human being and is given the mind of a human probably reminded Daniel of the man himself. Daniel had known Nebuchadnezzar personally. He had his tyrannical side, but he was a man like other men. The visionary combination of beast and human points to the ambiguity of all empires (and we'll come back to that later).

The identity of the second and third beasts is less clear and actually does not matter much (as Daniel himself realized in his eagerness to enquire about the fourth). They function to create space between the present (the Babylonian Empire) and the more distant future (the fourth beast). The fourth beast in chapter 7, seen in the light of all that is foreseen in detail in chapters 8, 10–11, is almost certainly a portrayal of the rule of the Greek Seleucid Kingdom in the second century BC, with its climactic era of persecution under Antiochus IV Epiphanes. And in light of chapter 8, the second and third beasts would seem to be representative of the Medes and Persians, two kingdoms that had separate histories and geographies but were united in the fully established Persian Empire. But it doesn't matter right now. Further explanation comes in chapter 8.

Daniel felt he could ignore the first three beasts. After all, he and his people were living and surviving quite well under the dominion of the first, so the second and third might not represent too great a threat. But that fourth beast! It was of a different order altogether.

It seemed too terrible to contemplate, and yet Daniel wanted to know. Even if it was in the distant future, what lay ahead for God's people if such a fearsome beast emerged?

> "Then I wanted to know the meaning of the fourth beast, which was different from all the others and most terrifying, with its iron teeth and bronze claws—the beast that crushed and devoured its victims and trampled underfoot whatever was left. I also wanted to know about the ten horns on its head and about the other horn that came up, before which three of them fell—the horn that looked more imposing than the others and that had eyes and a mouth that spoke boastfully. As I watched, this horn was waging war against the holy people and defeating them, until the Ancient of Days came and pronounced judgment in favour of the holy people of the Most High, and the time came when they possessed the kingdom.
>
> "He gave me this explanation: 'The fourth beast is a fourth kingdom that will appear on earth. It will be different from all the other kingdoms and will devour the whole earth, trampling it down and crushing it. The ten horns are ten kings who will come from this kingdom. After them another king will arise, different from the earlier ones; he will subdue three kings. He will speak against the Most High and oppress his holy people and try to change the set times and the laws. The holy people will be delivered into his hands for a time, times and half a time.'" (Dan 7:19–25)

Various historical interpretations have been made, which by the very fact that there are several of them suggests that it is right to see here not so much a single unique historical point of reference but a recurring pattern. Human empires rise and fall, overlap with each other, go to war with each other, and so on. And at different times in history especially vicious regimes arise that seem to concentrate evil to its most potent virulence. This fourth beast represents such ultimate manifestations of evil, anti-God, anti-human forces that exude arrogance, breathe out violence, and wreak devastation and destruction on an enormous scale causing intense suffering to the people of God at such times.

The features of the "little horn" are detailed. They include:

- blasphemous arrogance in speaking against God;
- oppression of the saints, God's "holy people";
- changing times and laws (this may have meant the banning of Jewish festivals, but speaks more generally of social and moral upheaval and chaos);
- waging war against the saints almost to the point of extinction, until God himself intervenes.

Such a picture fits more than one regime or individual tyrant in the long history of Jews and Christians. The first such moment in history after Daniel's vision in Babylon was undoubtedly the persecution of the Jews under the Greek Seleucid Kingdom, and the "little horn" was perceived as Antiochus IV Epiphanes. The early Christian church could see the increasing persecution by the Roman Empire under the guise of this fourth beast, and some suggest that Paul had the "little horn" in mind when he spoke of the "man of lawlessness" in 2 Thessalonians 2. It is tragic and sobering to know that some Jewish interpreters have seen the fourth beast in the rise of Christian Europe after the conversion of the Roman emperor, which became so destructively persecuting of the Jews in later centuries. And the twentieth century saw the massive oppressive violence of both Nazism and Communism in which the attempted extermination of Jews and Christian believers reached industrial scales. And what does the twenty-first century hold? Perhaps Christians in the Middle East will give us some insight into the ravages of a "fourth beast" in their heartlands.

The Vindication of God's People (vv. 26–27)

The last line of verse 25 is a word of hope. The people of God will suffer, indeed they will be permitted to suffer as God "delivers" them into the hands of such monsters as the fourth beast represents.

And it may well be that such a period of intense suffering will herald an ultimate, eschatological era of satanic and human opposition to God, such as we see depicted in Revelation. But there is a limit, set by God himself. It will be "for a time, times and half a time." It is surely pointless to try to give this precise numerical or chronological meaning, either in terms of length of time or of specific dates. The real point is that, however long the suffering of the saints may be, it will be temporary and it will be terminated. God is in control and God is the ultimate judge in the court of human history. And that court is moving to its verdict.

> "'But the court will sit, and his power [of the little horn of the fourth beast] will be taken away and completely destroyed forever. Then the sovereignty, power and greatness of all the kingdoms under heaven will be handed over to the holy people of the Most High. His kingdom will be an everlasting kingdom, and all rulers will worship and obey him.'
>
> "This is the end of the matter. I, Daniel, was deeply troubled by my thoughts, and my face turned pale, but I kept the matter to myself." (Dan 7:26–28)

Verses 26–27 amplify verse 18. God's divine verdict will first of all negatively destroy the powers of blasphemous evil and oppression. The temporary power given to this bestial regime will be taken way, and its destruction will be both total and permanent ("completely destroyed forever"). This does point towards the picture of the eradication of evil that we see in Revelation.

But the rule and power that had been so viciously usurped by the fourth beast will not simply be taken back by God himself. Rather, the right and power to govern throughout the whole earth will be given to the people of God. But who are they? They are those who were symbolized in the "one like a son of man"—the human being whose rule was authorized in the very presence of God in verses 13–14. His rule is theirs. Their rule is his. And he is as human as they are.

There is much mystery here, but it seems to point in at least two directions. First, the reign of God (the everlasting kingdom of the Most High, v. 27) will be mediated through the rule of the saints, which points to a restored creation in which God's original intention for humanity is realized, for the saints are the redeemed humanity of God, exercising God's rule within creation. And second, this reign of the saints will be connected with the investiture and authority of the heavenly figure who, though human ("like a son of man"), comes with the clouds of heaven and receives divine worship.

Mystery enough, at any rate, to trouble Daniel, and menace enough to turn him pale with fear (7:28). The vision has a happy ending but a terrifying plot before that ending is reached.

THE THREE KINGDOMS

What lessons can we learn for our instruction and encouragement? I think we can discern three kinds of "kingdoms" in this chapter. There are the kingdoms represented by the beasts from the sea. There is the simultaneous kingdom of heaven, above and behind that earthly realm, hidden but in ultimate control. And there is the kingdom of the saints, an apparently future reality that will emerge only when the bestial kingdom is destroyed forever.

The Bestial Kingdoms

In his vision Daniel perceives the bestial evil that lies behind the world powers of his own day, and throughout history. This kind of reported vision is given the name "apocalyptic." Daniel 7–8 and 10–12 are early examples of the genre, which is also found in Ezekiel and of course in the New Testament book of Revelation. The word means literally "unveiling," and that is what is happening. God is pulling back the curtain to show what is going on behind and underneath all the human constructed image and glory of human kingdoms and empires.

That kind of unveiling can work in different ways. Sometimes it may expose something that seems awesome and terrifying and expose it as a fraud, not worth being scared of at all. That moment in *The*

Wizard of Oz when Dorothy's little dog Toto pulls the curtain away from behind the façade of terrifying sights and sounds to expose a frightened old man is just such an "apocalypse." Sometimes God's people need to see idols for what they truly are—powerless and useless. That is what the "unveiling" of Babylon and Babylon's gods accomplishes in Isaiah 40–48, especially in chapters 46–47.

But in the other direction, apocalypse pulls away the façade of apparent benevolence that human governments like to construct and exposes the depths of evil, lies, corruption, and violence that lies behind the facade, showing the fingerprints of satanic evil all over the reality underneath. And that is what happens here.

Perhaps this came as a genuine shock to Daniel (v. 28 suggests it may have been). He had lived through the relatively constructive reign of Nebuchadnezzar. Daniel was not naïve—Nebuchadnezzar could threaten to cremate dissidents. But Daniel had served this human government for a lifetime and even had at least one opportunity (in ch. 4) to influence it in the direction of social justice. And, as we saw, he was probably praying for Nebuchadnezzar and seeking the welfare of the city where God had put him, in line with the instructions of Jeremiah 29:7.

But suddenly, he is shown that same kingdom—the government of a man he respected and prayed for—as a beast of prey (in fact a beast and a bird, both carnivorous), to be followed by others even worse. It cannot have been easy to reconcile the familiar human government he served with this bestial, devouring force that his "apocalyptic" unveiling placed so vividly before his frightened sleeping eyes.

But this is the double-sided reality of political power in this world, and as biblical Christians we ought to be far more alert to it than we often are. Biblical "apocalypse" opens our eyes. The New Testament gives us a similar duality of perception.

Paul recognized that government is appointed by God and has the responsibility of administering justice (Rom 13). For that reason he urged Christians to pray for governing authorities, none of whom in his day were Christians (1 Tim 2:1–2). And he could use his Roman citizenship when it served the cause of the gospel and instruct Christians to see the paying of taxes as part of their duty to God (Rom 13:6–7; verses which some Christians seem to have lost from their Bibles in their hostility towards any kind of taxation). Peter, likewise, even while Christians were suffering persecution, urges them to submit to human authorities and to honour the emperor (1 Pet 2:13–17).

But at the same time, Paul had a robust theology of "principalities and powers," which he perceived as spiritual forces that, among other things, lie behind structures of political and economic power in human society and, in their rebellion against God, can easily turn human power in satanically evil directions. If 2 Thessalonians 2 is a veiled reference to the potentially persecuting power of the Roman emperor, then he understands Daniel's vision very well. He was also well aware of the blasphemous idolatry of the cult of emperor worship that had already taken hold in the first century AD. A phrase like "our great God and Savior," which in Titus 2:13 clearly refers to Jesus Christ, is one that Paul has deliberately and subversively stolen from that imperial cult, since it was a phrase already being applied to the Roman emperor. And, as has often been pointed out, we must balance the positive view of the state in Romans 13 with the apocalyptic depiction of it in Revelation 13, where Daniel's imagery of beasts is developed to expose the satanic and devouring potential of human empires.

Now we need to be careful in how we handle this double picture. It is NOT being said that human governments have an appearance of doing good things (law and order, justice, business, welfare, etc.), but *actually* they are utterly evil in reality. It is NOT saying that governments can do nothing good, but are entirely composed of satanic deception and evil. That would be to buy into the kind of obsession with conspiracy theories that are so abundant around the world.

No, the Bible recognizes the proper and positive place of different forms of human political order in society, even in a fallen world—from dictatorships to democracy and everything in between. Because people are made in the image of God and because of God's common grace, governments can do what is right and good at least some of the time. But *at the same time* there is this underlying ambiguity about all governments, regimes, and empires, the same ambiguity that runs through humanity itself since the fall. We are simultaneously capable of good and evil: capable of constructive invention and creative beauty, but capable also of destructive violence and degrading ugliness; capable of reflecting something of the glory of our Creator, but capable also of repeating the blasphemous rebellion and boastful God-hatred of the evil one.

Part of our Christian calling is to have the wisdom of discernment of *both* realities that will be present in any manifestation of political power, at local, national, or global levels. Paul saw that the Roman Empire could be both a power for good and constructive achievements under God's sovereign governance of history and *at the same time* a source of satanic evil, built on the evils of slavery and lethal military and civil violence against all who opposed it. Are we prepared to accept the same evaluation of the modern empires we have seen in the past few centuries?

One of my friends in India has a grandmother who lived during the British Raj—possibly the greatest manifestation of Western colonialism on the planet at the time. He tells me that in the years after India's independence in 1947, she (along with many others) would complain that things were better under the British rule than under India's own successive governments (even with their remarkable secular and democratic constitution). "We should ask the British to come back," she used to say. "They are Christians. They will forgive us." She recognized that there were positive aspects of the British Empire that had brought benefits to the country. And yet we know full well that there were dimensions of naked racist superiority, violent suppression at times, and horrendous economic exploitation that fuelled the wealth of Britain's industrial revolution while impoverishing India for a long time. And in the same era, of course, British and French colonial self-interest fostered, fed, but finally betrayed both Arabs and Jews in the Middle East, contributing to the most lasting and destructive conflict of the past hundred years.

As a British citizen, I can exercise that kind of discriminating evaluation of the British Empire. I can see it as a mixture of constructive benefits and sometimes horrifying duplicity, violence, and greed. Are we able to exercise the same kind of discernment around the decades of American hegemony in world affairs? Are we able to avoid the simplistic binary options of being (from the outside) "pro-American" or "anti-American"? We can surely acknowledge all that has benefited the world and contributed to human well-being while facing up to the economic and political self-interest that has generated corporate and foreign policy activities that have colluded with tyranny and oppression elsewhere. Daniel's vision calls on us to open our eyes and see the world, neither with naïve approval of "our own side" nor with equally naïve dismissal of every political ambition and action as satanic and irredeemably evil, but rather with the "split-screen" that brings God's perspective to bear on the ambiguity of all human life.

And that leads to our second kingdom.

The Heavenly Kingdom

Daniel is given the privilege of a glimpse into the heavenly reality that lies "above and behind" world history, both contemporary and (from his point of view) future. It is similar to the invitation that John received to go through that "door open in heaven" and see the universe from the perspective of the throne room of God (Rev 4–7).

Again, we need to be careful. Neither Daniel's nor John's vision is merely a vision of *the future*. There is, of course, a predictive element. Through this vision Daniel is able to alert his own people to a future that would bring terrible times of testing—a vision which also prepared them to be able to meet it, knowing that even such a future remained under the control of the God who had revealed it. The same purpose underlies the book of Revelation. But in both books this is more than mere prediction. This is "unveiling"—showing the reality of what is going on in the present. And that reality is that God is still on the throne.

So history proceeds. Human empires come and go. Kings, presidents, and prime ministers do what they do. But ultimately God remains the supreme governor and final judge. And nothing will be overlooked or swept under the carpet. "The books were opened" (Dan 7:10). This is the Auditor-in-Chief, the one to whom all hearts are open, all desires known, and from whom no secrets are hidden. This is the God who sees and knows, who looks, considers, and assesses all that is done by every human being on earth (Ps 33:13–15), and not only their actions but their thoughts and motives.

All earthly authority then—even that which is used boastfully and destructively—is delegated and derivative, subject to being revoked and terminated. And even when human powers are doing their worst, the kingdom of God is at work.

We need to cultivate an awareness of this heavenly dimension to all that happens on earth. It is not a form of escapism. It is not opting out of reality into fantasy. On the contrary, it is bringing the true reality of the reign of God to bear on the fantastic imaginings, posturings, and plunderings of men behaving badly. It is to live in the world of Psalm 2 and to look for the signs of the reign of God in the midst of the turmoil of the nations. The kingdom of God is not only a future hope ("Thy kingdom come"), but a present reality ("Thine is the kingdom").

So then, just as our first point alerts us to perceive the bestial, satanic element in the affairs of human power and authority at work, so this point alerts us to perceive the heavenly and divine dimension of the same realities. God is at work in the midst of the ordinariness or the chaos of history. Heaven rules, as Daniel pointed out to Nebuchadnezzar (Dan 4:26).

The "Saintly" Kingdom

We return in conclusion to the most mysterious part of Daniel's vision—the "one like a son of man." As we have seen so far, this term essentially and simply means a human being. But critically, it is a human being as opposed to the ravening beasts. God's rule will be, in the proper sense of the word, "humane."

But then we saw further that in the interpretation of the dream, this human being is a representative person, incorporating the people of God, the saints/holy ones of the Most High. And that symbolic fusion of identity functions in two ways:

- Their destiny will be his—namely, suffering, persecution, and violence.
- His destiny will be theirs—namely, glorious vindication and everlasting reign on earth.

Now we know from the Gospels that this figure in Daniel 7 was immensely influential on the self-consciousness of Jesus. "The Son of Man" was his most frequent way of referring to himself. He used it in a number of different ways, as New Testament scholars have pointed out, but some of his Son of Man sayings clearly draw from the imagery of Daniel 7. The clearest example comes during his trial. When the High Priest asked Jesus if he was the Messiah, Jesus answered:

> "You have said so," Jesus replied. "But I say to all of you: From now on you will see the Son of Man sitting at the right hand of the Mighty One and coming on the clouds of heaven." (Matt 26:64)

And that claim (a combination of Ps 110 and Dan 7) is, of course, repeated often in the rest of the New Testament, where the ascended Christ is pictured "at the right hand of God," i.e. in the place of supreme government of the universe. The universal reign of God over "all nations and peoples of every language" will be exercised through the Son of Man, the crucified, risen, and ascended Jesus of Nazareth.

But just as Jesus, as Son of Man, suffered and gave his life before his vindication, glory, and eternal reign, so it will be for those who belong to him, who share his identity and destiny: suffering, then vindication and eternal reign. That combination is clearly stated in Daniel 7:27. But we should not read into this some kind of proud superiority by which Christians will lord it over the rest of the world's population. That kind of arrogance (which fuelled Christendom and one of its bestial outcomes—colonialism and imperialism), is precisely what this text sets itself against. No, "the holy people of the Most High" will be the whole redeemed humanity from every tribe and language and people and nation, who will, as John said, "be a kingdom and priests to serve our God, and they will reign on the earth" (Rev 5:10).

The future, in other words, belongs not only to the Son of Man (the Lord Jesus Christ) but to the son of man—that is, human beings. The creature God created in his own image to exercise dominion over creation will at last do so in the way God intended and in a way that reflects God and serves God on God's cleansed earth.

That seems to be the vision that encourages the writer to the Hebrews. He reflects on the glory of humankind in the words of Psalm 8.

> "What is mankind that you are mindful of them,
>   a son of man that you care for him?
> You made them a little lower than the angels;
>   you crowned them with glory and honour
>   and put everything under their feet."

> In putting everything under them, God left nothing that is not subject to them. Yet at present we do not see everything subject to them. But we do see Jesus. (Heb 2:6–9)

We were created to exercise godly dominion over the rest of creation. But our sinful rebellion has left us in a position of partial servitude to the creation we were supposed to rule—the servitude of idolatry (as Paul outlines in Rom 1:18–23). So we do not yet see the rightful rule of humanity over creation. But, adds Hebrews, "we do see Jesus!" For in his humanity and deity combined rests the true sovereignty over all creation, which we will one day share with him.

Meanwhile, the four beasts continue their arrogant and destructive work, as do the four horsemen of John's vision (Rev 6:1–8). But they do so under the ultimate control of the one on the throne. And in the midst of such times, we remind ourselves that when we pray, "*Yours* is the kingdom, the power and the glory, for ever and ever," we know that it is also the case that, in Christ and because of Christ, *ours* is the kingdom that cannot be destroyed.

CHAPTER 8

A RAM, A GOAT, AND AN ENDING

Animals again! Daniel certainly has some weird dreams! In the last chapter he sees four gruesome beasts rising up out of a churning sea. Here he sees a two-horned charging ram and a unicorn he-goat in mortal combat. Surely this is the stuff of fantasy or of a deranged mind!

But not so fast. It may seem strange, but it is not very different from some of the ways we use animals in our own cultures.

For example, first of all, we regularly personify animals, turning them into caricature humans. Sometimes we do this in simple metaphors for certain human behaviour. We talk about lame ducks, fat cats, loan sharks, and children who are cheeky monkeys. Walt Disney built his empire on Mickey Mouse and *The Jungle Book* and *The Lion King*. And more recently we have a genre of computerized fantasy in virtual worlds where human, animal, and mythical creatures all combine, as in *Avatar*. And children's literature is full of humanized animals from Peter Rabbit and Jemima Duck to Rupert the Bear and Paddington.

But secondly, we also "animalize" nations. We portray whole nations through the image of an animal that seems to express some aspect of its own self-image or uniqueness. There are the British bulldogs (or the British and Irish Lions when it comes to rugby), the American (and Albanian) eagle, the French cock or rooster, New Zealand kiwis, and so on.

So what Daniel does in this chapter with a ram and a goat is a familiar kind of symbolism. He is "seeing" real nations and historical events but using the animal imagery to make some important points and ask some challenging questions. In other words, the imagery is fantasy, but what he is talking about is reality. And for that reason we need to ask what it has to say to us today as Daniel's dream comes to us as part of our revealed Scriptures.

A PATTERN OF EMPIRES (8:1–12, 20–25)

> In the third year of King Belshazzar's reign, I, Daniel, had a vision, after the one that had already appeared to me. In my vision I saw myself in the citadel of Susa in the province of Elam; in the vision I was beside the Ulai Canal. (Dan 8:1–2)

The date puts us in the same period as the king of chapter 5. So we are still in the Babylonian Empire, but only just. Daniel, an old man by now, must have known that Babylon's power was waning fast. The writing was on the wall. The closing verse of chapter 5 and the opening verses of chapter 9 show us what came next and that Daniel was very aware of the times and of God's sovereign hand in the present and future.

Daniel tells us that the vision reported here in chapter 8 came "after the one that had already appeared to me," which means the one in chapter 7. That consisted of a terrifying sequence of four beasts coming up from the sea. It represented four successive human kingdoms and was clearly a mutation of the pattern of four that we saw in Nebuchadnezzar's dream statue in chapter 2: gold, silver, bronze, and iron mixed with clay. And in both those earlier dreams, that pattern of empires had been destroyed by God's own supreme power: in chapter 2 by the rock not hewn by human hands and in chapter 7 by the one like a son of man who receives heavenly authority and everlasting rule.

Now if we want to make precise historical identifications of the four kingdoms, things get a bit complicated. We can be clear about the first: the head of gold (in ch. 2) and the eagle-winged lion (in ch. 7) clearly refer to Nebuchadnezzar's Babylon. And from the detail supplied in chapters 10–11, it seems that the arrogant, violent, and blasphemous fourth kingdom was the Greek-speaking Seleucid

Empire that ruled from Antioch in Syria, and its "little horn" was Antiochus IV Epiphanes. This would mean that the second and third kingdoms would be the originally separate kingdoms of the Medes and the Persians, respectively. However, chapter 8 binds the Medes and the Persians together (v. 20; something that King Cyrus of Persia did in fact accomplish), which suggests that the Medes and Persians together constitute kingdom number two, while the Greeks come in as kingdom number three.

But beyond that, since the book of Daniel also looks forward to the establishment of the kingdom of God in a uniquely climactic way in the context of a fourth kingdom, it was natural for early Christian interpretation to identify that fourth kingdom with the Roman Empire in which God became incarnate in Jesus of Nazareth who announced, "the kingdom of God is at hand. Repent and believe the gospel."

Didn't I say it was complicated? This all means that we can envisage two possible sequences as both being compatible with the text of Daniel, depending on the precise location of the interpreter.

1	Babylon	Babylon
2	Medes	Medes and Persians
3	Persians	Greece (Seleucids)
4	Greece (Seleucids)	Rome

And given this flexibility, it seems best (as I've said before) to treat the symbolism of the statue and the beasts as portraying an underlying pattern within history. Empires rise and fall as they successively overreach themselves in arrogance. And sometimes they reach a pinnacle of climactic evil and violence against God and God's people. But eventually they are overthrown by God. And in the end—the ultimate end, as distinct from the many partial "endings" that history illustrates—God will finally destroy all that opposes him and establish his own reign fully and forever.

So, here in chapter 8 Daniel's vision portrays the next two major powers that would rule over the people of Israel in the years to come: the empire of the Medes and Persians that had been unified and rapidly expanded by Cyrus and then the kingdom of the Seleucid portion of the Greek Empire that had been established after Alexander the Great of Macedon conquered the Persian Empire.

Let's take the sequence of actions in Daniel's dream alongside the explanation that Daniel is given in the second half of the chapter by an angelic figure in his vision (vv. 15–18).

The Two-Horned Ram (vv. 3–4 and 20)

> I looked up, and there before me was a ram with two horns, standing beside the canal, and the horns were long. One of the horns was longer than the other but grew up later. I watched the ram as it charged toward the west and the north and the south. No animal could stand against it, and none could rescue from its power. It did as it pleased and became great.
>
> The two-horned ram that you saw represents the kings of Media and Persia. (Dan 8:3–4, 20)

Here we have the empire of the Medes and Persians. The kingdom of the Persians was more recent but grew larger than that of the Medes, which is why the two ram's horns are described as they are. Cyrus of Persia brought the two kingdoms together, and after him it is known simply as the Persian Empire. In 539 BC Cyrus defeated and entered Babylon, apparently without a fight, bringing the Babylonian Empire to an end (as noted in Dan 5:31, where it is likely that "Darius" there refers to Cyrus).[1]

Cyrus then went conquering rapidly in all directions (as noted in Isa 41:2–3, where his feet scarcely touch the ground). From his capital in Susa he spread the sovereignty of Persia over the whole

---

1. There is a fairly strong case for regarding "Darius" in the book of Daniel as the same person as Cyrus. The term "Darius" is a throne name rather than a personal name. The issues are discussed in the major commentaries. Those who take this view would agree with the NIV footnote on Daniel 6:28 which reads, "So Daniel prospered during the reign of Darius, that is, the reign of Cyrus."

Middle Eastern region, including regions we now know as Turkey, Palestine, Israel, Lebanon, Syria, Jordan, Egypt, Iraq, and of course Iran, the modern state that was Persia. The empire he established went on to rule the region for 200 years, including a period of sustained conflict with Greece. It was the Persian Empire that Greek forces from Athens and Sparta drove back from their attempt to spread their power into Europe at the battles of Marathon (490 BC), Thermopylae and Salamis (480 BC).

The One-Horned Goat (vv. 5–7 and 21)

As I was thinking about this, suddenly a goat with a prominent horn between its eyes came from the west, crossing the whole earth without touching the ground. It came toward the two-horned ram I had seen standing beside the canal and charged at it in great rage. I saw it attack the ram furiously, striking the ram and shattering its two horns. The ram was powerless to stand against it; the goat knocked it to the ground and trampled on it, and none could rescue the ram from its power.

The shaggy goat is the king of Greece, and the large horn between its eyes is the first king. (Dan 8:5–7, 21)

Here we have the conquests of Alexander the Great. Alexander was the young king of Macedon, a kingdom in northern Greece which had risen to power in the century after the "golden age" of Athens and its great rival, Sparta. In a period of ten years from 333 to 323 BC, Alexander swept across the Middle East, slicing through the Persian Empire like a knife through butter. He established Greek rule in a vast region stretching from the Aegean Sea to the borders of India (at which point, it seems, his soldiers refused to go any further).

The Four Horns (vv. 8 and 22)

The goat became very great, but at the height of its power the large horn was broken off, and in its place four prominent horns grew up toward the four winds of heaven.

> The four horns that replaced the one that was broken off represent four kingdoms that will emerge from his nation but will not have the same power. (Dan 8:8, 22)

Alexander died suddenly in 323 BC, at the height of his power and tragically still in his thirties. Before his death he divided his empire among four of his generals: Cassander (who ruled over Macedonia and Greece); Lysimachus (who ruled over Thrace and Asia Minor); Seleucus (who ruled over northern Syria, Mesopotamia, and the eastern regions); and Ptolemy (who ruled over Egypt, Palestine, and southern Syria). In relation to the ongoing history of Israel, only the last two were significant, as the small province of Judah came under the control of first the Ptolemaic rulers of Egypt and then later the Seleucid dynasty in Syria.

So, the world became Greek for the next 250 years or so, spreading the Greek language and culture throughout that whole region, until Greece itself was conquered by Rome, and the world turned Roman. That is the world we find in the New Testament—a world of Roman power but Greek language and culture.

The small homeland of the Jews, which had been a province of the Persian Empire (as we find it in the books of Nehemiah and Ezra), thus came under the power of the Greeks. But as throughout its history, it was caught between rival powers to the north and the south. For about 125 years the dominant power was the Ptolemaic dynasty ruling from Egypt to the south. But in 198 BC Palestine came under the control of the Seleucid dynasty ruling from Antioch in Syria to the north. And it was then that the time of terrible trouble for the Jews began.

The Little Horn (vv. 8–12 and 23–25)

> Out of one of them came another horn, which started small but grew in power to the south and to the east and toward the Beautiful Land. It grew until it reached the host of the heavens, and it threw some of the starry host down to the earth and trampled on them. It set itself up to be as great as the commander of the army

of the LORD; it took away the daily sacrifice from the LORD, and his sanctuary was thrown down. Because of rebellion, the LORD's people and the daily sacrifice were given over to it. It prospered in everything it did, and truth was thrown to the ground.

In the latter part of their reign, when rebels have become completely wicked, a fierce-looking king, a master of intrigue, will arise. He will become very strong, but not by his own power. He will cause astounding devastation and will succeed in whatever he does. He will destroy those who are mighty, the holy people. He will cause deceit to prosper, and he will consider himself superior. When they feel secure, he will destroy many and take his stand against the Prince of princes. Yet he will be destroyed, but not by human power. (Dan 8: 9–12, 23–25)

This describes one of the rulers of the four parts of the Greek world. Out of the Seleucid dynasty in Syria came a man called Antiochus IV. He took the name Epiphanes, signifying that he considered himself a manifestation of divine power—an illusion he indulged to its fullest extent. There is clearly an echo in these verses of the description of the little horn in Daniel 7:8, 11, 20–21, and 24–25. He ruled from 175 to 163 BC.

Antiochus Epiphanes acted with incredible hostility, hatred, and arrogance towards the Jews in Jerusalem and the surrounding region. He became, indeed, for God's people at that time, the very embodiment of blasphemous evil and the cause of enormous and prolonged suffering and oppression. We need to explore that a bit further in our next section.

A PORTRAIT OF EVIL (8:10–12, 23–25)

Those verses (Dan 8:10–12 and 23–25) summarize the wickedness of Antiochus Epiphanes and show us some clear and distinctive features of his sin. There is a potent combination of arrogance, viciousness, and deceit. Or to be more precise,

- he sinned against God (vv. 10–11),
- he sinned against God's people (v. 24),
- and he sinned against God's truth (vv. 12b and 25).

He embodied a toxic mixture of three serious sins: blasphemy, persecution, and lies, all of which bear the marks of satanic evil.

The detail of his activities is contained in 1 Maccabees 1, which you can read if you have access to an NRSV Bible with the Apocrypha included. It is a fearsome catalogue of destruction, abuse, murders, desecration of holy places, people, and books, and what today would be called "crimes against humanity." The chapter ends with these words:

> But many in Israel stood firm and were resolved in their hearts not to eat unclean food. They chose to die rather than to be defiled by food or to profane the holy covenant; and they did die. Very great wrath[2] came upon Israel (1 Macc 1:62–64).

Now, although Antiochus Epiphanes is the single historical figure in view in Daniel's vision, there is no doubt that he is a kind of archetype. That is, he represents a reality that has surfaced at different times in history. He is typical of something that happens again and again. There is a pattern here. That coalition of anti-God, anti-church, anti-truth forces and intentions faced the people of Israel in the Old Testament, has faced the Jewish people and the Christian church at different times in past centuries, and still faces the people of God in many parts of the world today. Jews have seen Antiochus Epiphanes as a pre-figuring of the horror of pogroms under "Christian" nations in Europe, culminating in the Holocaust. Christians have suffered from tyrannical regimes that sought to stamp out the Christian faith and church, from Roman emperors to atheist communist states that banned Bibles and all other symbols of Christian profession, to the brutal excesses of ISIS, Boko Haram, and Al Shabab.

---

2. This refers to the wrath of Antiochus, not the wrath of God. The book does not interpret the suffering of the Jews under the Greeks as God's judgment on them for sin.

Those are the extremes. But it has to be said that less violent forms of hostility can embody those same three features in more subtle ways. In rapidly secularizing Western cultures, we can see hatred of God, attacks on Christians, and deception and lies about both. Now of course we must immediately confess that the church has been guilty of the most enormous wrongdoing that has wrecked many lives—thinking of the child-abuse scandals that have been so widely reported in recent years but stretch back decades and constitute a terrible, damnable offence. But while such abuse by the church gives plenty of ammunition to her enemies, there is surely also a more deeply rooted spiritual hostility that manifests itself in militant atheism, discrimination against Christians in the workplace, judicial privileging of sexual preference rights over moral conscience rights, and a whole culture of deception and suspicion in which people demand truth but trust nobody to deliver it—least of all God or his representatives.

So when and where will it all end? That's the question God's people have asked for generations, and it is another part of the message of this chapter. Daniel's angelic interpreter mentions it three times.

A PREVIEW OF "THE END" (8:15–19)

> While I, Daniel, was watching the vision and trying to under-stand it, there before me stood one who looked like a man. And I heard a man's voice from the Ulai calling, "Gabriel, tell this man the meaning of the vision."
>
> As he came near the place where I was standing, I was terri-fied and fell prostrate. "Son of man," he said to me, "understand that the vision concerns *the time of the end*."
>
> While he was speaking to me, I was in a deep sleep, with my face to the ground. Then he touched me and raised me to my feet.
>
> He said: "I am going to tell you what will happen later in *the time of wrath*, because the vision concerns *the appointed time of the end*. (Dan 8:15–19, italics mine)

Notice those three phrases in italics: "time of the end," "time of wrath," and "the appointed time of the end." There is a variation in the expressions, but clearly they mean that what Daniel is seeing in his vision is a significant historical moment that can be called "the end." But what does that mean?

Well, first of all, obviously, it cannot mean "The End of the World," since we are all still here two thousand years later! It seems to mean something a bit more like the final frame of a long movie, when the words The End come on the screen. When we see that, we know that it does not mean the end of the world! Rather we understand that it is the end of the whole plot, with all its characters, actions, joys, tragedies, and whatever else that made up that particular movie. *That* sequence, *that* story, has come to its end. And if it was a good movie, we should feel a sense of satisfaction, of fulfillment, of resolution to all the complexities of what we have been watching in the previous hour or two.

We need to understand how the Bible itself uses this language of an "end," and of "fullness" (in v. 23 we read that "rebels have become completely wicked").

In Genesis 15:16 God told Abraham that he was going to give the land of Canaan to his descendants—but not yet. Rather, says God, "In the fourth generation your descendants will come back here, for the sin of the Amorites has not yet reached its full measure." In Hebrew that reads "the sin of the Amorites is not yet full." So God would not have been justified in acting in punishment against them at the time of Abraham. But that time would come. The sins of that whole culture became so degraded (including child sacrifice) that they reached a "fullness" which led to the conquest of Canaan by Israel. And Deuteronomy 9 makes it clear that in that event God was using Israel as the agent of his moral judgment on the wicked nations in the land. So, for that generation of Canaanites, "the end" had come. It was the end for them.

But God had threatened that he would do exactly the same to Israel if they behaved in the way the Canaanites had done (Lev 18:24–28;

20:22–24). Tragically, that is exactly what Israel did do—generation after generation of idolatry, injustice, and oppression. Until eventually God said, "Enough is enough. It's time to bring this to an end." So the prophet Amos uses the imagery of harvest to make this point. Just like the harvest comes when the fruit is ripe, so the time is ripe for Israel— ripe for punishment (Amos 8:2). And indeed, for that generation of the Northern Kingdom of Israel it was indeed "the end." Samaria was destroyed in 721 BC, and the northern tribes were scattered in exile. Not the end of *the* world, but certainly the end of *their* world. An even more climactic "end" was the destruction of Jerusalem in 587 BC. Ezekiel describes it repeatedly as "the end" in Ezekiel 7:2–9. It was indeed the end for his generation who died in exile. But not the end of the world, nor the end of God's purposes for Israel and the nations.

In the New Testament, Paul regards the intense suffering of new Christian believers as evidence of the same pattern at work; that is, it was an illustration of the fullness of sin and wrath being worked out in that generation (2 Thess 2:16). And the language that Jesus uses to portray what happened in AD 70—namely another occasion when Jerusalem and its temple were destroyed, this time by the Romans— portrays it as a time of terrible distress that would point forward to "the end" (Matt 24).

These various events in the Bible, then, function as previews or prefigurations of the ultimate End, when the powers of evil reach their worst. They are sign-posts reminding us that there will be times when evil appears to triumph, and such triumph will someday reach its final peak, and will then be finally and forever destroyed by the power of God alone.

So are we living in "the end times"? That is a question I often get asked, sometimes by those who seem anxious that if we are, it is a frightening prospect, and sometimes by those who seem to want to test my orthodoxy in case I don't share the same view of the rapture, tribulation, and millennium as they hold. My answer usually is, "Yes we are, and we have been ever since Jesus was raised from the dead."

For that indeed is how the New Testament uses the concept of end times, or to be more accurate in its terminology, "the last days." If you take a look at these texts, you will see clearly that the apostles believed that the resurrection had ushered in the final great act of God's work on earth. Because God had raised Jesus from the dead, they knew they were already living in "the last days" or "the last hour" (Acts 2:17; Heb 1:2; 1 Pet 1:20; 1 John 2:18).

In the light of these text, the end has, in a sense, already been anticipated. Evil has been defeated at the cross; the risen and ascended Christ is reigning; the Holy Spirit has been poured out. All these are signs and proof of "the last days"—as Peter claimed on the day of Pentecost.

And yet, of course, we know that the great movie drama of history has not yet come to "The End." That still lies ahead when Christ returns. And until Christ does return and we reach that climactic "End" (which will in fact be a new beginning, the coming of the new creation, as in Rev 21–22), we may yet experience other "endings" in the great sweep of human history—endings that the catalogue of "end times" in the Bible (including Antiochus Epiphanes) helps us to anticipate, understand, and endure. In other words, within the era of "the last days" (i.e., from the resurrection until the return of Christ), there may be many "end times" before we reach the ultimate End that only God knows and will decree.

For example, it looks like we are in the midst of the slow collapse of the dominance and self-assured superiority of Western civilization (predominantly European and North American) in the world. There are many signs of it. We still have an astoundingly arrogant and (in my view) blasphemous worship of the false gods of mammon and consumerism. We still sacrifice astronomical sums of money (and lives) on the altar of militarism, war, and violence-meeting-violence. We heedlessly pursue unsustainable levels of economic consumption and ecological carelessness that are leading to the destructive effects of climate change. And we are struggling to cope with the rise and assertiveness of new powers in the geo-political arena. Meanwhile our population is getting both smaller and older, while the populations of the majority world are burgeoning with youth. It may well be "the end times" for the great Euro-American Western hegemony.

But would the end of Western civilization mean the end of the world? The only biblically justifiable answer to that is, maybe, but maybe not. Only God knows. People thought the world would end at AD 1000. A millennium had passed. Time up. People thought that the terrifying Black Death that ravaged Europe in the fourteenth century, when an estimated 30–60 percent of the population perished, must surely signal the end of the world. Martin Luther was convinced that the wars and rumours of wars convulsing Europe in his own day were proof that the end of the world must come in his generation. There have been various catastrophic "ends" all through the course of history, including the ones in the Bible. But God has not yet decreed any of them to be the final, ultimate end. But one day he will.

One day Christ will return. And that day, according to the book of Revelation, will be preceded by the apparent triumph of evil and great suffering for God's people. The whole point, then, of a vision such as Daniel's, or indeed of the book of Revelation, is not to try to calculate and predict precise timetables, but rather to be ready at any time and to be faithful at all times. And that is where the encouragement of this chapter lies, a word of encouragement to which we finally turn.

A WORD OF ENCOURAGEMENT (8:13–14, 26–27)

But how long do we have to wait for "the end"—in whatever sense we mean that term? That is an understandable question which gets some answer in the middle of the chapter and a more encouraging one at the close.

> Then I heard a holy one speaking, and another holy one said to him, "How long will it take for the vision to be fulfilled—the vision concerning the daily sacrifice, the rebellion that causes desolation, the surrender of the sanctuary and the trampling underfoot of the LORD's people?"

> He said to me, "It will take 2,300 evenings and mornings;
> then the sanctuary will be reconsecrated." (Dan 8:13–14)

The worst moment of the reign of terror of Antiochus Epiphanes was when he abolished the daily sacrifices in the temple and in their place set up a defiling image of some kind (12:11). The questioner in verse 13 wants to know how long such desecration will last. The answer is mysterious. "2,300 evenings and mornings" could mean that number of whole days, which would be approximately six and a half years. Or "evenings and mornings" could refer to the two sacrifices that took place at that time every day in which case the number would imply 1,150 actual days, that is, approximately three years. That was approximately the length of time between the appalling moment when Antiochus erected an altar to Zeus in the temple and sacrificed pigs there (in 167 BC) and the cleansing of the temple after the Maccabean revolt (in 165 BC, celebrated in the Jewish feast of Hanukkah). Probably, as is often the case with numbers of this sort in apocalyptic literature, we are not meant to expect precise arithmetical chronology. Rather, the words imply a limited period of relatively short duration.

The main point is: the desecration of the temple and "the trampling underfoot of the LORD's people" will not last forever. The reign of the little horn, the "fierce-looking king, a master of intrigue," will come to an end. His time will come, as it always does and always will, for the enemies of God and God's people. And his destruction will come about by God's hand, as is implied in the closing words of verse 25: "Yet he will be destroyed, but not by human power." The suffering will be great, but the end will come. And that is the encouragement that God's people have needed at many times in their history, in the Old Testament and the history of the church. God remains in control, and those who try to destroy God's people will themselves be ultimately destroyed.

In closing, however, let's go back to the beginning, to Daniel's weird vision. It was filled with the imagery of animals: a ram and a he-goat, fighting with fierce horns. It is a picture that symbolizes those many human kings and conquerors who have charged around, butting and trampling their way through history.

The Bible also ends with animal imagery. John, like Daniel, has a prolonged vision. We should read Revelation 4–7 as a single whole vision. He sees the throne of God. It is surrounded by thrones of twenty-four elders (probably representing the whole people of God, Old and New Testament) and by four living creatures, with the heads of a lion, an ox, a human, and an eagle (probably representing the whole created order). And surrounding all of these are the innumerable hosts of angelic creatures. The whole scene is one of worship and of the exercise of divine government throughout the whole created universe.

But, rather like the beasts in Daniel's visions in Daniel 7 and 8, John sees four horses riding out (Rev 6:1–8). These are not pictures of terrible things that will happen only at some distant point in the future (as they are sometimes portrayed: the "four horsemen of the Apocalypse"). No, they portray conquest, war, famine, and death—realities that were as devastatingly present in John's own day in the Roman Empire as they have been throughout human history and still are today. These horses, apparently wild and uncontrolled animals like Daniel's beasts, have been riding through history bringing devastation in their wake for countless centuries.

But are they in fact out of control? No! For who is summoning them? Each of them receives an authorizing command "Come" from the throne of God. They are under orders. And where are they coming from? They ride out as the seals are opened on the scroll in the hand of the one on the throne. That scroll represents the whole purpose and plan of God throughout human history. They are actors in a script written by someone else, not directors of their own drama. And, most of all, who has the authority to open the scroll, that is, to interpret and control the whole destiny of history, including the horsemen?

When John had asked that at first, he was dismayed that nobody was worthy to take such authority; no human participant in the story of the scroll has the authority to interpret and control the whole scroll itself. But wait! There is one who is worthy. John is told to look for a lion, or rather *the* Lion—the Lion of Judah, the Root of David (the one who fulfills all the promises of Old Testament Israel; Rev 5:5). But when John did in fact look, what did he see? "A Lamb, looking as if it had been slain, standing at the centre of the throne" (Rev 5:6).

The Lion morphs into a Lamb—what an amazing combination of images, surpassing even Daniel's! The one who will triumph and rule like the lion-king is the one who gave his life as the crucified Lamb of God. And of course, in all this imagery and its surrounding description, John is seeing a portrait of the crucified and risen Jesus of Nazareth, the Lion and the Lamb.

So in the midst of John's world of rampaging horsemen, that is, in the midst of evils with human, natural, and satanic causes (from our limited perspective), just as in Daniel's world of beasts and empires and endings, there is this tremendously encouraging assurance in both books that the government of the universe is in God's hands and (in Revelation) in the hands of the one who died and rose again for our salvation.

The God of Daniel, the God of John, is still on the throne and he will remember his own. And God will ultimately defeat and destroy all evil including the Evil One himself and so deliver his people forever.

And that leaves just the very last verse of the chapter, which in some ways is my favourite!

> I, Daniel, was worn out. I lay exhausted for several days. Then
> I got up and went about the king's business. I was appalled by
> the vision; it was beyond understanding. (Dan 8:27)

It's the honesty I love: "worn out . . . exhausted . . . appalled." Well, we can relate to that, if we can exercise any kind of imagination about what it was like to have such a vision. And the fact that Daniel himself says, even after having some angelic coaching, that the vision "was beyond understanding" surely means we should not be over hasty or over confident in claiming total accuracy and precision in the interpretation we ourselves put on this and Daniel's other visions. As we saw, there is a certain flexibility about how the pattern of four might connect with actual history, and there is likely some general "rounding" in the numbers that occur here and elsewhere. Like Daniel, we "get the picture." But we need not pin down every detail.

But what I most love is the simple down-to-earth comment, "Then I got up and went about the king's business." Daniel went back to the office the next day! Back to his desk, back to the day job (after the visions of the night), back to the place God had put him decades earlier, to get on with life and work and all the government responsibilities he had been entrusted with. The ordinariness of this response is astonishing.

Daniel had just had this incredible vision. It was appalling and scary, yes, but it was also prophetic and, in some senses at least, exciting. He had seen the future! BUT, he did not go around ranting like some wild prophet of doom. Nor did he set up a lucrative "end-times" ministry, complete with websites, movies, and books (well, perhaps one book). No, he just "got up and went about the king's business."

- He doubtless adjusted his worldview to take into account (even more than he already had throughout his life), the sovereignty of God and the transience of human empires.
- He anticipated with fear the terrible evils of a world totally under the feet of a regime opposed to God and God's people.
- He knew that the end would come someday, somehow, in God's own time and God's own way.

. . . and he went back to work.

There is a wonderfully mature balance about that. On the one hand, the fact that he was in government service, fully committed to working for what we would now call "the secular authorities," did not blind him from recognizing that underneath the positive and constructive dimensions of the state lay a "beast" with idolatrous tendencies and a frightening capacity for violence, persecution, and lies. He had spiritual discernment as well as ethical commitment and integrity in the workplace.

But on the other hand, and at the same time, the fact that he had become very aware of the potentially "bestial" (and we might add, satanic) spiritual dimensions that are at work within the social, political, and economic structures of the state did not make him decide to opt out of secular employment altogether, reject any involvement in political life, and inhabit a marginalized world of spiritual piety. No, he understood only too well the spiritual dimensions of the present and future, but he took that understanding with him *into* his work. He went about the king's business, knowing that he was, at the same time, going about the business of the true King of kings, serving the One whom John would later describe as "the ruler of the kings of the earth" (Rev 1:5).

The challenge for us, surely, is to be able to open both our minds and hearts to the great, sweeping vision of this biblical view of history—past, present, and future—and yet get on with the life and work God has called us into, with that same combination of realism and assurance born of faith in the God of Daniel.

MODEL PRAYER, MYSTERIOUS PREDICTIONS

"Dial 999 for intercessory prayer," I used to tell students when I was teaching the Old Testament—999 being the telephone number used in the UK for emergency services (the equivalent to 911 in the USA). The reason is that several very instructive examples of profound confessional and intercessory prayer are found in chapter 9 of several Old Testament books. First there is Deuteronomy 9, where we read Moses's own recollection of his prayers on behalf of Israel at the two great moments of apostasy and rebellion, at Sinai (Exod 32–34) and Kadesh Barnea (Num 14). Then there is Nehemiah 9, when Nehemiah leads the people of Israel in a great prayer of confession after the reading of the law in chapter 8 and before the covenant renewal in chapter 10. Ezra has a similar but shorter prayer also in Ezra 9. And then, here in Daniel 9 we have one more outstanding example of biblical prayer in action.

It would be a very worthwhile exercise to read those other chapter nines before reading through Daniel 9. You will undoubtedly see common phrases and themes, and you will also notice how the later prayers of Nehemiah, Ezra, and Daniel are all saturated with earlier Scriptures.

DANIEL'S PROBLEM (9:1–3)

In the first year of Darius son of Xerxes (a Mede by descent), who was made ruler over the Babylonian kingdom—in the first year of his reign, I, Daniel, understood from the Scriptures, according to the word of the LORD given to Jeremiah the prophet, that the desolation of Jerusalem would last seventy years. So I turned to the Lord God and pleaded with him in prayer and petition, in fasting, and in sackcloth and ashes. (Dan 9:1–3)

The date matters. Without going into the detailed arguments (which can be read in the commentaries), there is a good case for affirming that the "Darius" of verse 1 is the same person as Cyrus the Great, who unified the kingdom of the Medes with that of the Persians to create the Medo-Persian Empire. In 539–538 BC he had conquered the city of Babylon and taken over the empire that Nebuchadnezzar had founded. So this entry in Daniel's prayer journal occurs during that momentous first year of the new imperial reality.

Babylon had fallen! Was this not what the exiled Jews had longed for ever since they had been dragged from their homeland two generations earlier? Was this not what the prophets Isaiah, Jeremiah, and Ezekiel had all foretold? If Cyrus was the LORD's anointed one as Isaiah 45:1 had remarkably affirmed, should he not now usher in a whole new age of freedom, blessing, and prosperity for God's people? And yet, might not the new empire turn out to be just as bad as the one it replaced? A mixture of hopes and fears must have filled the air among the exiles of Judah, including any of Daniel's friends who were still alive.

Think, for a moment, about what Daniel had *experienced* in his long life. He must have been in his eighties by this stage. At an early age, in 605 BC, he had been seized and carried off with his three young friends into exile in the strange foreign land that was to be his home till he died. He had not personally witnessed the destruction of Jerusalem in 587 BC, but he would have shared in the shock, grief, and numb devastation of the whole Jewish community in Babylon when the news arrived (see Ezek 25:15–27, 33:21–33). He had witnessed the rise to power of Nebuchadnezzar, including the dazzling glory of the city of Babylon that he developed. Daniel had served in the government of the man who had destroyed Daniel's city and beautified his own. And as the power of Babylon had risen, so had the position of Daniel in its senior government service. He had experienced personal career success and great prestige. The story of Joseph finds its echoes in the story of Daniel—from captivity to high office, while maintaining his faith, his integrity, and his life of prayer to the God of Israel.

And think about what Daniel *knew* by this stage of his life, from the revelations God had given him through the dreams of Nebuchadnezzar in chapters 2 and 4, and his own visions in chapters 7 and 8. He knew the "beastly" spiritual dimension that lay behind the human political reality of the political and imperial world order. But he also knew the "heavenly" reality of the sovereignty of the God of heaven, none other than the Lord God of Israel. And he knew that the kingdom of this God would ultimately be victorious. The enemies of God and God's people would be destroyed. There would be an end to the persecution and suffering of his people. The reign of God would be extended over all the earth. Daniel was a man of intense personal engagement in the social and political world of his day, exercising all his skill and abilities in that realm. At the same time, Daniel was a man of intense prophetic insight into the spiritual dimensions of the present and the assured outcomes of the future.

So why not just sit back and wait for it all to happen as predicted? Go for a walk in the Hanging Gardens of Babylon. Sing a few more praise psalms with his friends down at the synagogue. Relax. Let go and let God.

Not Daniel. From chapter 6 we know that even into the Persian Empire he was still committed to serving the king. He was a practical man, and the day job with all its seniority and responsibility still occupied his time. But from these verses we see that he was still committed to studying the Scriptures. He was also a praying man, and he blended his prayers to God with searching for a word from God. In that respect he typifies what we know happened among the Jewish people in exile. Their temple—the place where they had been accustomed to encounter God—had been destroyed. So they turned instead to meet God in the Scriptures and prayer, the staple ingredients of synagogue worship ever since.

So why was Daniel so intense in his study of Scripture and prayer? Answer: because of the problem that was weighing so heavily on his mind. The problem of Israel itself. The problem of Jerusalem. What about them? We might ask. Surely by now they have become irrelevant. Israel no longer exists—at least not as an independent people in charge of their own destiny in their own land. And Jerusalem no longer exists—nothing more than a heap of charred ruins and rubble a very long way away. Ah, but no. They could not be so easily dismissed from Daniel's mind or prayers. For Israel was not just any people; Jerusalem was not just any city. They were not mere statistics in Nebuchadnezzar's catalogue of conquered nations and cities. The name of Yahweh the God of Israel was invested in this people and city. And the prophetic word of the same God was clear about an ongoing future for both.

So, that being the case (that the people and the city had an identity and a destiny bound up with the name of Yahweh, the Lord God of Israel), how could God possibly abandon them and also remain true to himself and his word? The problem came down to an issue for the honour and reputation of God himself in the world. God must act, and act soon, if God wanted to defend his own name. There must be a future. For Daniel, as we have already seen (remember those open windows in chapter 6?), Jerusalem (even Jerusalem still in ruins) was a symbol of the future, not a casualty of the past. The big question was, how long? When would God act? What could be expected? And in that frame of mind, Daniel had turned to the Scriptures.

And specifically he turns to the book of Jeremiah. This indicates two things. First, it gives some strength to my suspicion that Daniel and his friends would have heard the reading of the letter that Jeremiah sent to the exiles way back in the early years between the deportation of 597 BC and the final destruction of the city in 587 BC. As I said earlier, there is no proof of that, of course, but the way those four young lads settled down in Babylon in exactly the way Jeremiah urged the exiles to do strongly suggests that they did. Secondly, it shows that there was a scroll (or scrolls) of the prophecies of Jeremiah circulating among the exiles in Babylon. We know that Baruch wrote such a scroll when Jeremiah was in hiding from the anger of King Jehoiakim. Baruch's first scroll was burnt (Jer 36), but Jeremiah instructed him to write it all out again to replace the first scroll, and doubtless Baruch went on to add, collect, and edit his written collection of the word of the God through the prophet Jeremiah, even when both Jeremiah and Barurch were taken off with the party of Judeans who fled to Egypt. At some point a copy of that scroll must have reached the exiles in Babylon, where it would have been carefully preserved and copied. It was such a scroll that Daniel has in his possession and turns to once again in order to hear the voice of his God.

Now there are two places in Jeremiah that speak of Babylon's rule lasting seventy years,[1] in Jeremiah 25 and 29. They come from different dates and have significantly different purposes.

1. *Jeremiah 25:1–11.* This word came in 605 BC, a very significant year for Daniel. For that was also the first year of the reign of Nebuchadnezzar, the year when he imposed his power over Judah by taking some hostages captive from Jerusalem to Babylon—among them Daniel and his three friends, as young boys. If Daniel had heard that prophecy at the time it would have made him realize that, without some unlikely change of heart in the pagan king, he and his friends would spend the rest of their lives in Babylon.

---

1. "Seventy years" is most probably a "round number." The actual exile itself (from the fall of Jerusalem to the decree of Cyrus allowing the Jews to return to their land) was approximately fifty years, from 587 to 538 BC. If we look for a period of approximately seventy years, then two periods would fit: (1) from 605 BC (the definitive date of Nebuchadnezzar's reign after defeating the Egyptians at Carchemish) until 538 BC (the date of the fall of Babylon to Cyrus); (2) from 587 BC (the date of the destruction of the temple) to 516 BC (the date of the completion of the rebuilding of the temple). Daniel seems to be working with option (1) in assuming that Babylon's seventy years are coming to an end through the victories of Cyrus. Zechariah 1:12–16 seems to see the seventy years in terms of option (2).

> Therefore the LORD Almighty says this: "Because you have not listened to my words, I will summon all the peoples of the north and my servant Nebuchadnezzar king of Babylon," declares the LORD, "and I will bring them against this land and its inhabitants and against all the surrounding nations. I will completely destroy them and make them an object of horror and scorn, and an everlasting ruin. I will banish from them the sounds of joy and gladness, the voices of bride and bridegroom, the sound of millstones and the light of the lamp. This whole country will become a desolate wasteland, and these nations will serve the king of Babylon seventy years. (Jer 25:8–11)

The main thrust of this passage is that, after generations of refusing to listen to the warnings of the prophets, Judah fully deserved the judgment of God that was about to fall on them. Seventy years of Babylon meant seventy years of judgment on Israel.

2. *Jeremiah 29:1–4.* This is the letter that Jeremiah wrote to the exiles soon after the first major deportation in 597 BC. God told them that even though it was Nebuchadnezzar who had carried them off into exile, it was in fact God himself who had taken them there (note v. 4, 7, 14). And furthermore, God was with them there, for they could pray to him there just as surely as they could in the temple in Jerusalem. So let them settle down there for the next two generations. And while they are there, let them pray for, and seek the welfare of, Babylon—a shockingly surprising message, which Daniel and his friends had been carrying out. Then comes the seventy-year message again.

> This is what the LORD says: "When seventy years are completed for Babylon, I will come to you and fulfill my good promise to bring you back to this place. For I know the plans I have for you," declares the LORD, "plans to

prosper you and not to harm you, plans to give you hope and a future. Then you will call on me and come and pray to me, and I will listen to you. You will seek me and find me when you seek me with all your heart. I will be found by you," declares the LORD, "and will bring you back from captivity. I will gather you from all the nations and places where I have banished you," declares the LORD, "and will bring you back to the place from which I carried you into exile." (Jer 29:10–14)

The main thrust of this passage is clearly a surprising hope for the future, even in the context of judgment. God *would* restore them. And for that reason, the Israelites are urged to show full repentance by seeking the Lord once again with all their heart. Seventy years for Babylon meant hope for Israel when that time was up.

The double thrust of *both* these texts in Jeremiah then (the reality of deserved judgment, and the hope for forgiveness and restoration based on a whole-hearted, fresh seeking of God), are woven together in Daniel's meditating mind, and both themes emerge now in his great prayer in chapter 9.

Daniel's problem (the pain of exile and its impact on God's reputation) had been caused by God acting in judgment. The solution Daniel sought, therefore, could only come from God himself, by God acting in restoration. That is why he turns to God in prayer. Indeed, the word Daniel uses to describe his prayer in Daniel 9:3, (in Hebrew; "I *sought* the Lord God") is exactly the word that God urged the exiles to do in Jeremiah 29:13: "You will seek me and find me when you seek me with all your heart."

DANIEL'S PRAYER (9:4–19)

When Daniel starts to pray, we are immediately aware that he has a lot more of the Scriptures in his mind than Jeremiah only. If you have a cross-reference Bible, you will see many references to earlier books of the Bible in so many of the phrases Daniel uses. This is, in the best sense, liturgical prayer. It follows a form that we find elsewhere (like Nehemiah 1 and 9, and Ezra 9), and is saturated with scriptural echoes, from Leviticus and Deuteronomy, from the Psalms, and of course from Jeremiah. Indeed, it would be worth taking a moment to read the following two texts right now: Leviticus 26:40–45 and Deuteronomy 30:1–10. And then listen for the similarities when you read Daniel's prayer straight afterwards.

And yet, of course, just because it is full of scriptural phraseology does not mean that it is not personal prayer. This is Daniel's own, urgent, intense, intimate engagement with God. But as he enters into that work, the words of his mouth echo the words of Scripture in his heart, the words of God himself. It's a good model to follow.

What Daniel Confessed

I prayed to the LORD my God and confessed:

"Lord, the great and awesome God, who keeps his covenant of love with those who love him and keep his commandments, we have sinned and done wrong. We have been wicked and have rebelled; we have turned away from your commands and laws. We have not listened to your servants the prophets, who spoke in your name to our kings, our princes and our ancestors, and to all the people of the land.

"Lord, you are righteous, but this day we are covered with shame—the people of Judah and the inhabitants of Jerusalem and all Israel, both near and far, in all the countries where you have scattered us because of our unfaithfulness to you. We and our kings, our princes and our ancestors are covered with shame, LORD, because we have sinned against you. The Lord our God is merciful and forgiving, even though we have rebelled against him; we have not obeyed the LORD our God or kept the laws he gave us through his servants the prophets. All Israel has transgressed your law and turned away, refusing to obey you. (Dan 9:4–11a)

And here's another good model to follow. Did you notice how often Daniel says "We . . . our." Daniel does not stand outside his people and confess *their* sin in an accusatory way. Rather, he identifies himself with his people. Indeed, at the end of his prayer, in verse 20, he says, "While I was speaking and praying, confessing *my* sin and the sin of my people." Now Daniel had been a young lad at the time Nebuchadnezzar snatched him from Jerusalem. In any literal or physical sense, he had not been personally involved in the catalogue of wickedness and rebellion and disobedience that he lists in his prayer. Yet he confesses it as his own, along with his people. He feels himself so bound up with his own people, in their past as much as their future, that he can summarize sins that had taken place over many generations and count himself as part of it all.

And did you pause to count how many different ways Daniel describes his people's sin? I can count at least ten: sinned . . . done wrong . . . been wicked . . . have rebelled . . . turned away (v. 5) . . . not listened (v. 6) . . . shame . . . unfaithfulness (v. 7) . . . have not obeyed (v. 10) . . . has transgressed (v. 11). These are all different words in Hebrew. This is no quick and shallow apology, "Sorry, Lord, we messed up a bit there." This is deep awareness of the endemic, incorrigibly evil ways of a whole nation (note "all Israel," v. 11) for many generations. This is a history of stubborn rebellion and rejection of all warnings and pleadings by successive prophets. This is genuine contrition before their covenant God.

But why now? Why at this precise point in Daniel's long life? And particularly, why does Daniel turn to confession of sin at the very moment when he has worked out from the Scriptures that the promised return of his people to their land must be getting very close, since Babylon's seventy years are up? Should he not be out celebrating with whatever friends have survived as long as he has? Would thanksgiving and praise, rather than confession of sin, not be the right response to what he has found in Jeremiah?

Once again, Daniel surprises us. He saw that the state of his own people was far from ready for the restoration that lay just around the corner. I wonder if he also knew the Scriptures of Isaiah 40–55. Those chapters are full of joyful hope for Israel's future when God would bring them back from Babylon. But they are also very realistic: God does not hesitate to explain (again) why they were in exile in the first place. It was because of their sin and rebellion (Isa 42:18–25; 43:22–28). They stood in dire need of forgiveness, and that would be accomplished (according to Isa 53) through the self-sacrificial suffering and death of the mysterious servant of the Lord. Both Isaiah and Daniel understood that, even though Cyrus would be God's means of bringing the Israelites back to Jerusalem, at a deeper level God needed to bring them back to himself. They needed not only to be lifted out of exile but to be forgiven for their sin.

So that is what Daniel prays for here. He confesses the depth of Israel's sin, as the foundation of repentance on which alone any hope for the future could be built. And only if there were a future for Israel could there be a future for the world as well. For although Daniel does not articulate this point, we know from the wider Scriptures that God's ultimate plan for Israel was that they should be the means by which God would fulfil his promise to Abraham that all nations on earth would find blessing through him. That story needed to continue. And Israel's present sinful condition (like the failed, blind, and deaf servant of Isa 42:18–25) stood as an obstacle to God's long-term and worldwide purposes. Israel needed to be restored so that God could continue his mission for the whole earth. And Daniel's longing for the kingdom of God to be established and acknowledged on earth among the kingdoms of mankind led him to confess the sins and failures of the redeemed community of God's people.

And with that thought in place, another one comes along. Why is Daniel listing Israel's sins, rather than Babylon's?

Jeremiah 25 not only saw the seventy years of Babylon as judgment on Israel's sin but also saw the completion of those seventy years as *the starting point of God's judgment on Babylon*. Jeremiah's words continued:

"But when the seventy years are fulfilled, I will punish the king of Babylon and his nation, the land of the Babylonians, for their guilt," declares the LORD, "and will make it desolate forever. I will bring on that land all the things I have spoken against it, all that are written in this book and prophesied by Jeremiah against all the nations. They themselves will be enslaved by many nations and great kings; I will repay them according to their deeds and the work of their hands." (Jer 25:12–14)

Now, in the light of those verses which he had just read, we could very easily imagine Daniel filling his prayer with a catalogue of all *Babylon's* "deeds and the work of their hands." He'd lived there all his life! Who better to remind God of the arrogance, corruption, oppression, violence, and injustice of Babylon than Daniel, who had seen it all first-hand. He could give God plenty of ammunition with which to "repay them."

And yet, at the moment when he knows *Babylon's* judgment is about to begin, he ignores that pagan evil empire and focuses entirely on *the sin of God's people* in the midst of it. What lesson is there in that for us?

It seems to me that there is a tendency in Christian circles sometimes to be highly critical of the world around us while being naïve, self-excusing, or downright triumphalistic about the church. It may have something to do with a "Hollywood" culture of bad guys and good guys, and we're the good guys. Self-righteousness is such an easy sin to slip into, almost as easy as self-pity. Condemnation of the world goes easily hand in hand with wallowing in our own righteousness and the suffering it may bring upon us from the world.

Interesting, therefore, is it not, that Jeremiah told the exiles to pray for the world around them (the pagan city where God had put them, Jer 29:7), while Daniel, even though he knew full well the sins of the pagan world around him, chose rather to confess the sins of God's own people? There is even something subversive here of a too simplistic application of the emotions of the Psalms—understandable though they are in their own context. Psalm 137 curses Babylon while Psalm 122 says "pray for the peace of Jerusalem." Jeremiah commands us to pray for the peace of Babylon and Daniel confesses the sins of Jerusalem. Perhaps some churches need to redress their balance in the light of this and spend more time praying for the world and lamenting the sins of the church.

What Daniel Affirmed

"Therefore the curses and sworn judgments written in the Law of Moses, the servant of God, have been poured out on us, because we have sinned against you. You have fulfilled the words spoken against us and against our rulers by bringing on us great disaster. Under the whole heaven nothing has ever been done like what has been done to Jerusalem. Just as it is written in the Law of Moses, all this disaster has come on us, yet we have not sought the favour of the LORD our God by turning from our sins and giving attention to your truth. The LORD did not hesitate to bring the disaster on us, for the LORD our God is righteous in everything he does; yet we have not obeyed him." (Dan 9:11b–14)

Prayer is not just asking for things. In fact, Daniel does not begin to ask for anything until verse 16. He continues to affirm the facts. The facts about Israel's sin are clear enough, and he still has them very much in mind. But alongside those sombre facts, Daniel is reaffirming the truth he has lived by all his life—the sovereign justice of God in all his doings. The last sentence quoted above (v. 14b), is a summary of the whole prayer so far—"the LORD our God is righteous in everything he does; yet we have not obeyed him." And that repeats what he said earlier on in the prayer: "You, LORD, are righteous, but this day we are covered in shame" (v. 7).

God was right in 587 BC to allow Babylon to conquer and destroy Jerusalem. But even though it was an act of God's judgment, it gave God no pleasure whatsoever. On the contrary, Jeremiah weeps the tears of God himself over the suffering, death, and devastation. The book of Lamentations exposes the sheer horror of it all. But that terrifying and traumatic event was the consequence of sin and rebellion—rebellion against God in the spiritual and moral realms and rebellion against Babylon in the political realm (which Jeremiah had repeatedly urged them not to do). It was an act of God's just judgment after centuries of warning going all the way back to Moses. That is the point of these verses. God was acting within the terms of the Sinai covenant, acting in faithfulness to his threats as well as his promises. That is God's nature as God—to be faithful to his own word in all its dimensions.

But in that simple fact lay also Israel's hope (and ours). For God's righteousness and faithfulness will be in operation also in the act of forgiveness and restoration. And that is where Daniel now turns.

But before we go on to the final movement of Daniel's prayer, we should pause to note the importance of this middle section. Daniel is not pleading with God to pretend it all hadn't happened. He is not trying to excuse Israel, as if to say, "We didn't really mean it. It was all just a big mistake. We'll try to do better." He is not trying to "play on God's emotions" as a child might whimper before an angry parent, hoping that by looking pitiful they might escape punishment. No, Daniel has faced up to the stark facts about Israel. But he is also holding up and holding on to the strong facts about God. Yahweh, the God who is righteous in all that he says and does, will therefore also be faithful to his promises to his people, and through his people to the world. The God of justice is the God of forgiveness and mercy.

It is never easy to hold those last two affirmations together in our minds at the same time, and yet it is vital that we do, especially in prayer. Daniel does so in close proximity. Look what he says in verse 7: "Lord, you are righteous." And look what he says two verses later in verse 9: "The Lord our God is merciful and forgiving."

Of course, standing where we do in the flow of the great drama of Scripture, we now have the supreme fact of the cross of Christ to help us to know, grasp, and trust in both sides of those affirmations. For it was there that the supreme justice of God and the supreme mercy and forgiveness of God were simultaneously outpoured. It was there that God bore in himself in the person of God's own Son the consequences of our sin and rebellion and opened the door of mercy and forgiveness. Daniel's prayer shows that he knew the depth of the character of the God he was praying to, because he knew the story of God's actions in the history of his own people. Our prayer has an even stronger foundation since we know how that story of Israel reached its climax and fulfilment in the death and resurrection of Israel's Messiah. Let our prayer be a constant affirmation of the biblical truth (from both Testaments) about the God to whom we are praying.

What Daniel Asked

"Now, Lord our God, who brought your people out of Egypt with a mighty hand and who made for yourself a name that endures to this day, we have sinned, we have done wrong. Lord, in keeping with all your righteous acts, turn away your anger and your wrath from Jerusalem, your city, your holy hill. Our sins and the iniquities of our ancestors have made Jerusalem and your people an object of scorn to all those around us.

"Now, our God, hear the prayers and petitions of your servant. For your sake, Lord, look with favour on your desolate sanctuary. Give ear, our God, and hear; open your eyes and see the desolation of the city that bears your Name. We do not make requests of you because we are righteous, but because of your great mercy. Lord, listen! Lord, forgive! Lord, hear and act! For your sake, my God, do not delay, because your city and your people bear your Name." (Dan 9:15–19)

I'm sure you'll agree that this is powerful intercessory prayer. There is great passion in the words and the repetitions. The English translation tries to express that through the use of exclamation marks. But there is more than just rhetoric and emotion here. There are further features of this model prayer that we can take to heart.

It is clear, from his concluding requests (emphasised by those exclamation marks), that Daniel's fundamental prayer is that God should forgive his people and restore them, along with their city and his temple ("your desolate sanctuary"). As we contemplate the state of God's people today—the state of the church around the world and in our own countries—that is a prayer we ourselves may rightly pray, and probably much more often than we do. Not that we stand in the same position as Israel in exile awaiting physical restoration to their land and city or the rebuilding of a physical temple. But rather in the sense we considered above, namely, that in so many places and so many ways those who claim to be God's people are scarcely fit for purpose, the purpose for which God called us into existence, to serve God's mission in the world. We need to be restored, in humility and penitence, and we need to cry to God to do so.

But if that is our prayer, if we resonate with the longing of Daniel's heart, we must pay attention to the foundations on which he prays it. What basis did Daniel have for asking God to look and listen, to forgive and act?

First of all, we can see at once what he did NOT base his request on. "We do not make requests of you because we are righteous, but because of your great mercy" (v. 18). Daniel does not plead with God on the basis of any merits in himself or his people. There is absolutely no sense of entitlement in his prayer ("We deserve a break here, Lord"). On the contrary, any response will have to flow from the unmerited grace of God alone. Very probably the beautiful "Prayer of Humble Access" in the Anglican Book of Common Prayer intentionally alluded to this verse in Daniel.

We do not presume to come to this thy Table, O merciful Lord, trusting in our own righteousness, but in thy manifold and great mercies. We are not worthy so much as to gather up the crumbs under thy Table. But thou art the same Lord, whose property is always to have mercy.[2]

Having made that negative point, here are three things that Daniel mentions, which go right to the heart of the God he is praying to: God's consistency, God's reputation, and God's covenant.

1. *God's consistency*: Daniel begins by reminding God of his actions in past history, of which the greatest was, of course, the exodus. That was the monumental act of redemption by which Yahweh God had proved his power over all the gods of Egypt (including Pharaoh) and had delivered his people from political, economic, social, and spiritual oppression. It was the event upon which Yahweh's fame as God was based (v. 15; and see Exod 15:14–16). And it was the event upon which Israel's faith in the redemptive love, faithfulness, and mighty power of their God was forever founded. So Daniel simply asks God to be consistent with all his "righteous acts" in the past, going back to the exodus itself. God need only do what God consistently does: be himself and act accordingly.

2. *God's reputation*: If Yahweh's fame had been built on his mighty acts of deliverance in the past, what would the world be thinking of him in the present, now that his people were in the disgrace of exile and his city and temple were in ruins? They were "an object of scorn," and therefore so was Yahweh their God. That was exactly the dilemma that Ezekiel addressed (Ezek 36:16–32). The name of the God of Israel was "profaned" (treated as common and despised) among the nations because of the disgrace of the people of Israel. Their shame was his shame. Therefore, through Ezekiel, God promised to act, not only to cleanse and restore *them*, but ultimately to clear *his own* name and restore his own reputation. That is what Daniel prays for here, in tactfully reminding God that the city and the

---

2. This prayer was first published in the first Book of Common Prayer of the Church of England in 1549 during the reign of Edward VI.

people "bear your Name." Their destiny and his name were bound together for good or ill. Let it now be for good.

3. *God's covenant*: Did you notice how many times Daniel uses the word "your"? It tolls through the final sentences of his prayer like a bell: "your people . . . your city . . . your holy hill . . . your desolate sanctuary . . . your city . . . your people . . . your Name." As I said before, this is not just rhetorical or emotional emphasis. This is profound theology. At the heart of the covenant relationship between Yahweh God and Israel was that intensely personal and possessive relationship: "I will be your God and you will be my people," with the reciprocal response, "You will be our God and we will be your people." This is beautifully affirmed by both covenant partners in Deuteronomy 26.

> You have declared this day that the LORD is your God and that you will walk in obedience to him, that you will keep his decrees, commands and laws—that you will listen to him. And the LORD has declared this day that you are his people, his treasured possession as he promised, and that you are to keep all his commands. (Deut 26:17–18)

> That was the relationship, established in the covenant at Sinai on the basis of the redemption accomplished in the exodus, to which Daniel here appeals: "Lord, remember who we are. Remember who we belong to." He is echoing the same appeal that Moses made centuries earlier (read Deut 9:26–29 and notice there too the multiple use of the word "your" in Moses's prayer).

What a remarkable prayer is recorded here in Daniel 9 for our learning and use! It gives us such a powerful model for our own praying, taking its place alongside so many of the Psalms which perform the same function. This is the kind of prayer that goes to the heart of God and finds God even more ready to answer than we are to pray—which is what Daniel discovers before he has even said Amen.

DANIEL'S PROSPECT (9:20–27)

> While I was speaking and praying, confessing my sin and the
> sin of my people Israel and making my request to the LORD my
> God for his holy hill—while I was still in prayer, Gabriel, the man
> I had seen in the earlier vision, came to me in swift flight about
> the time of the evening sacrifice. He instructed me and said to me,
> "Daniel, I have now come to give you insight and understanding.
> As soon as you began to pray, a word went out, which I have come
> to tell you, for you are highly esteemed. Therefore, consider the
> word and understand the vision. (Dan 9:20–23)

God's instant answer to Daniel's praying (even before he had
finished!) is an example of God's promise of what life will be like in
the new creation, "Before they call I will answer; while they are still
speaking I will hear" (Isa 65:24). This does not imply, of course, that
Daniel's prayer was pointless (why pray if God has the answer ready
the moment you start?). That is far too "wooden" an interpretation of
what happens here. The point rather is that the relationship between
Daniel and God had become so mutual and intimate through that
thrice-daily conversation (Daniel was a man "highly esteemed" [or
"greatly loved"] in heaven itself! 9:23; 10:11, 19) that God knew
what the thrust and content of Daniel's prayer would be even as he
began to pray. That does not make his prayer unimportant; we have
already seen how profoundly relevant it is as a model for us and all
God's people as we engage with God in prayer over the confusing
affairs of the world and the church. And in some mysterious way God
weaves the prayers of his people into the means of his governance of
world history.

What then, would God say in answer to Daniel's prayer?
Remember: Daniel had understood so far from the scroll of Jeremiah
that Babylon's seventy years were coming to an end and that Israel's
return to their homeland was therefore imminent. But he sees that
not as a cause for rejoicing only, but rather as a stimulus to confess

the sin of his people—even on the point of that return—and to ask for God to act in mercy and forgiveness. What has God to say now about that "seventy" and that forgiveness? Gabriel gives God's answer, which, as he also points out, would need "insight and understanding." How right he was!

> "Seventy 'sevens' are decreed for your people and your holy city to finish transgression, to put an end to sin, to atone for wickedness, to bring in everlasting righteousness, to seal up vision and prophecy and to anoint the Most Holy Place.
>
> "Know and understand this: From the time the word goes out to restore and rebuild Jerusalem until the Anointed One, the ruler, comes, there will be seven 'sevens,' and sixty-two 'sevens.' It will be rebuilt with streets and a trench, but in times of trouble. After the sixty-two 'sevens,' the Anointed One will be put to death and will have nothing. The people of the ruler who will come will destroy the city and the sanctuary. The end will come like a flood: War will continue until the end, and desolations have been decreed. He will confirm a covenant with many for one 'seven.' In the middle of the 'seven' he will put an end to sacrifice and offering. And at the temple he will set up an abomination that causes desolation, until the end that is decreed is poured out on him." (Dan 9:24–27)

Remember when Peter asked Jesus if he should forgive somebody up to seven times, and Jesus replied (more or less), "Not seven times, but seventy times seven. Stop checking, ticking, and counting, and expand your thinking!" Something like that happens here. Daniel (and Jeremiah) are thinking "seventy years," but God says, "You need to think a lot further ahead than that. Try seventy 'weeks' of years!" (The NIV translates "weeks" as "sevens" to make the point clear). That amounts to literally 490 years, but again it is most likely that such significant numbers (seventy, and weeks), are rounded, approximate, and symbolic. It is telling us that although something important was about to happen approximately one long lifetime since the rise of

Babylon (Jeremiah's seventy-years prophecy), something even more important would have to happen in order to answer Daniel's prayer to the fullest extent, in approximately half a millennium (Daniel's seventy sevens). He needed not only faith but also patience and long-term vision.

Part of the reason why I think we should take the seventy sevens (v. 24), and then the seven sevens, sixty-two sevens, and a final seven (vv. 25–27), in an approximate sense (sketching relative periods of time), rather than trying to work out precise chronological dates within our calendar system, is that many people down through the centuries have tried to work out exactly what dates and what events match a literal sequence of 49 years, 434 years, and 7 years. And they have come to all kinds of different solutions, mainly depending on what date is assumed to be the starting point (what date and what person is meant by "From the time the word goes forth to restore and rebuild Jerusalem"? Jeremiah's prophecy? Cyrus's edict?). You can read all the various options on offer in the larger commentaries if you like that kind of thing (Ernest Lucas is particularly detailed and helpful). But frankly, like Lucas, I think the attempt to square Gabriel's words as if they were precise predictions of detailed chronological events and persons is probably missing the point.

Another reason for not trying to be too dogmatic and one-eyed in pinning down these enigmatic predictions is that they seem to operate at different levels. It seems to me that there is a difference between what Gabriel is talking about in verse 24 from what he then goes on to add, with a fresh start, in verses 25–27.

Verse 24

Daniel had prayed that God would deal with Israel's sin, and Gabriel answers in verse 24, "He will. But not merely in the coming return from exile. Beyond that, in about 500 years time, God will act so decisively that he will bring about not just a temporary restoration of a still sinful people to their land, but a complete solution to the whole problem of sin in itself."

Verse 24 falls into two halves, with two groups of three verbs, the first group negative, the second group positive. What does the future hold? Basically, an end to sin and the establishment of God's justice.

First of all, it is "decreed"—that is, it is God's unbreakable will and commitment—that something will happen within the people of Israel and in Jerusalem that will

- finish transgression . . .
- put an end to sin . . . [and]
- atone for wickedness.

And secondly, what happens at that time

- will vindicate God's justice and bring everlasting righteousness,
- will be the fulfilment of the scriptural prophecies, and
- will "anoint a most holy"—which may refer to a place (the temple) or a person (translations vary, between "most holy place" and "most holy one").

It is difficult, in my view, to read verse 24 as a fitting description of any events that took place in the centuries after the fall of Babylon other than the events of the life, death, and resurrection of the Lord Jesus Christ. Certainly the New Testament writers view the cross as the ultimate "putting an end to sin" and "atoning for wickedness," and the resurrection as the ultimate vindication of God and God's anointed one. And all these things happened (as Paul puts it), "in accordance with the Scriptures" (1 Cor 15:1–3).

Verses 25–27

These verses are much more enigmatic, and it is here that so many commentators come up with so many different possibilities. On the whole, I think it seems very likely that we are back in the period of time running up to the terrible blasphemy and persecution of Antiochus IV Epiphanes, and especially his desecration of the temple in 167 BC (which is probably what v. 27 refers to). If that is so, then we need to recognize that the words "Anointed One" in verses 25 and 26 do not refer to Jesus *the* Messiah (as seems to be implied by the use of the capital letters in the NIV). In both cases the word in Hebrew is "an anointed one" (without the definite article). And the Hebrew word *māsîah*, ("anointed one") referred to anyone who was anointed to perform a particular task or service for God. Isaiah used it to describe even the pagan king Cyrus because God had raised him up to fulfil his purpose for Israel (Isa 44:28–45:1). It may be that Cyrus is the one referred to in verse 25, approximately "seven weeks" of years after the prophecies of Jeremiah that Jerusalem and the temple would be restored. Or if "the time the word goes out to restore and rebuild Jerusalem" refers to the decree of Cyrus himself, then "an anointed one" could refer to one of the early leaders of the restored community such as Joshua or Zerubbabel who were instrumental in initiating the rebuilding of the temple (see Haggai).

Then would follow a much longer period (sixty two weeks of years), when another "anointed one" will be "put to death and have nothing" (v. 26). Some see this as a reference to the murder of the High Priest Onias III in 171 BC—which occurred shortly before the climax of the excesses of Antiochus Epiphanes. Once again, we read the word "the end." Antiochus would do his worst. He would set up in the temple an idolatrous statue, the "abomination that causes desolation." He would humiliate and murder countless numbers of God's people. But his time will be relatively short in comparison to the other symbolic numbers—a mere final "week." There is "an end that is decreed," and it will come upon him, as upon all tyrants who take their puny stand against the living God.

Conclusion

So then, it seems to me that what we have here is a schematic sketch of history to come, not a detailed chronology within which we can dogmatically assign dates, persons, and events. Indeed, trying obsessively to do that will probably distract us from the main point of the text. But even though the details may be hazy or open to differing plausible theories, there is enough overall shape to the scheme to help us see the message that Gabriel was bringing in his answer to Daniel's prayer. That message is broadly this.

Daniel had prayed that God would act in forgiveness on the basis of his confession of sin. And God promises that he will do so. But that forgiveness operates at two levels. On the one hand, the return of Israel to the land after the exile was perceived as at least a partial declaration of God's forgiveness and restoration of his people. Isaiah 40–55 preaches that message powerfully. But on the other hand, it was clear even then to Daniel and the prophets of the postexilic era that Israel was still a sinful people, in need of constant repentance and forgiveness. But in the end, declares Daniel 9:24, that state of affairs will not last forever. God will act to finish transgression, bring an end to sin, and make atonement for wickedness. Only God could ultimately and totally accomplish that, and as we stand on this side of the cross and resurrection of Christ, we are privileged to look back, just as Daniel looked forward, to see that indeed he did. "It is finished!"

And Daniel had also prayed that God would vindicate his own name and reputation. That too would happen, but as history progressed there would be repeated and even climactic challenges to the God of Israel (vv. 25–27). His people would be hunted, persecuted and slaughtered. His temple would be desecrated yet again. Terrible times lay ahead in the distant future. But the prayer of Daniel and the prayers of countless more of his people would not be forgotten. There would be an end to such times of tribulation, and God would remain faithful to his long-term promise and purpose for his people in the world.

So God's answer to Daniel's prayer was a mixture of encouragement and warning. It was, like so much of the rest of the book, a call to trust in the sovereignty of Yahweh the God of Israel in the midst of historical events that seemed to deny it. The ultimate fulfilment of what Daniel prayed for, and the ultimate realization of what he saw in his dreams and visions, lay in the distant future (from his location in history). But that's all right. God is in control, and as one of the

Psalms that Daniel would have known put it, "a thousand years in your sight are like a day that has just gone by, or like a watch in the night" (Ps 90:4). Let Daniel then join with all the generations of his people who had made the Lord their dwelling place and would continue to do so to this day (Ps 90:1).

The same psalm speaks of God turning human beings back to dust (Ps 90:3). That indeed was where Daniel and his whole generation would end their days, asleep in the dust of death. But that would not be the end of his story, as we shall see in our final chapter.

FINALE AND FAREWELL

The reason for combining Daniel chapters 10, 11, and 12 together is not simply so that we can keep this book shorter with a neat number of ten chapters. It is because these three chapters of Daniel are, in fact, one single, climactic, visionary experience that Daniel had near the end of his earthly life. It would be a good idea to read all three chapters together at one go before joining me in considering their message. Don't give up halfway through chapter 11! Be like Daniel, and persevere to the end.

The three chapters fall into three clear sections:

- 10:1—11:1 Daniel's preparation and encounter with Gabriel[1]
- 11:2—12:4 A preview of the history leading up to Antiochus IV Epiphanes
- 12:5–13   Closing promises to Daniel

DANIEL'S FINAL VISION (10:1–11:1)

The whole vision is given in the form of a testimony (rather like Nebuchadnezzar's in ch. 4), though it is introduced initially in the third person (10:1), in an editorial note that tells us both that the vision was trustworthy and what it was substantially about, namely, "a great war." The note of conflict, among earthly kingdoms and in the heavenly realms, runs through the whole section. As often before, we have so much to learn simply from observing Daniel himself as a

---

1. The angel Gabriel is not named here, but the angelic speaker refers to his own activity in "the first year of Darius the Mede" (11:1), which indicates he is the same speaker as the Gabriel who was sent to Daniel in 9:21 in that year, and the same angel as in 8:15–16.

man, even before we focus on the content and meaning of his vision. At least three things stand out in chapter 10.

Daniel's Prayer: Mourning on Earth, Warfare in the Heavens

In the third year of Cyrus king of Persia, a revelation was given to Daniel (who was called Belteshazzar). Its message was true and it concerned a great war. The understanding of the message came to him in a vision.

At that time I, Daniel, mourned for three weeks. I ate no choice food; no meat or wine touched my lips; and I used no lotions at all until the three weeks were over. (Dan 10:1–3)

Daniel was a man of prayer. We knew that already from chapter 6. But here his prayers have taken on an intensity of emotion and purpose. We are not told immediately why he had chosen to mourn and fast for three weeks, but later we find out (v. 12) that he was struggling to gain some understanding of what was going on in the international arena. This would have included a professional interest, of course, given that he was involved in government administration at the highest level. But clearly Daniel was as aware as he had been throughout his life that God, his God, the God of his people Israel, was also involved in the affairs of empires—or rather, God was sovereign over all human empires. So he was seeking to discern the spiritual realities behind the earthly contingencies that swirled around him. Already God had given him visions that alerted him to the "bestial" dimensions of human empires (ch. 7). He had something of a preview of the accelerating evil that would happen in the coming years when the Persian Empire, whose beginnings he had just witnessed, would be carved up into the competing Greek/Hellenistic kingdoms (ch. 8). But as he tells us himself, all of this was still "beyond understanding" (8:27). So Daniel prays on, seeking God's further insight into the world he knew and the story he was living in. His prayer life was not a means of escaping *from* the world but of bringing God *into* the world. Or, as we saw in chapter 6, the windows of his room were open towards Jerusalem, not to let his prayers out, but to let the God of Israel in.

And now, right towards the end of his life, Daniel seems almost desperate to understand God's plan and purpose—perhaps, we might think, so that he can die with a measure of peace, hope, and assurance. That is the aim of his mourning and fasting. And that was what God eventually grants him, as we shall see, in the closing verse of the book.

Unlike some earlier visions, which seem to have taken place at night in the form of dreams within which God spoke to him through angelic messengers, this one takes place in the midst of his working daytime and in the company of others. The account in 10:4–9 has some similarity to the experience of Saul of Tarsus on the road to Damascus (Acts 9:7) in that there were others present who were overawed by the presence of God or God's angel but took no part in the event (Daniel's companions simply ran away in terror, 10:7). But the main difference is that it was the risen Lord Jesus Christ who appeared to Saul, while the person who appears to Daniel is clearly an angelic figure of great magnitude, splendor, and power, one who has been sent as a messenger of God. With great courage, Daniel manages to gaze at the "man" long enough to describe his appearance in some detail (10:5–6), but when he spoke, with a "voice like the sound of a multitude" (which makes me think of the noise of a sports stadium in full throat), Daniel collapses, prone, to the ground.

> A hand touched me and set me trembling on my hands and knees. He said, "Daniel, you who are highly esteemed, consider carefully the words I am about to speak to you, and stand up, for I have now been sent to you." And when he said this to me, I stood up trembling.
>
> Then he continued, "Do not be afraid, Daniel. Since the first day that you set your mind to gain understanding and to humble yourself before your God, your words were heard, and I have come in response to them. But the prince of the Persian

kingdom resisted me twenty-one days. Then Michael, one of the
chief princes, came to help me, because I was detained there with
the king of Persia. Now I have come to explain to you what will
happen to your people in the future, for the vision concerns a
time yet to come." (Dan 10:10–14)

Now we hear from the angel what Daniel had been doing those
three weeks. It was a very intentional effort, on which he had "set his
mind," with a clear purpose: "to gain understanding," and "to humble"
himself. Daniel's prayer was purposeful and persistent and (as we saw
in ch. 9) based on the deep humility of confessing the sin of himself
and his people. Daniel may well have wondered why it was that God
seemed to be taking so long in answering his prayer and giving him
the understanding he longed for. The explanation is quite a surprise.

It was not (explains the gleaming messenger, with a hint of
apology in his words), that God had not given an answer. On the
contrary, Daniel's prayer had been heard, and a response given, on
the "first day" he began to pray. The delay was not God's fault. Nor
was it the messenger's fault. He had sped on his way, *but* he had been
resisted by "the Prince of the Persian kingdom"—a resistance that
had lasted for twenty-one days, the whole length of time Daniel had
been praying. Only when "Michael, one of the chief princes" came
along to help, was Gabriel (for it is almost certainly he) freed up,
so to speak, to complete his mission by coming to Daniel. What is
going on here?

Well the honest answer to that question is, I don't really know in
any detail (and probably we are not meant to try to invent the details).
But what is clear is that Daniel's prayer on earth is connected to
spiritual conflict in the "heavenly realms" (using the word "heaven"
here not merely as the "place" of God's dwelling, but the whole realm
of created spiritual beings, including those who do God's will as his
messengers and agents, and those that have rebelled against him and
turned to evil). There is a cosmic conflict that lies behind all that
goes on below on the earth, and it involves spiritual forces that can

be called "princes," or in New Testament terms, "principalities and powers." The Bible does not tell us very much about these spiritual powers, but it does affirm their existence. Some of them, as here, seem to be associated with particular nations and to be involved in the political and military fortunes of those nations. Whatever they are, they are created beings and remain subject to the Lord of lords and King of kings, the sovereign creator God. Deuteronomy 32:8–9, in affirming that the Most High God has a unique relationship with Israel as his covenant people, also says that God has assigned other nations their specific inheritance "according to the number of the sons of God" (Deut 32:8, NIV footnote). The expression "sons of God" (which is probably the correct reading of the difficult Hebrew text) often refers to angelic beings in the OT.

Daniel's prayer, then, has connected in some way with that realm of spiritual power and spiritual conflict. Why would the angelic "prince of the Persian kingdom" have resisted the messenger whom God had sent to bear his word to Daniel (v. 13)? Because that word speaks of the defeat of Persia by the Greek Empire of Alexander the Great (11:2–4), and once God's word is spoken, it will accomplish what he decrees. So the prince of Persia tried to prevent the word going forth, until Michael—the angelic defender of God's own people— overcame him. So the conflict on earth mirrors the conflict in the spiritual realms, and Daniel is now made aware of that (though it would have been part of his worldview already).

Where does this lead us as regards our own prayer life? Certainly, like the apostle Paul, we need to be aware that we are engaged in a spiritual battle as we submit to and serve the kingdom of God. That conflict is clearly there in the ministry of Jesus himself, and he made sure his disciples understood the nature of the battle we are in. As Paul put it, "our struggle is not against flesh and blood, but against the rulers, against the authorities, against the powers of this dark world and against the spiritual forces of evil in the heavenly realms" (Eph 6:12). And in that struggle, our warfare and weapons also are spiritual. "The weapons we fight with are not the weapons of the world. On the contrary, they have divine power to demolish strongholds. We demolish arguments and every pretension that sets itself up against the knowledge of God, and we take captive every thought to make it obedient to Christ" (2 Cor 10:4–5).

However, it is questionable whether the Bible, with the limited information it gives us about these spiritual powers, intends that we should focus our minds or our prayers specifically on them. We certainly need to understand that our prayers do engage with spiritual realities beyond what we can see and that spiritual warfare is going on behind and around all that we are involved in as we serve the kingdom of God in this world. But we are told to put on the armour of God and pray to God, not to get involved with those powers themselves directly. There is a theology and practice of spiritual warfare that includes trying to identify and name "territorial spirits" and then to engage with them in detailed confrontational practices. Although popular in some circles as a mission strategy, I do wonder how much biblical foundation such practices can claim. We should also be wary of excessive claims that can be made by some "experts" in such tactics. Sometimes it sounds as if God is waiting for the result of our spiritual warfare, as if the success of God's mission of salvation depends on us going about things in the right way. But on the contrary, as God made plain to Moses and the Israelites, the battle is the Lord's and it is God who will win it (Exod 14:13–14)—or rather, has already won it through the cross and resurrection of Christ (Col 2:15). We are called to participate in the ongoing conflict, but the decisive victory is already won.

As far as Daniel is concerned, it is noticeable that even though he is fully aware now of the existence of these spiritual forces and "princes," and even though he knows that some of them will oppose and some will support the word and works of God, he himself is not instructed, and makes no effort, to engage in battle with them directly himself. That is a realm of activity that he leaves to them and to God. He prays to his God and entrusts the outcome to him. Perhaps that too is the best model for us.

Daniel's Humility: Helpless on Earth, Esteemed in Heaven

Daniel is ruthlessly honest about himself. There is nothing heroic about his posture in this account. We don't imagine him calling his friends with a casual, "Hey, guys, I've just been chatting with Archangel Gabriel." On the contrary, he stresses the overwhelming nature of the event and how it reduced him to a quaking wreck on the ground. Indeed, there is an almost comic sequence of postures. First he is flat on his face (v. 9), then he gets to his hands and knees, still trembling (v. 10), then he manages to stand up (v. 11), only to bow face to the ground again (v. 15). Look how he describes his state of mind and body throughout the encounter:

- I had no strength left, my face turned deathly pale and I was helpless. (v. 8)
- I am overcome with anguish because of the vision, my lord, and I feel very weak. How can I, your servant, talk with you, my lord? My strength is gone and I can hardly breathe. (vv. 16–17)

Three times he needed a touch from God's messenger to give him strength and enable him to speak (vv. 10, 16, 18). Daniel was an elderly saint. He had a lifetime of experience and wisdom to call on. He had walked the corridors of human power since his youth, and spent part of every day in the presence of God in prayer. And yet there is no sense of his own status or confidence in his own ability to cope with any eventuality.

Perhaps I should not have put those words "and yet" at the beginning of that last sentence. A better connection would have been, "And that is why . . . ." For surely the closer we come to God in daily conversation, the more our self-importance shrinks. The more we understand of the majesty of God and the surprising abundance of his loving grace, the more humility comes very naturally. Daniel seems like an embodiment of the desire expressed in the hymn,

Let holy charity mine outward vesture be,
And lowliness become mine inner clothing;
True lowliness of heart, which takes the humbler part,
And o'er its own shortcomings weeps with loathing.[2]

But if that is how Daniel saw himself, it was not quite how God saw him. Three times he is reassured with the words "You are highly esteemed" (9:23; 10:11, 19). The Hebrew is an intensive form, more literally, "greatly loved." Now God does not have favourites, but the Bible assures us that there is an intimacy with God that is available to those who cultivate their relationship with him. It is a relationship in which, without losing any of the deep humility and unworthiness that comes from walking close to God, a person can have moments of knowing that God is pleased with them. Such moments were surely Christ's own earthly experience, especially, of course, at the moment of his baptism when he heard precisely those words from his Father, "This is my Son, whom I love; with him I am well pleased" (Matt 3:17).

One of my favourite verses, particularly in my years as a younger Christian, is Psalm 25:14, "The friendship of the LORD is for those who fear him" (NRSV). There is a reassuring ring to it. Like many Christians, I have often laboured under a feeling of unworthiness, of "never matching up" to God's expectations of me or even my own expectations of myself. There is a well-researched and documented state of mind known as "imposter syndrome," in which, no matter how hard a person works or how much success they achieve, they always feel a bit of a fraud internally. The success is "outside," but the fraud lurks "inside." I think there is a spiritual equivalent, and Satan enjoys plaguing Christians with it. I have experienced it at various points in my life and Christian service. But genuine humility does not mean going around feeling like a fraud or imposter. It means simply knowing who and what you are in the presence of God and trusting

---

2. Bianco da Siena, "Come Down, O Love Divine," trans. Richard Frederick Littledale (1867).

in *God's* verdict on your life, not your own. And from time to time, God has given me "Daniel" moments (not meaning visions like his, for which I'm grateful!), when I have felt a deep sense of the Lord's smile and his assurance that he is pleased with what I'm trying to do for him. It's not arrogance. It never leads to boasting (to myself or others), but it is a moment of "the friendship of the Lord," and such moments are precious.

Daniel's Understanding: Sought on Earth, Given from Heaven

"Where does he get all this?" They asked that about Jesus, too. The answer he would have given, of course, would have been that he "got it" from his heavenly Father, whose words he spoke and whose works he was doing (John 5:16–30). And yet there is no doubt that Jesus must have studied the Scriptures very thoroughly for himself, in such depth that even at the age of twelve he was able to engage in discussion with the learned teachers of the Torah in the temple. He received from God, but he received it also through his study on earth.

Those of us who preach will sometimes get a grateful or admiring response along the lines of "I don't know how you do it, making the Bible come alive so clearly like that!" My usual reply to comments like that is a quiet, "Well, it's God's Word. All I do is just let it out." And that's true of course. But I also know that many hours of hard work, thought, and prayer went into the preparation of the sermon.

We can see that combination of God's gift and human effort in Daniel in these chapters. From the very start, Daniel's angelic visitor had told him, "I have come now to give you insight and understanding" (9:22). The visions that he had and the meanings they held were not something he just "dreamt up for himself." They came from God through God's messengers. Yet at the same time, Daniel is told to "consider the word and understand the vision" (9:23b). He spent three weeks of prayer and fasting before receiving the message contained in chapters 11 and 12. And when the angel comes to him at the end of that time he begins by saying, "Since the first day that *you set your mind* to gain understanding and humble yourself before your God, your words were heard" (10:12; italics added). To put it simply, what we read in the second half of the book of Daniel (his visions and their meaning) is a mysterious combination of divine revelation and human mental effort. Not either without the other.

In the training seminars for biblical preaching that Langham Partnership organizes in many countries around the world, we often confront the attitude, "I don't need to prepare to preach. I rely on the Holy Spirit." There are some who even argue that any kind of preparation in advance is "unspiritual," a sign of lack of faith in the Holy Spirit. They justify this opinion by quoting the words of Jesus, "do not worry about what to say or how to say it. At that time you will be given what to say, for it will not be you speaking, but the Spirit of your Father speaking through you" (Matt 10:19–20). What they overlook is that Jesus was talking about occasions when his disciples would be arrested and hauled into court (the verse begins, "When they arrest you"). At such moments they would not have time to prepare their defence. But they need not worry, for the Holy Spirit would enable them to speak. So Jesus was talking about a prisoner in court, not a preacher in church. No, we need to *work hard* in diligently studying God's Word, as Paul instructed Timothy (1 Tim 4:13–15; 2 Tim 2:15), while at the same time praying and depending on God's Spirit to help us both in the preparation and in the preaching itself. The result will be a combination of God's gift and our effort, as it was here for Daniel.

HISTORY, HYBRIS, AND HOPE (11:2–12:4)

So at last we come to the message itself—the last message that Daniel received. It portrays a history that would stretch into the future beyond Daniel. It reinforces the theme of his earlier visions that the end of the Babylonian exile was not the end of the sufferings of Israel; even back in their own land there would come a time of intense persecution and suffering. But it also reinforces the great affirmation of earlier visions that in the end, God's kingdom will triumph and the people of God will not merely survive but will indeed rise again to everlasting life—and Daniel would not be deprived, not even by death, of his share in that ultimate glorious future.

History: Divine Control but Human Choices

Daniel's angelic visitor begins with a surprisingly dismissive comment about the remaining years of the Persian Empire. A single verse (11:2) is enough to summarise about 200 years of an empire that ruled from the Aegean Sea to the borders of India! We are told that there will be a few more Persian kings until one comes who will attack Greece. In fact two Persian kings attempted to conquer Greece in the early years of the fifth century BC but were beaten back in some critical battles in 490 and 480 BC. Then another single verse (v. 3) suffices to mention Alexander the Great (the one-horned charging goat of ch. 8) and his conquest of Persia in the mid-fourth century BC. So by the time we reach verse 4 we have arrived in the four separate kingdoms that emerged in the so-called Hellenistic era. If a thousand years in the Lord's sight are as a single day, then perhaps it is not surprising that two verses are enough to cover several centuries!

That epoch of Greek cultural dominance over the whole region lasted another two hundred years until Rome conquered Greece and extended its rule over the Eastern Mediterranean and Middle Eastern region. Only two of the four Hellenistic kingdoms, however, impinged upon the life of the Israelites in Judea: the kingdom of the Ptolemies, who ruled in Egypt and then the kingdom of the Seleucids, who ruled in Syria. In Daniel chapter 11 these are referred to, respectively, as the king of the South and the king of the North. Since the land of Palestine lay in between the two rival kingdoms, the fate of the Jews seemed to be at the mercy of one or the other. That is the way chapter 11 proceeds, outlining the cycle of plots and schemes and battles between the two powers in the South and the North. We really don't need to spend time on the details (you can check them out in larger commentaries). The main thrust of the chapter is to lead up to the climax of the story—the reign of the Seleucid king Antiochus IV Epiphanes (11:21–39), who was featured in the previous visions (7:23–25; 8:23–25; 9:26–27).

But before focusing on him, notice an important feature of this narrative: the balance in tension between the sovereignty of God's control of events (it is God, through his angel who is explaining what will happen) and the freedom and responsibility that humans have for their own choices and actions.

On the one hand, we read that certain things will happen "at the appointed time" (vv. 29, 35), and that "what has been determined must take place" (v. 36). But on the other hand, three times in chapter 11 we read that this or that king "will do as he pleases" (vv. 3, 16, 36). The phrase is applied at the beginning of the sequence to Alexander the Great and at the end to Antiochus. So it embraces all the human participants in the story. There is therefore no room for the accusation that, because God presents the history to come in the form of a prophetic vision, the characters are mere puppets on strings, manipulated by divine power to act without any choices or decisions of their own. On the contrary, they act freely and they are responsible for their actions since they can be judged and punished for them. And most of the time it seems that these human kings and commanders, just like the spiritual forces in opposition to God, are acting against God and God's people in their ambitious vying for earthly power and greed. And yet God remains in control. Neither Daniel, nor his angelic messenger, nor the whole book makes any effort to resolve the tension between these twin realities. The Bible simply affirms both of them. People do what they choose to do, in pursuit of their own chosen goals, for good or ill. Yet God remains sovereign and works out the course of history over the centuries to fulfil God's own purposes of redemption and grace on the one hand and ultimate judgment of the wicked on the other.

This, of course, is a tension to which the whole Bible bears witness. We cannot slide out of the tension either into dualism (the unending struggle between good and evil with no resolution) or into fatalism (the view that all human actions are mere out-workings of a cosmic fate, such that personal freedom of choice and moral responsibility are mere illusions). Daniel, like the rest of the Bible, simply tells us: people choose their courses of action and bear the consequences, but God knows and sees and ultimately works all things according to his own purpose.

Persecution: Lethal but Limited

In this mysterious combination of divine appointment and human freedom, the climax will come in the overwhelming evil, violence, oppression, and sacrilege that marked out the rule of Antiochus IV Epiphanes. Some details are listed in 11:31–35. Three things stand out.

First, the people of God will suffer. That in itself is not surprising; the Bible indicates that this is a regularly recurring reality. Now, sometimes such suffering is, we might say, self-inflicted, when it takes the form of the judgment of God in response to continued rebellion and wickedness. That was certainly how the prophets interpreted the terrible suffering of the people of Jerusalem and Judea under the Babylonian siege that ended in the destruction of Jerusalem and the exile. We saw that very clearly in Daniel's prayer in chapter 9. But the Bible makes it equally clear that sometimes suffering cannot and should not be explained in those terms. The Hebrews in Egypt, for example, are not said to be suffering there because of God's judgment on their own sin, but because of the sinful oppression of the Egyptians. And that is the case here, too. There is no hint in Daniel that the "wrath of Antiochus" was an expression of the wrath of God against Israel. Rather, they were the victims of an evil regime that set itself up against the God of Israel and his people. They could cry out in pain and anguish, but they are not called to repentance.

Second, such suffering can divide God's people. Indeed, the tactics of their enemies can be precisely to create such division. It seems that Antiochus used both intense persecution and violence on the one hand, along with seductive flattery and deception on the other hand, to tempt some of the Jews to collaborate with him, while others remained firm in resisting him even to death. At such times there is a great need for people who will understand what is happening and give good guidance and leadership to the rest of the people. Such persons are here referred to as "the wise" (vv. 33–35). They themselves, however, will not necessarily escape the terrible, purging fires of persecution.

> With flattery he will corrupt those who have violated the covenant, but the people who know their God will firmly resist him. Those who are wise will instruct many, though for a time they will fall by the sword or be burned or captured or plundered. When they fall, the will receive a little help, and many who are not sincere will join them. Some of the wise will stumble, so that they may be refined, purified and made spotless until the time of the end, for it will still come at the appointed time. (Dan 11:32–35).

Third, however, the suffering of persecution has a limit. It will come to an end. Or rather, it will come to many "ends." As we saw in chapter 8, the word "end" in a book like Daniel does not necessarily mean "the end of the world as we know it." We know that eventually there will come a definitive, ultimate end to this world of evil. Or more accurately, there will come an end to evil so that the world can be restored to the goodness, beauty, joy, and peace that God intends for it. But even before that time, periods of intense suffering do not last forever. There is an ebb and flow in the history of persecution and oppression of God's people. Daniel's visions stress that such an "end" will come, in the appointed time, even to the excessive, blasphemous, and violent arrogance of Antiochus. Again and again this chapter points out that there will be a limit to the suffering—it *will* happen, but it will be only for a limited time, or within God's "appointed time" (11:24, 27, 29, 35, 36, 40).

Such an assurance does not lessen the suffering, but it does give hope. But hope is allowed its questions. And the most oft-repeated question of God's suffering saints is "How long, O Lord?" It echoes right through until the closing chapters of the whole Bible, where it receives the same assurance of God's sovereign control and God's ultimate redemptive justice (Rev 6:9–11).

As I have been writing this chapter I have been spending a week of fellowship and retreat with colleagues in Langham Partnership. One couple among our leadership team are Syrians living and working in Lebanon. We read Psalm 119 together during the course of the week, and when we read the *kaph* section, the wife commented that verse 84 was being prayed intensely by Syrian Christians, whether still in Syria or as refugees in Lebanon:

> How long must your servant wait?
> 　　When will you punish my persecutors? (Ps 119:84).

Of course they pray for the perpetrators of the terrible violence inflicted by ISIS, that God would either bring them to repentance or restrain them. Of course they are willing even to exercise costly love in caring for the families of some of those fighters who are living in the camps in Lebanon. But as they struggle to live and work and witness as Christians to the vast numbers in desperate need, they daily ask the Lord that burning question—"How long will this go on? How long must we wait for an end to all this destruction, death, dislocation, and suffering?" They do not seek vengeance, but they do long for God to act in justice—with a longing often expressed in the Bible and assured of God's answer.

Future Hope: Resurrection and Judgment

But what of those for whom that answer comes too late, those who have perished in the "time of distress" (12:1)? That ultimate question—the enigma of the unjust death of the saints in times of persecution—drives the book of Daniel to its climax with an unambiguous promise of personal resurrection (12:2). I say "unambiguous" because up to this point the Old Testament has given hints and hopes that death would not be the end of God's covenant relationship with faithful believers, but there are very few clear and specific promises of a resurrected life.[3] The following texts point in that direction, but without any detail:

- Psalm 16 affirms that God will not abandon the psalmist in death. Somehow even his body will "rest secure" and he will find "life," "joy," and "eternal pleasures" in the presence of God. But how that might happen is not explored.

- Psalm 49:15 claims that God will rescue his faithful one from the fate of the wicked, which is Sheol, the grave. Does that mean he will be preserved from death, or after death?

- Psalm 73:23–24 expects that God will receive the Psalmist with honour/glory, "afterwards"—which many assume to mean, after death.

- Job 19:25–27 includes the famous line, "I know that my redeemer lives," and seems to anticipate that, even if he dies, Job will see himself vindicated before God. But the text is notoriously difficult to translate with certainty.

- Isaiah promises that God will eventually "destroy the shroud that enfolds all peoples" (meaning death), for "he will swallow up death forever" (Isa 25:7–8). So God's people can look forward to the day when "your dead will live, LORD; their bodies will rise—let those who dwell in the dust wake up and shout for joy" (Isa 26:19).

---

3. People often ask why there is so little teaching about life after death, resurrection, eternal life, etc. in the Old Testament. I think one reason is that God wanted Israel to be very different from surrounding cultures where there seems to have been a morbid fascination, even obsession, with death and the afterlife. In Egypt, for example, people who could afford it (especially Pharaohs), would spend their entire lifetime and vast amounts of money preparing their future "home" in the world of the dead. The evidence is still there, in the pyramids, the tombs, the mummies, etc. The Old Testament directs attention away from obsession with death and affirms the goodness of life, life in this good creation, and calls on people to live now in the presence of God "for all its worth," so to speak. For Old Testament Israel, death is an evil and an enemy. What lies beyond it is a mystery. But Yahweh, the LORD God, is Lord over death as over life (Deut 32:39; 1 Sam 2:6), and was known to have the power to raise back to life those who had recently died (1 Kgs 17; 2 Kgs 4) so they could live in trust in him for whatever lay beyond.

Apart from these, other references to resurrection are corporate or representative. Israel as a whole will be raised up when they repent and turn back to God (Hos 6:1–2). When they return from exile, it would be like an army of dead bones being restored to life (Ezek 37:11–14). And the Servant of the Lord—who shares Israel's identity representatively, after he has given his life for others—"will see his offspring and prolong his days" and be triumphantly vindicated by God (Isa 53:10–12).

Here at the end of the book of Daniel, however, the promise is clear and unambiguous.

> Multitudes who sleep in the dust of the earth will awake: some to everlasting life, others to shame and everlasting contempt. Those who are wise will shine like the brightness of the heavens, and those who lead many to righteousness, like the stars for ever and ever. (Dan 12:2–3)

Death has become not a never-ending shadowy existence in a gloomy underworld of Sheol, but simply "sleep in the dust of the earth." And the future is not closed off by death, either for those who have suffered it unjustly under persecution or for those who have perpetrated great evil on earth—but seemed to "get away with it" by dying before facing justice. For the resurrection described here is discriminating. For some it will bring "everlasting life," for others "shame and everlasting contempt." The God who acts in vindication and redemption will also act in judgment. Resurrection, therefore, not only vindicates the righteous, it also vindicates the justice of God.

Two things should still be said, however. First, this does indeed provide great hope and reassurance for individual believers in the face of suffering and death. But it is not merely individual. Those to whom this promise of everlasting life comes are not just assured of their own personal future bliss. Rather, they will participate in the corporate redemption of God's people. The two verses about resurrection must be read in the light of the first verse: "At that time your people—everyone whose name is found written in the book—will be delivered" (Dan 12:1). Elsewhere the Bible will make clear that God's ultimate purpose is a whole new creation in which the redeemed humanity—God's people from every tribe and nation and language—will dwell in the fullness of resurrection life eternally.

Second, while the promise is clear, the details are not. We are not told what it will be like to "awake" from the sleep of death. We are not told what our bodies will be like in that time of "everlasting life." We might want to ask a lot of questions—as Daniel probably did—but instead he is told to "roll up and seal the words of the scroll until the time of the end." Answers must wait. However, the "time of the end" has invaded history already. For that is exactly how the resurrection of Jesus Christ is described. The astonishing message of the first disciples was that an event they all believed would happen "at the last day" (as Martha replied to Jesus about her dead brother Lazarus, John 11:24) had been anticipated on that first day of the week when God raised the crucified Christ to risen, bodily life—"the firstfruits of those who have fallen asleep" (1 Cor 15:20). On that day God brought into history in advance a guarantee of what will ultimately be a reality for all God's people. The resurrection of Jesus is the model of what resurrection will mean for all of those who are in him by faith. For the same power of God that raised Jesus from the dead "will transform our lowly bodies so that they will be like his glorious body" (Phil 3:21).

FAREWELL DANIEL—FOR NOW (12:5–13)

The words of the messenger (probably the angel Gabriel, as we saw earlier), which began way back in 10:11, have come to an end, and Daniel is left standing by the riverside alone. But not quite alone, for his vision has not quite finished and he has some unanswered questions.

> Then I, Daniel, looked, and there before me stood two others, one on this bank of the river and one on the opposite bank. One

of them said to the man clothed in linen, who was above the waters of the river, "How long will it be before these astonishing things are fulfilled?"

The man clothed in linen, who was above the waters of the river, lifted his right hand and his left hand toward heaven, and I heard him swear by him who lives forever, saying, "It will be for a time, times and half a time. When the power of the holy people has been finally broken, all these things will be completed."

I heard, but I did not understand. So I asked, "My lord, what will the outcome of all this be?"

He replied, "Go your way, Daniel, because the words are rolled up and sealed until the time of the end. Many will be purified, made spotless and refined, but the wicked will continue to be wicked. None of the wicked will understand, but those who are wise will understand.

"From the time that the daily sacrifice is abolished and the abomination that causes desolation is set up, there will be 1,290 days. Blessed is the one who waits for and reaches the end of the 1,335 days.

"As for you, go your way till the end. You will rest, and then at the end of the days you will rise to receive your allotted inheritance." (Dan 12:5–13)

The book comes to an end in a way that is both puzzling (hardly a surprise after all we have read so far) and yet also strangely comforting and reassuring. Indeed, surely the fact that Daniel himself says "I heard, but I did not understand" relieves us of becoming obsessively determined to work out with mathematical precision the connections between Daniel's vision and either events in contemporary history or a timetable for the so-called "end times." When one of the two men in this final vision asks his question "How long . . . ?," and when Daniel himself asks "What will the outcome of all this be?" the answers are almost certainly deliberately mysterious. All attempts to work out an exact meaning for the "times" of verse 7 and the "days" of verses

11–12 seem to end in confusion. They point to coming suffering and desolation of God's people, but they continue to give assurance of God's ultimate control to make sure that "all these things will be completed."

Beyond that, Daniel's instruction sounds like the famous words, "Keep calm and carry on." The twice repeated "Go your way" is not a brusque dismissal but a simple assurance that Daniel can go back to his work, back to his prayers, back to whatever of his life was left, "till the end." His own personal "end" would come soon no doubt. But for him too it would be merely a sleep, the rest that God promised to his people, in life or in death. And for him, as for all those who remain faithful to God, in Babylon, in Persia, in Jerusalem—God's people in all places and in all times who are faithful in life and obedient even unto death—the promise of the final verse remains God's assurance. And it is no purely spiritual, immaterial promise. The language of "allotted inheritance" spoke clearly of Israel's portioning out the land that God gave them and points to an earthly future by God's redeeming power. We will share in the reality of the new creation, the new heaven and new earth that God promises (Isa 65:17; Rev 21:1–5).

For all of us then, if we know the God of Daniel as our God, through faith in his Son, the Son of Man, the Lord Jesus Christ, the promise of God's word comes: "You will rest . . . you will rise . . . you will receive."

With such a word ringing in our ears, we can indeed, like Daniel, go in peace, to love and serve the Lord.

In the name of Christ, Amen.

SCRIPTURE INDEX

SUBJECT INDEX

How to Preach and Teach the Old Testament for All Its Worth

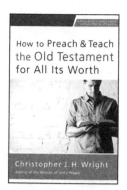

Many preachers ignore preaching from the Old Testament because they feel it is outdated in light of the New Testament and difficult to expound. On the other hand, some preachers will preach from the Old Testament frequently but fail to handle it correctly, turning it into moralistic rules or symbolic lessons for our spiritual life. In *How to Preach and Teach the Old Testament for All Its Worth*, Christopher J. H. Wright proclaims that preachers must not ignore the Old Testament. It is the Word of God! The Old Testament lays the foundation for our faith and it was the Bible that Jesus read and used.

Looking first at why we should preach from the Old Testament, the author moves on to show the reader how they can preach from it. Covering the History, Law, Prophets, Psalms, and Wisdom Literature, interspersed with practical checklists, exercises, and sermons, Wright provides an essential guide on how to handle the Old Testament responsibly.

The Mission of God's People

A Biblical Theology of the Church's Mission

Chris Wright's pioneering 2006 book, *The Mission of God*, revealed that the typical Christian understanding of "missions" encompasses only a small part of God's overarching mission for the world. God is relentlessly reclaiming the entire world for himself. In *The Mission of God's People*, Wright shows how God's big-picture plan directs the purpose of God's people, the church. Wright emphasizes what the Old Testament teaches Christians about being the people of God. He addresses questions of both ecclesiology and missiology with topics like "called to care for creation," "called to bless the nations," "sending and being sent," and "rejecting false gods." As part of the Biblical Theology for Life Series, this book provides pastors, teachers, and lay learners with first-rate biblical study while at the same time addressing the practical concerns of contemporary ministry. *The Mission of God's People* promises to enliven and refocus the study, teaching, and ministry of those truly committed to joining God's work in the world.

Available in stores and online!

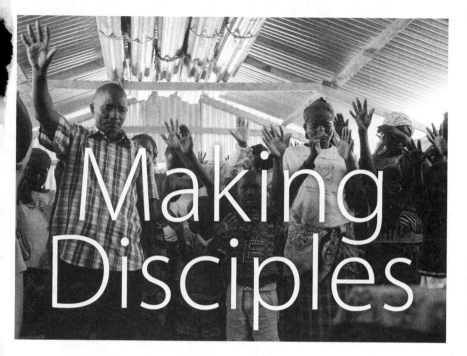

Making Disciples

Around the World — Christianity is exploding with growth in numbers

Yet — Believers are struggling to grow in Christ

That's Why Langham Exists

Our Vision

To see churches in the Majority World equipped for mission and growing to maturity in Christ through the ministry of pastors and leaders who believe, teach and live by the Word of God.

www.langham.org

FOUNDED BY JOHN STOTT

Langham®
PARTNERSHIP